Eradicating Child Maltreatment

ERADICATING CHILD MALTREATMENT

Evidence-Based Approaches to Prevention and Intervention Across Services

Edited by Arnon Bentovim and Jenny Gray

Foreword by Harriet Ward

Jessica Kingsley *Publishers*
London and Philadelphia

First published in 2015
by Jessica Kingsley Publishers
73 Collier Street
London N1 9BE, UK
and
400 Market Street, Suite 400
Philadelphia, PA 19106, USA

www.jkp.com

Library of Congress Cataloging in Publication Data
Eradicating child maltreatment : evidence-based approaches to prevention and intervention across services / edited by Arnon Bentovim and Jenny Gray.
pages cm
Includes bibliographical references and index.
ISBN 978-1-84905-449-2 (alk. paper)
1. Child welfare. 2. Child abuse. 3. Child abuse--Prevention. I. Bentovim, Arnon. II. Gray, Jenny.
HV713.E73 2015
362.76'7--dc23
2014021851

British Library Cataloguing in Publication Data
A CIP catalogue record for this book is available from the British Library

ISBN 978 1 84905 449 2
eISBN 978 0 85700 823 7

Printed and bound in Great Britain by Bell & Bain Ltd, Glasgow

Contents

FOREWORD

Harriet Ward

Historically, there have been times when it was possible to assume that child abuse and neglect did not occur. In nineteenth-century America, the assertion that children might need to be protected from abuse or neglect by parents and others who had responsibility for them was regarded as so outrageous that the case that led to the New York Society for the Prevention of Cruelty to Children in 1874 was prosecuted under animal welfare legislation. In the UK, for nearly a century, the issue shifted in and out of the public consciousness, at one point being a major source of concern, and then forgotten or ignored for lengthy periods. The London Society for the Prevention of Cruelty to Children was founded in 1884, at a time when concerns were beginning to be raised about the prevalence of physical and sexual abuse and neglect; its activities sparked off debates concerning the limitations of the father's right to chastise his children as he saw fit. The rights debate was almost always framed from the father's perspective, rarely ever the mother's, and certainly not the child's. However, throughout the first half of the twentieth century, apart from concerns raised following the death of Denis O'Neil at the hands of his foster carers in 1945, the issue was largely forgotten or hidden, and professionals could have been forgiven for assuming that child abuse and neglect simply did not happen in supposedly civilised countries.

Kempe and colleagues' seminal paper on 'The battered-child syndrome', published by the Journal of the American Medical Association in 1962, marked the point at which the prevalence of child abuse and neglect could no longer be ignored (Kempe 1926). Since then, the work of the International Society for the Prevention of Child Abuse and Negelct (ISPCAN), the UN Committee on the Rights of the Child, and numerous other national and international bodies have made it clear that the maltreatment of children is a very real issue in every country. A wealth of empirical research has also shown that the long-term impact of childhood abuse and neglect on health and well-being, and the costs to society of widespread prevalence, are such serious issues that they cannot be left to local or national initiatives to resolve. The maltreatment of children needs to be faced and addressed on an international basis.

In 1978 Henry Kempe, the founder of ISPCAN, argued that societies and professionals with safeguarding responsibilities needed to go through a number of stages until they reached a position in which it was possible to guarantee that 'every child is wanted, loved and cared for, sheltered, fed and receives first class preventative services and health care' (Kempe 1978). We are still very far from that position today.

Nevertheless there have been a number of advances towards this goal. The promotion of children's rights encapsulated in the United Nations Convention on the Rights of the Child (UNCRC), international initiatives to prevent female genital mutilation, trafficking and sexual exploitation of children and the introduction of legislation banning physical abuse in a number of countries have undoubtedly been steps in the right direction.

Many of the theoretical and practical issues explored in *Eradicating Child Maltreatment: Evidence-Based Approaches to Prevention and Intervention Across Services* mark further stages in our understanding of child abuse and neglect and how it might be addressed. Conceptualising abuse as a public health issue that has to be tackled on a population-wide basis by promoting what is known about successful, sensitive parenting is a huge step forward, because it makes it clear that abusive parenting is not an isolated aberration, but one end of a spectrum of parental practices. Such a universal approach reinforces the message that addressing child abuse and neglect is the responsibility of all professionals who work with children, and that this demands close inter-agency working. Introducing a common-elements approach to training professionals and enhancing their everyday working practices marks a further step towards introducing evidence based practice. This book should be read by all who have an interest in the well-being of children, for the material that it covers marks a further advance on the journey towards ensuring that every child is wanted, loved and cared for.

Harriet Ward, CBE
Professor of Child and Family Research, Loughborough University

References

Kempe, C.H. (1978) 'Recent developments in the field of child abuse'. *Child Abuse and Neglect 2,* 4, 261–267.

Kempe, C.H., Silverman, F.N, Steele, B.F. Droegemueller, W. and Silver, H.K. (1962) 'The battered-child syndrome.' *Journal of the American Medical Association 181,* 1, 17–24.

Reference

Chapter 1

INTRODUCTION

Jenny Gray

The impetus for this book came from a national conference, *Eradicating Child Maltreatment. Intervening with Children and Families: Policy and Practice*, held at the Institute of Health, Great Ormond Street Hospital, London in November 2012. The conference, organised by Child and Family Training UK, The Michael Sieff Foundation and The Lucy Faithfull Foundation, brought together a number of key professionals to present on how this goal might be achieved by taking a public health approach, with evidence-based interventions at primary, secondary and tertiary levels. The presenters' work is set out in the chapters of this book.

The conference took as its starting point the seminal work of Dr Henry Kempe and colleagues who described 'the Battered Child Syndrome' in 1962. Their influential paper had focused the attention of the professional world and society itself on the phenomenon of child maltreatment and it initiated a global process of recognition, response and intervention to child maltreatment. It made a major impact on policy and practice in England leading to the establishment of the British Association for the Study and Prevention of Child Abuse and Neglect (BASPCAN) in 1979.

In London in 1978 Henry Kempe, who had founded the International Society for the Prevention of Child Abuse and Neglect (ISPCAN) in the previous year, gave the keynote address at its Congress. He set out the following six stages that he considered professionals and society needed to go through to reach a world state where children were free from violence:

⊿ Stage 1: Denial of physical or sexual abuse

⊿ Stage 2: The Battered Child Syndrome is recognised

➤ Stage 3: Physical abuse is better managed, with attention being given to neglect and failure to thrive

➤ Stage 4: Recognition of emotional abuse, deprivation and neglect

➤ Stage 5: Serious plight of sexually abused child is recognised

➤ Stage 6: Guaranteeing each child is wanted, loved and cared for, sheltered, fed, receives first class preventative services and healthcare.

The 2012 *Eradicating Child Maltreatment* conference took place in the very same lecture theatre at Great Ormond Street Hospital as the 1978 congress. It was fitting therefore that the 2012 conference was considering whether the idea of eradicating child maltreatment by reaching Henry Kempe's sixth stage was a wishful fantasy or if it was possible to become a practical reality.

The conference recognised that interventions at primary, secondary and tertiary levels should be informed by the wealth of research evidence available and whilst more research is necessary, especially on the effectiveness of interventions, there is no excuse for not making best use of what we know already. Indeed we owe it to the children and families we work with and to society. A common elements approach to training was considered to provide a digestible way of equipping all professionals to work together using effective interventions. Key to change at both national and international levels is a political commitment to making policy which uses evidence-based approaches to support professionals' ongoing work in developing systems to eradicate child maltreatment.

This book presents a series of chapters that address each of these issues and provides a blueprint for action. Bentovim in Chapter 2 sets out the burdens and costs as well as the determinants of maltreatment. He then addresses the challenging question of how effective the policies and practices in different countries are and makes the case for prevention, not only because it is the right of children to be free from violence but also because the evidence strongly suggests that treating and later trying to remedy the effects of child maltreatment are both less effective and more costly than preventing it in the first place.

Woodman and Gilbert in Chapter 3 consider the role of health services in responding to child maltreatment within the context of the child protection system in England. They present the evidence base for health practitioners taking a broader approach to intervention and support when there are child maltreatment-related concerns. They argue that this approach is required to ensure that children and families get the help they need, particularly given the high demand for family support services, which is currently not able to be met by children's social care.

Barlow in Chapter 4 examines the importance of the parent–infant relationship for later infant development, and the impact of 'atypical' or anomalous parent–infant interaction that takes place during this period. She argues that the research strongly points to the need for assessment and intervention, which begins in pregnancy and continues throughout the first postnatal year, and describes a new perinatal care pathway located in children's social care. This development is critically important as infants under one year of age account for 11 per cent of children who are the subject of a child protection plan in the England with neglect (49%) and emotional abuse (25%) accounting for nearly three quarters of these (Department for Education 2013). Barlow reminds us that infants are highly dependent on their caregivers to enable them to optimise their rapidly developing nervous system, and also to promote their ability for affect regulation via the attachment relationship. As a result, maltreatment that occurs during this period has a disproportionate effect on the child's development.

Prinz in Chapter 5 argues that the successful prevention of child abuse and neglect requires a broader approach than the sole focus that historically has focused on providing programmes for only the highest-risk families. This chapter offers a framework for parenting and family support that combines prevention of child maltreatment with other prevention goals. It demonstrates the value of a blended prevention approach that introduces interventions at every level to support parents coming to terms with the responsibilities of parenting through to those who are experiencing significant difficulties. He introduces the idea that such interventions need to be tested on a population-wide basis.

In Chapter 6 Chorpita and his colleagues describe their training approach, which demonstrates that evidence-based approaches can be widely accessible through an analysis of the common elements across different approaches regardless of theoretical approach. In developing this approach Chorpita, Bernstein and Daleiden (2011) identified 395 evidence-based protocols in a review of over 750 non-pharmacological treatments tested in controlled clinical trials. No one practitioner could be expected to become an expert in using a significant number of these different protocols, never mind in all of them. They therefore did all the heavy lifting by distilling out the common elements from these protocols and producing training resources to enhance the practitioner's everyday work with children experiencing mental health problems and their families.

Bentovim and colleagues have applied the Chorpita approach to child maltreatment. Bentovim and Elliott's paper (2014) describes how they analysed a number of gold standard interventions in child maltreatment and surveyed the literature to identify further good evidence outcome studies. Using this knowledge they identified the common elements across the various types of maltreatment and then a team of professionals used this work to develop intervention modules targeting abusive and neglectful parenting and the associated impairment of children's health and development.

Bentovim in Chapter 7 describes how this approach can be made available for front-line practitioners through the use of the training resources *Hope for Children and Families Modular Systemic Interventions: Targeting Abusive Parenting and the Associated Impairment of Children. Building on Strengths, Modifying Difficulties* (Bentovim 2014) whilst Chapter 8 demonstrates through a case example how these *Hope for Children and Families* resource materials can be used in practice.

Child sexual abuse remains a major concern despite its being the subject of Henry Kempe's C. Anderson Aldrich Lecture in 1977 (Kempe 1978). UK studies (Cawson *et al.* 2000; Grubin 1998; Radford *et al.* 2013) suggest that:

- 1 in 6 children have been sexually abused by the age of 17

- 8 out of 10 children know their abusers

- a minority of abuse is by parents/step-parents

- the vast majority of child sexual abuse is not reported to the police.

Findlater in Chapter 9 describes a comprehensive multi-level approach to eradicating child sexual abuse. There four essential targets: offenders/potential offenders, victims/potential victims, specific situations in which abuse has occurred/is more likely to occur and communities/families. In addition there are three levels of prevention: primary, secondary and tertiary. He argues that there are therefore 12 points of focus for prevention efforts. He calls for the widespread adoption of approaches at every level, to prevent sexual abuse through educational approaches and to provide channels to identify and intervene with victims, perpetrators and families.

The Special Representative of the Secretary-General on Violence against Children, Marta Santos Pais (Office of the Special Representative of the Secretary-General on Violence against Children 2013) in her recent Global Survey assessing progress since the 2006 United Nations Secretary-General's *World Report on Violence against Children* found that whilst progress has been made it is 'too slow, too uneven and too fragmented to bring violence against boys and girls to an end' (p.xiii). She is clear that:

> *Preventing and ending violence against children requires a global effort on an unprecedented scale – an effort that includes political leaders as well as ordinary citizens, and children as well as adults. The cost of inaction – for every child, and for nations' social progress – is simply too great to be tolerated. (p.vii)*

Chapter 10 reviews the contribution of each chapter in this book to supporting the implementation of the policy and practice recommendations set out in the *World Report on Violence against Children* presented in 2006 to the United Nations by Pinheiro, the independent expert leading the study. It is our intention that this book will make a meaningful contribution to the continuing massive global effort required to end violence against children.

References

Bentovim, A. (ed.) (2014) *Hope for Children and Families Modular Systemic Interventions: Targeting Abusive Parenting and the Associated Impairment of Children. Building on Strengths, Modifying Difficulties.* London: Child and Family Training. Available at www.childandfamilytraining.org.uk accessed on 13 March 2014.

Bentovim, A. and Elliott, I. (2014) 'Hope for children and families: Targeting abusive parenting and the associated impairment of children.' *Journal of Clinical Child and Adolescent Psychology 1*, 16, 270–285.

Cawson, P., Wattam, C., Brooker S. and Kelly, G. (2000) *Child Maltreatment in the United Kingdom. A Study of the Prevalence of Child Abuse and Neglect.* London: NSPCC.

Chorpita, B.F., Bernstein, A. and Daleiden, E.L. (2011) 'Empirically guided coordination of multiple evidence-based treatments: An illustration of relevance mapping in children's mental health services.' *Journal of Consulting and Clinical Psychology 79*, 4, 470–480.

Department for Education (2013) *Characteristics of Children in Need in England, 2012–13*. London: Department for Education. Available at www.gov.uk/government/uploads/system/uploads/attachment_data/file/254084/SFR45-2013_Text.pdf, accessed on 14 April 2014.

Grubin, D. (1998) *Sex Offending against Children: Understanding the Risk*. Police Research Series Paper 99. London: Home Office.

Kempe, C.H. (1978) 'Sexual abuse, another hidden pediatric problem. The 1977 C. Anderson Aldrich Lecture.' *Padiatrics 62*, 3, 382–389.

Kempe, C.H., Silverman, F.N, Steele, B.F. Droegemueller, W. and Silver, H.K. (1962) 'The battered-child syndrome.' *Journal of the American Medical Association 181*, 1, 17–24.

Office of the Special Representative of the Secretary-General on Violence against Children (2013) *Toward a World Free from Violence. Global Survey on Violence against Children*. New York: United Nations. Available at http://srsg.violenceagainstchildren.org/sites/default/files/publications_final/toward_a_world_free_from_violence.pdf, accessed on 14 April 2014.

Pinheiro, P.S. (2006) *World Report on Violence against Children*. Geneva: United Nations.

Radford, L., Corral, S., Bradley, C. and Fisher, H. (2013) 'The prevalence and impact of child maltreatment and other types of victimization in the UK: Findings from a population survey of caregivers, children and young people and young adults.' *Child Abuse and Neglect 37*, 10, 801–813.

Chapter 2

BURDENS AND CONSEQUENCES
OF CHILD MALTREATMENT

Arnon Bentovim

Introduction

Kempe's identification of the sequential recognition of different forms of maltreatment in the community represented a milestone in the process of recognition and responding to child maltreatment. This process will hopefully lead the way to its eradication. A further milestone was the publication of *The World Report on Violence against Children – United Nations* (Pinheiro 2006). This report followed an extensive two-year period of consultation regionally and nationally through expert thematic meetings, liaison with the committee on the UN Rights of the Child, and an advisory panel including the voices of children and young people.

Pinheiro wrote in his introduction, 'The full range and scale of all forms of violence against children is only just becoming visible, as was the evidence of the harm it does' (Pinheiro 2006, p.26). The report includes a statement by the late Nelson Mandela:

> *The children must, at last, play in the open velds, no longer tortured by the pangs of hunger or ravaged by disease, or threatened with the scourge of ignorance, molestation and abuse, and no longer required to engage in deeds whose gravity exceeds the demands of their tender years. (Nelson Mandela, quoted by Pinheiro 2008, p.26)*

The study was the first United Nations study to engage directly and consistently with children, underlying and reflecting their status as rights holders, and their right to express views on all matters that affect them and have those views given due weight.

The central message was that 'no violence against children is justifiable, and all violence against children is preventable' (Pinheiro

2006, p.26). Pinheiro points out that in contradiction to the human rights obligations entered into by many countries in the international community, which recognises children's developmental needs, much violence against children remained legal, state authorised and socially approved. The study aimed to provide a turning point to end the justification of violence against children, whether accepted as 'traditional or disguised as discipline'. Whatever the justification violence needed to stop. The study also marked the recognition of extreme forms of violence against children, not included in the initial definitions of various forms of abuse. This includes:

A sexual exploitation and trafficking

A female genital mutilation

A the worst forms of child labour

A the impact of armed conflict, ethnic conflict

A the involvement of children and young people in such conflicts as victims or organised into roles to take part in violence, sometimes against their own families and others

A the impoverishment of families, and failures to support family life and to provide the basic needs for children are associated with all such forms of exploitation.

The full spectrum of violence against children comprises those children exposed to physical, sexual and psychological abuse in their homes, in school, in care, in the justice systems and in their communities. The spectrum also includes more recently identified concerns about exploitation. As well as active forms of violence and abuse, there are also concerns about the pervasive neglect of children's needs, the failure to respond to their needs – e.g. the Harvard Neglect Project's concept of a failure of 'serve and return' – the absence of meaningful interaction. A degree of neglect is 'Normal' in family life, implying that at such times the child has to develop their own resources, rather than expecting a parent will attend to their every need. Care can only be 'good enough'. Serious neglect in a family context is where children's needs are unmet, with resulting harmful effects on health and development, and serious neglect in institutional care is when there is extensive harm to children's health and development, including brain development (Center on the

Developing Child (Harvard University) 2012). A key element in the international recognition and response to child maltreatment and to its eradication is the adoption of a children's rights perspective.

A children's rights perspective

Reading *et al.* (2009), writing in the series of reviews of child maltreatment in the *Lancet*, have pointed out that the basic response of child protection systems has generally followed a conventional medical approach of diagnosis and treatment. That is, to identify, assess and intervene to prevent further harm. They argue that although this approach has achieved considerable progress, it does not necessarily include primary prevention, to prevent the occurrence of child maltreatment in the first place. They point out that as understanding grows of the factors which make child maltreatment more likely to occur, which we review at a later point in this chapter, it is becoming increasingly clear that a primary preventative public health approach is required. Reading *et al.* (2009) argue that a consideration of children's rights strengthens public health and child protective approaches.

Children's rights are delineated in the principles and articles of the UN Convention on the Rights of the Child (UNCRC). Crucially these rights include:

⋏ the provision of services

⋏ participation in society

⋏ rights of protection and care.

The UN committee on the Rights of the Child argues that all three types of rights are inseparable and should be implemented as a package rather than selectively. Reading *et al.* point out that UNCRC obtains its power to influence policy and enforce accountability by being a legal instrument rather than a moral code, even though based on ethical and moral foundations. These principles can be brought to bear on a public health and protection approach, to help reduce prevalence and consequences of maltreatment, and eventually to contribute to eradication. The introduction of the Assessment Framework in the UK marked a shift from a focus on protection of children who had been maltreated, taking a holistic view of whether the needs of the child in all areas of their functioning were being met, whether parenting supported the child, and the influence of individual and family factors on the capacity to provide adequate parenting. This approach puts the need for protection in the context of whether the overall needs of the child are being met – an approach which brings together the three limbs of the children's rights perspective: provision of services, participation in society and rights of protection and care.

Gilbert *et al.* (2009a) in their *Lancet* paper on the burden and consequences of child maltreatment in high income countries point out that a broader perspective on child welfare rather than a focus on child protection may be more successful in reducing the incidence of child maltreatment in the community – an important step towards eradication. Woodman and Gilbert explore these issues in Chapter 3 of this book.

Failures to recognise and report abuse and violence against children

It is universally recognised that only a small proportion of acts of abuse and violence against children is reported and investigated, and few perpetrators are held to account. In many parts of the world there are no systems available to record or thoroughly investigate reports of violence against children. The study by Gilbert *et al.* (2009a) emphasises the fact that official statistics based on reports dramatically underestimate the true magnitude of the problem.

There are various explanations for the lack of reporting, which include: silence in the face of a significant power discrepancy between the perpetrator and the child; fear of the consequences of reporting; fear related to stigma attached to reporting violence, particularly where patriarchal notions of family 'honour' are valued above human rights and wellbeing of females. Persistent social acceptance of some types of violence against children is a major factor, laws condoning 'reasonable' or 'lawful' corporal punishment reflect societal approval of violence when disguised as discipline. The absence of reliable data in many countries makes assessing the process towards tracking the level of maltreatment challenging.

Pinheiro (2006) points out that data gathered for the international UN study revealed that very few children – the estimated figure was only 2.4 per cent – were legally protected from corporal punishment. A report of a school-based student health survey revealed that between 20 and 65 per cent of school age children reported having been verbally or physically bullied in school in the previous 30 days.

A recent United Nations Children's Fund (UNICEF) global study of independent human rights institutions for children – *Championing Children's Rights* (UNICEF 2013) has reported on progress through the global emergence of bodies 'promoting children in public decision making and discourse'. Over 200 public institutions are now reported, which monitor and promote children's rights through scrutiny of governments, influencing public policy and intervening on behalf of individual children.

The issue of how child maltreatment is defined

The definition of child maltreatment is central to how it is recognised, managed and prevented. For example, there has been considerable debate about whether young people involved in prostitution, who may be under the required minimum age to give informed consent, should be considered victims of child abuse, or as part of a network of perpetrators of an organised criminal activity. It is now recognised that such young people are subject to significant exploitation, and such exploitation is part of a spectrum of violence against children and child maltreatment in general.

Child maltreatment is generally defined as any 'act of commission or omission by a parent or other caregiver that results in harm, potential for harm or threat of harm to a child'. Harm itself does not need to be intended, definitions can range from those which focus on the specific act, or the specific form of harm caused to children by parents or carers. Thus the following basic forms of child maltreatment are recognised:

- ⅄ **Physical abuse** is defined as the intentional use of physical force or implements against a child that results in or has the potential to result in physical injury.

- ⅄ **Sexual abuse** is defined as a completed or attempted sexual act; some form of sexual contact which attempts to interact sexually with a child. Non-contact forms of sexual grooming are also recognised.

- ⅄ **Psychological or emotional abuse** is intentional behaviour that conveys to a child that he or she is worthless, flawed, unloved, unwanted, in danger or valued only in meeting another's needs.

▲ **Neglect** is failure to meet a child's basic physical, emotional, medical/dental or educational needs, failure to provide adequate nutrition, hygiene or shelter or failure to ensure a child's safety.

▲ **Witnessing intimate partner violence** includes any incident of threatening behaviour, violence or abuse between adults who are or have been intimate partners of family members, irrespective of sex or sexuality.

These definitions do not include notions of 'collective harm and exploitation', for instance caused through placement in institutional care, harmful policies and laws, avoidable war, conflict, failure of governance or social disruption (Reading *et al.* 2009). Gill in 1975 was reported as attempting to provide a more comprehensive definition, which focused on:

Inflicted gaps or deficits between potential and actual circumstances of living which would facilitate the optimum development of children, to which they should be entitled and to their actual circumstances, irrespective of the sources or agents of the deficit. (p.83)

Thus any act of commission or omission by individuals, institution, government of society together with their resultant conditions which 'deprive children of equal rights and liberties and/or interfere with their optimal development constitute, by definition abusive or neglectful acts or conditions' (p.75). Although it may be helpful to subsume maltreatment as an aspect of overall child wellbeing, the disadvantage is that the concept can be too broad and encompassing. This makes epidemiological measurement impossible, it becomes difficult to create a focus to target, and compromises attempts to assess the success of any intervention.

The UN study (Pinheiro 2006) adopted the definition of:

The intentional use of physical force or power, threatened or actual, against a child by an individual or group that either results in, or has a high likelihood of resulting in actual or potential harm to the child's health, survival, development or dignity. (p.28)

The inclusion of the abuse of power broadened the definition to include acts of commission or omission that resulted in emotional harm and allowed social, political and economic violence to be incorporated. The addition and use of the term exploitation broadens the scope of maltreatment from simple violence; it offers the possibility of operationalising the basic definition to enable epidemiological measurement and monitoring. The focus on intentional harm helpfully defines epidemiological and public health monitoring and links specific policy responses to a children's rights-based approach. Extending the boundaries to encompass social and environmental harm would be much more difficult to define epidemiologically or through public health monitoring, although, as Reading *et al.* (2009) point out, from a child's perspective the source of harmful action may be indistinguishable. They argue that drawing together a rights-based and public health approach can be complementary and when harnessed in concert they can act as a highly effective instrument of change in policy, professional activity and public values.

Recent research from the Kempe Centre presented at the European Regional Conference of the International Society for the Prevention of Child Abuse and Negelct (ISPCAN) (Fluck *et al.* 2013) is testing the impact of introducing a *differential response* when child protection agencies investigate allegations of maltreatment, as an approach to reforming traditional child protection services. They are testing the value of this approach by evaluating an alternative response pathway which differs from the more usual investigation response pathway by offering a welfare approach, engaging the family, seeing what services would be required, promoting family engagement with the case worker. It is testing whether evaluating the needs of the family, rather than investigating the presence of specific forms of maltreatment, results in adequate protection and family satisfaction. Preliminary results indicate that the alternative response approach results in parents feeling more satisfied and feeling they have received help, in comparison to the investigation pathway parents who reported feeling more worried and angry. It was observed that safety was not compromised. This approach, which overtly embraces a children's rights perspective, eliminating a maltreatment-substantiation decision creates the opportunity for more human relational interaction. Such an approach requires the screening out of situations where there is clear evidence of a child being seriously harmed and in need of active protection, a minority compared to the overwhelming incidence of neglect in the United States. Woodman and Gilbert in Chapter 3 discuss this issue from a health perspective, and note to date differential response approaches have not been so successful.

It is therefore argued that the potential legal status of a children's rights convention, plus the strength of a public health approach, could provide the scientific rigour behind monitoring, identifying risks and assessment of preventative intervention, and strengthen the arm of health and social care practitioners. The children's rights perspective has had an important role in focusing concerns about sexual exploitation, trafficking of children, and involvement in abusive interaction through the internet. Findlater in Chapter 9 discusses a comprehensive approach to preventative approaches to child sexual abuse.

The provision of universal services and adequate financial support for families can go a considerable way to ensure that parents have adequate resources to bring up their children. In such a context, where services are available, it becomes a more straightforward task to demonstrate the compulsory intervention is justified within the terms of the European Convention on Human Rights. Child welfare legislation is gradually incorporating children's rights principles, the need for children to have a voice in assessment and court proceedings, and considering that the child's welfare is of paramount important. These principles are being given greater and greater prominence. The outcome of intervention can be considered in terms of the health and wellbeing of a child, and also whether it upheld the child's rights.

Reading *et al.* (2009) examine studies of young children in institutional care in Europe. These have become a major concern in terms of the damaging effects of the high levels of neglect and abuse which can be perpetrated within institutional care, and the failure to recognise the rights of children to a family life, either their own families, or a culturally appropriate alternative. They point out that the state has a direct responsibility to the child to promote her or his rights, the child should have the right to make a direct call on the state, and to be heard in the development of legislation and policy, besides receiving adequate provision. Review of the process of promoting family care for the many children placed in institutions demonstrates the positive impact of providing for their rights to family life and protection. The process of changing the culture of a country from provision of institutional care to provision of family care through fostering and adoption is a significant contribution to eradication of maltreatment.

Measuring the frequency and severity of child maltreatment

Gilbert *et al.* (2009a) point out that in reviews of the incidence of different forms of abuse in their study, 80 per cent or more of maltreatment is perpetrated by parents or parental guardians. Sexual abuse is mostly perpetrated by acquaintances or other relatives, less by parents or parental figures. Reliable measurement of frequency and severity, and therefore of tracking whether progress is being made towards the goal of eradication, is not straightforward. The basic ways of assessing the frequency and severity of child maltreatment include:

- ▲ self-reports from victims old enough to comply with surveys

- ▲ studies based on parents reporting severe physical punishment or neglectful patterns of care

- ▲ official statistics from agencies investigating reports of abusive behaviour.

The gap between the low rates of maltreatment substantiated by child protection agencies and the tenfold higher rates reported by victims or parents underlines the fact that very few children who are maltreated receive official attention.

The recent observation in the UK when there has been extensive public focus about child protection issues as a result of the publication and publicity about major abusive cases, for example Victoria Climbié and Baby P (Peter Connolly) (Munro 2011), has resulted in significant increases in reporting of abusive concerns. This has resulted in child protection systems feeling overwhelmed and a significant increase in children being placed in the care system.

Gilbert et al. (2009b) point out that the discrepancies between official statistics and community studies are even more substantial when examined by the ages of maltreatment. There is an inverse relation between the rate of reporting and age for all categories of maltreatment apart from sexual abuse. There appears to be an increased risk of under-reporting by parents of younger children and under-detection of maltreatment by child protection agencies in older children.

In their Lancet paper on recognising and responding to child maltreatment Gilbert et al. (2009b) noted that the most frequent source of referral for investigation of child protection concerns come from the educational context. Younger children who had not been identified previously may present with impairment of health and development when they start school, suggesting that they have been subject to abuse, which leads to referral. Chapter 3 by Woodman and Gilbert updates their work in this field from a health perspective. Gilbert et al. (2009b) in their systemic review identified that of the 1 in 30 children who are physically abused by a parent, and who were investigated by social welfare services, only a small proportion were monitored in accordance with a child protection plan.

Sexual abuse is perpetrated with significant frequency, with a similar discrepancy between reports to authorities and actual experiences of abuse. Figures in the region of between 5 to 10 per cent of girls and 1 to 5 per cent of boys are exposed to penetrative sexual abuse during childhood, although figures that include any form of sexual abuse are much higher. Gilbert *et al.* (2009b) state that these estimates are supported by a result of a meta-analysis of worldwide studies and probably indicate a lower limit of the true rate of sexual abuse because of under-reporting.

Self-report studies in the UK and USA showed that 8–9 per cent of women and about 4 per cent of men reported exposure to severe psychological abuse, and around 9 per cent of children or their mothers reported neglect – persistent absence of care or instances in which a child was hurt. The prevalence of witnessing intimate partner violence during childhood ranged from 8–10 per cent to 24 per cent in the USA.

Detailed examination of reports indicate the high rate of *multiple types of maltreatment* and *ongoing risk factors* in the child, such as disability or chronic medical disorders, or in the parents such as alcohol misuse, indices of social adversity associated with multiple or chronic maltreatment, particularly neglect. Such multiple or cumulative factors make intervention in neglect particularly challenging, and the rates of neglect in the community remain stubbornly high. Finkelhor (2008) and his colleagues pointed out the way that maltreatment by parents or caregivers merges with other forms of victimisation: the more extensive the abuse experienced by a child, the more likely it is they were subject to further victimisation, so that being exposed to one type of maltreatment puts a child at higher risk of other types of repeated exposure to harm over time. The more frequent the exposure to different forms of maltreatment, the more likely is the severity of the maltreatment, and the severity of the impact on the child's mental health, and the likelihood that as such children and young people move into adolescence they will be responsible for harmful responses to others. This observation is confirmed in the Baltic Seas epidemiological studies (Svedin and Priebe 2007) The research model was to interview older school aged young people across the countries bordering the Baltic sea, demonstrating the harmful effects of cumulative victimisation on mental health and increasing risks of young people perpetrating harmful behaviour –

aggression and sexual behaviour against peers, contributing to peer and partner abuse.

This perspective indicates that an approach to eradication requires maltreatment to be thought of not as a single one-off event but a chronic condition, where cumulative forms of adversity, victimisation and associated mental health and disruptive behaviours become increasingly likely, maintaining a process of abuse and reabuse.

What are the factors which determine that child maltreatment is more likely to occur?

If a broad ranging public health/children's rights perspective is to be developed then it is essential to have a picture of what are the determinants of maltreatment. It is helpful to look at:

⋏ the characteristics of the victim

⋏ the characteristics of the parents and community

⋏ whether there has been evidence of change over time

⋏ different patterns from different countries to provide a more detailed picture of the determinants and, therefore, the remedies.

The *ecological model* is a conceptual approach which identifies the way in which factors such as personal history and characteristics of the victim or perpetrator, his or her family, the immediate social context and characteristics of the larger society, play a role in the determination whether child maltreatment is more likely to occur. The model recognises that a wide and complex range of factors increases the risk of abuse, can maintain a chronic process of maltreatment, or may alternately protect against abuse.

This model emphasises the combination of factors, acting at different levels, which influence the likelihood that abuse will occur, recur or cease, by describing *risk* and *protective* factors. This model has influenced the establishment of the Assessment Framework in the UK, and in other countries, described in detail in a later chapter. This marked the shift from a focus on protection to a holistic approach which encompassed the way that the needs of the child are met through parenting capacity and individual family and environmental factors.

Characteristics of the victim

Key elements of the potential victim associated with child maltreatment are the nature of the child and the characteristics of the child associated with his or her experience of parenting. The primary attachment between a parent and infant has a profound impact on the growing child's responsiveness, and how he or she will be responded to in turn. Attuned responsive parenting is the key protective factor. A secure attachment is associated with a better prospect for the unfolding potential of the child to function emotionally in a positive manner (Bentovim *et al.* 2009). Factors in the child or parent can undermine this process. The result of a mismatch and a failure to develop a secure attachment may lead to the development of insecure or disorganised attachment patterns. The resulting patterns of avoidance, clinging, or alternately clinging and rejecting can put a child at significant risk in the longer term, through evoking rejection and irritation in the carer. This process is examined in detail by Barlow in Chapter 4.

A factor which has been demonstrated to be particularly undermining to the establishment of secure attachment is the birth of a child with a disability or chronic health problems. In our own series of maltreated children identified at the Hospital for Sick Children (Glaser and Bentovim 1979) we noted an unusually high number of children who were subjected to physical or emotional abuse or neglect who also showed evidence of disability or chronic illness. We considered that this association was in part related to the particular population of children admitted to the hospital. However, community studies have demonstrated that a child with a disability is at increased risk of maltreatment. A study in the USA (Sullivan and Knutson 2000), demonstrated that the cumulative prevalence of any maltreatment is 9 per cent of non-disabled children, whereas it is 31 per cent of disabled children.

There are known risks of girls being sexually abused and boys being at greater risk of harsh physical punishment. Cultural views about girls and boys also contribute, over-valuing male children in some societies, girls being under-valued and therefore more likely to be seen as being an appropriate target for sexual responses. Girls are therefore more at risk of sexual abuse, whilst boys, if they fail to meet expectations, are likely to be subject to harsh punishment. Temperamental factors such as the higher activity levels and non-compliant responses in boys' behaviour may also play a role in perceiving them as unruly, justifying harsh parenting responses.

There are associated groups of children who are especially vulnerable in the community: children from ethnic minorities and marginalised groups, children living or working on the streets, children in institutions and detention and children living in communities in which inequality, unemployment and poverty are highly concentrated, child refugees and other displaced children (Pinheiro 2006).

Although we have discussed risk factors, there is growing awareness that some children are particularly resilient and have a variety of protective factors available including a history of good quality early care, or genetic factors associated with resilience. The Rutter *et al.* study on Romanian orphanages (Rutter *et al.* 2009) demonstrated in initial studies that the later the child was placed for adoption with good quality care, following removal from the orphanage, the more likely they were to have been exposed to poor care, neglect and significant early adversity. As a result they were more likely to show adverse effects despite good subsequent care. However, later studies (Rutter *et al.* 2009) demonstrated that there was a group of children who, despite exposure to extensive early adversity, showed far less in the way of longer term impairment of health and development. This is hypothesised as being related to genetic and epigenetic factors promoting resilience.

Characteristics of parents and community

Gilbert *et al.* (2009a) point out that it is a difficult task to identify the specific parental characteristics which increase the risk of child maltreatment. Many factors are inextricably clustered: poverty, mental health problems, low educational achievements, alcohol and drug abuse, and exposure to maltreatment as a child. These factors are strongly associated with parents who subsequently maltreat their children. Parents who are young, have low educational levels or have an inaccurate knowledge about children's development and unrealistic expectations of their children are also likely to be more of a risk to their children. Factors associated with the parent's experience of adversity and harmful life experiences may result in them having an impaired capacity to respond positively to an infant's seeking care. This can result in an inter-generational pattern of insecurity, which can result in a disorganised attachment process and increased risk. Impaired emotional regulation is an associated response to the cumulative set of factors associated with risks of abusive parenting; negative emotions, anger rejection and blame may be triggered by the infant and young child's normal needs. This was described as a 'Trauma Organised Systemic process' (Bentovim 1995) where a parent attempts to 'divest' themselves of overwhelming emotional states by 'investing' the child with characteristics which justify abusive action. This is a characteristic of individuals who themselves have developed emotional, disruptive or personality disorders, particularly of a borderline nature associated with their own life adversity. This may be complicated when there has been substance abuse, or when partner relationships increase the intensity of negative emotional states. (Bentovim *et al.* 2009).

Particular associations have been noted, for example, by Dixon, Brown and Hamilton Jiacritis (2005), who noted the increased risk of maltreatment when a parent themselves had been abused in their own childhood, and had a partner who was violent. A parent focused on their own emotional needs has significant difficulties in understanding the changing needs of the developing child and modulating their responses, which can result in the failure of attunement, attachment difficulties and subsequent neglectful and abusive parenting.

Other factors which are associated with higher risks include single parenthood, social isolation and socio-economic disadvantage. They are increased when there are partners who are transient and have no biological relationship with a child, when there is intimate partner violence. Neighbourhoods characterised by poverty, unemployment and a general sense of anomie within the community increase isolation, reinforce family stress and do not provide alternate sources of social support for children or parents.

Jaffee and his colleagues (2007) have described 'bi-directional interaction'. This attempts to delineate the way that genetic predispositions to respond in a particular way to environmental exposure or gene–environment correlation may have a significant part to play in whether maltreatment will occur. For example, they quote that a child may inherit a predisposition to exhibit externalising problem behaviours which may increase the odds of evoking harsh parenting.

No single risk factor is necessary or sufficient, no single risk factor in itself will predict whether maltreatment will occur. For example, although parental mental illness is clearly a risk factor, the majority of parents with mental illness do not behave abusively, and most maltreated children do not themselves have parents with a mental illness. So risk factors interact with each other and with protective factors in a complex fashion.

Therefore maltreatment is conceptualised as a multiply determined process, determined by forces at work in the individual, in the family, in the community and in the cultural contexts. These determinants modify each other. The question is what are the implications of this finding for intervention, for the eradication of maltreatment? It could be argued that general risk factors may be modifiable through policy changes such as providing better income levels for parents, ensuring good quality education and managing the socio-economic context of families in general. Targeting factors which occur very frequently can also be the target for intervention; for example, substance abuse of a parent is a common factor present in both couple violence and child maltreatment – a focus on substance abuse can have a significant impact.

The burden of child maltreatment

Introduction

The burden on the life of a child who has been maltreated is potentially extensive, with a major impact on the individual and on future family life, and is a burden on the community. There is a significant risk of death as a result of maltreatment. Children who have been maltreated develop psychiatric and medical disorders at significantly higher rates than non-maltreated children. The long-term negative health consequences of child maltreatment are not limited to the childhood years, ill effects last well into adult life; children who have been maltreated are at risk of mental health and medical disorders and have significant degrees of mental health problems such as long-term depression. There is an associated impairment in various aspects of cognitive, social and emotional development. This is associated with poorer educational achievements, lower earnings and higher risks of being engaged in criminal activities. Therefore child maltreatment has significant personal and societal costs.

Child death and maltreatment

The most tragic manifestation of the burden of child maltreatment is the many child deaths every year due to deliberate killing (homicide) or neglect (manslaughter) (Gilbert *et al.* 2009a). The World Health Organization (WHO) has estimated that 100,000 such deaths in children younger than 15 occur worldwide every year, between 0 and 6 per cent of all child deaths, and around 7 per cent of child deaths due to any injury. Substantial under-reporting occurs; biological parents are responsible for four-fifths of cases, step-parents for the remainder. Child homicide is most frequent in infancy, perpetrated by either parent, but for older children the perpetrator is usually a male. The rates vary, but peak incidence have been noted to coincide with periods of economic and political transition when community services were severely disrupted. A concerning figure in terms of eradicating maltreatment is that, despite improvement in child protection, there has been very little decrease in the rate of child homicides (Fox and Zawitz 2007; WHO Regional Office for Europe 2008).

Quantifying the impact and consequences of child maltreatment

Since Kempe's original observations drew attention to the Battered Child Syndrome, there has been interest in attempting to quantify the long-term consequences of child maltreatment. Gilbert *et al.* (2009a) summarised the evidence for associations between different types of maltreatment and outcomes related to education, mental health, physical health and violence or criminal behaviour. As a result of developments in the field, Gilbert *et al.* were able to bring together findings from cohort studies which prospectively ascertained whether children were maltreated or not, and were able to follow up those children over time to identify later outcomes. They were able to compare these findings to cross-sectional studies which measured maltreatment retrospectively on the basis of self-reporting in adolescence or adulthood. The advantage of prospective studies includes the fact that the relationship between maltreatment and subsequent outcomes are not affected by recall bias or memory on the basis of outcome. There is also the opportunity to adjust for social and individual confounding factors as they occur.

Education and employment

The impact on educational achievement has been demonstrated consistently through longitudinal studies. These have shown that maltreated children have lower educational achievements than their peers and are more likely to receive special education. The differences are substantial. In addition as in other areas, effects are cumulative. When maltreatment, for example neglect, is associated with failure to attend school or absence of encouragement, this in turn reflects on school performance. These associations were still present when adjustments were made for family and social characteristics. The New Zealand population cohort study by Boden, Horwood and Ferguson (2007) demonstrated the persistence of failures of educational achievements into adult life. In addition maltreatment has long-lasting economic consequences for affected individuals, abused and neglected. In prospective studies they were more likely to be carrying out menial or semi-skilled occupations, and significantly fewer remained in work.

Mental health

An extensive set of studies reviewed by Gilbert *et al.* (2009a) demonstrated that child maltreatment increases the risk of child mental health problems, including internalising disorders – anxiety and depression – and externalising disorders – aggression and acting out behaviour. Witnessing rather than experiencing violence is also associated with an increased risk of child mental health problems, although exposure to intimate partner violence is also associated with other family adversity. Evidence suggests that the different types of maltreatment are cumulative in their impact on later mental health, for example the work of Finkelhor (2008) already referred to. The most significant mental health problem associated with maltreatment in later life is an increased risk of depression in adolescence and adulthood (Sternberg *et al.* 2006). This effect is independent of other individual and family factors which increase the risk of depression. Around a quarter to a third of maltreated children at follow-up meet the criteria for major depression in their late 20s. This is a substantial burden.

Child maltreatment also increases the risk of post-traumatic stress disorder, associated with recurrent intrusion of frightening thoughts and memories, sleeping difficulties and detachment. Again both prospective and retrospective studies consistently show associations between different forms of abuse and post-traumatic stress, effects which can be long-lasting. Widom (1999) demonstrated that the risk of post-traumatic stress disorder was about twice as high as in a controlled group in cohort studies. It was noted that various factors increase the risk of post-traumatic disorder, including a lack of a supportive parent or caring figure, and continuing exposure to a family context where parents have substance abuse or problems with violence which perpetuates post-traumatic symptoms in children and young people. Penetrative sexual abuse appears to be unique in causing long-term harmful psychological sequelae.

Bentovim *et al.* (2009) noted the developmental process: children growing up in a context of adversity and abuse; evidence of disorganised attachments; long-term impacts on failure to manage emotional regulation; failures in developing a capacity for mentalisation related to a capacity to understand the thoughts and feelings of others and themselves, and the risk of developing personality functioning characterised by preoccupation with the individual's functioning, and difficulties understanding and perceiving children's needs.

The vulnerability to psychosis has been demonstrated by Tianari and colleagues (Tianari *et al.* 2004). They followed up with children who carried a high genetic loading for schizophrenia and who were adopted into a non-biological family. It was noted they were more likely to demonstrate a psychotic disorder if they were placed in a family with higher levels of dysfunction than if they were placed in a family with more positive characteristics. The link between child maltreatment and the triggering of psychotic illness has also been related to the cumulative impact of adverse life events from childhood (Varese *et al.* 2012).

There are concerns that both physical and sexual abuse are associated with the risk of attempted suicide. Again the impact of multiple adversities plays a role. Several cohort studies reported the relationship between suicidal phenomena and self-injurious behaviour. Exposure to severe physical abuse or penetrative sexual abuse is also reported to have a particular relationship with self-injurious behaviour. Self-cutting responses are reported to be strongly associated with sexual abuse but not with physical abuse or neglect (Evans, Hawton and Rodham 2005; McHolm, MacMillan and Jamieson 2003; Yates, Carlson and Egeland 2008).

Prospective studies note the cumulative effect of child maltreatment and the risk for substance abuse, alcohol problems in adolescence and adulthood (Simpson and Miller 2002; Widom, Marmostein and White 2006). This is confirmed for females, less clear for males.

Prevention of alcoholism and its associated health, safety and social problems for girls and young women is an important goal, including concerns about foetal alcohol syndrome and attachment failures. Again, multiple forms of abuse and other childhood adversities such as witnessing violence lead to an increase in the risk of self-reported alcohol and drug misuse in adulthood.

Physical health outcomes

Gilbert *et al.* (2009a) note that a number of longitudinal studies have reported strong associations between physical abuse, neglect and sexual abuse and obesity, which persists after accounting for family characteristics in individual risk factors (Noll *et al.* 2007; Thomas, Hyponnen and Power 2008). There is also some suggestion in retrospective studies of a link between child sexual abuse and eating disorders, for example bulimia and anorexia (Brewerton 2007).

The classic large cross-sectional ACE study by Felliti *et al.* (1998) correlated the presence of childhood adversity and later health effects. They too noted the cumulative effects of childhood adversities and their relationship with ischemic heart disease, cancer, chronic lung diseases, skeletal fractures and liver damage.

Aggression, crime and violence

In addition to a variety of painful experiences relating to child maltreatment, including psychological pain, depression, post-traumatic stress disorder and actual physical pain, abused and neglected children are at increased risk of becoming aggressive and inflicting pain and suffering on others and perpetrating crime and violence. The study by Skuse *et al.* (1998) and Salter *et al.* (2003) which followed up sexually abused boys from early childhood into adult life was planned to test the belief that if a male had been sexually abused they would be significantly more likely to perpetrate harmful sexual behaviour at a later stage. The research demonstrated that it was not sexual abuse itself which was the key factor, but the association with physical abuse, emotional rejection and observing physical violence towards a parent.

The work of Finkelhor (2008) demonstrated that the more stressful and traumatic events a young person was exposed to, the more likely they were around the age of 14 to demonstrate externalising behaviour towards other children and young people. Those boys who had themselves suffered the most extreme adversity were more likely to perpetrate interpersonal violence; those suffering less to attack property.

The evidence from these studies demonstrates that although event forms of abuse, physical and sexual, can be harmful in their own right – particularly penetrative abuse – when such events are associated with pervasive process forms of maltreatment – neglect and emotional abuse in an unsupportive context – there is a much higher likelihood of long-term negative impacts in the areas of education, mental and physical health, aggression and perpetuating the cycle of violence.

In turn understanding this process has clear implications for intervention which will be explored in future chapters exploring primary, universal, targeted, secondary, tertiary and blended prevention approaches (see Chapter 5 by Prinz for more details). Barlow discusses primary prevention in Chapter 4; Prinz a 'blended' form of prevention applied on a population basis in Chapter 5; Chorpita and colleagues an approach to making evidence-based approaches to intervention widely available in Chapter 6; Bentovim an application of this approach targeting abusive parenting and the impairment of children in Chapters 7 and 8 and Findlater a comprehensive preventative strategy for sexual abuse in Chapter 9.

The cost of child maltreatment

American studies have attempted to assess the actual cost to the community of child maltreatment. Fang *et al.* (2012) have attempted to put a financial cost to the failures in education, mental health, physical health and aggression, crime and violence. They estimated the costs of providing special education, the costs of short-term healthcare, the costs of longer-term healthcare and the losses in productivity. They also calculated the child welfare costs associated with the fact that educational attainment, physical health, mental health, aggression, crime and violence have inter-generational effects, and will impact on the individual but will also have a significant role in subsequent parenting difficulties. They estimated future child welfare costs and criminal justice costs and estimated that the financial burden to the community amounted to more than $200,000 for each individual being maltreated. They emphasise, therefore, on grounds not only of the burden to the individual but the financial burden to the community, that eradication of child maltreatment would be a major saving, both for individual and community health and for the financial wellbeing of society.

Childhood exposure to maltreatment: life-long health burdens

Moffitt and the participants of the Klaus-Grawe 2012 Think Tank (Moffitt and the Klaus-Grawe Think Tank 2013) have drawn together contemporary evidence on the impact of exposure to childhood maltreatment on biological functioning, and on the psychological and physiological effects which can in turn lead to adverse effects on lifelong health. They have brought together this information recommending that Stress Biology Research and Intervention Science can join forces to tackle the problem.

They examine the evidence base in relation to stress sensitive measures for the following biological functions:

▲ inflammatory reactions

▲ telomere–chromosome erosion

▲ epigenetic methylation and gene expression

▲ in the brain from neuro-imaging and neuropsychological testing.

They assert that this review examines the hidden effects of maltreatment which are emerging from Stress Biology Research in recent years. Stress-sensitive biomarkers of 'toxic stress' in young people are known to be associated with elevated risks for a variety of health concerns in midlife, elevated risk of heart disease, metabolic diseases, immune diseases and stroke (Danese and McEwen 2012; Miller, Chen and Parker 2011). The authors stress that understanding these effects can open the door to early prevention.

Treating adults who have contracted illnesses associated with such factors is less successful than identifying prevention targets that can be tackled successfully in early life before disease takes hold. Because of the change in birth rate, they argue children are an increasingly valuable economic commodity, and ensuring lifelong health and productivity of each child-citizen is becoming more important for the world economy than ever before. They argue that:

> *[If the] hypothesis that stressors such as violence which precipitate psychological problems for young people also undermine their life-long physical health, this would imply that the burden of adult and later life diseases could be reduced by successfully improving the psychological health of children. (Moffitt and the Klaus-Grawe Think Tank 2013, p.1620)*

The definition of violence to children/child maltreatment which they use in their review is:

A personal exposure to physical acts of intentional harm in the first 18 years of life, including physical or sexual maltreatment by parents or other caregivers, physical or sexual assault by other adults, exposure to parents or caregivers, domestic violence, bullying by peers or siblings, or violence within the context of an adolescent romantic relationship.
(Moffitt and the Klaus-Grawe Think Tank 2013, p.1625)

This definition builds on the definitions described earlier and each of these forms of victimisation can be defined.

Although stress is a normative aspect of development and can facilitate development by promoting coping and capacity, stress can overwhelm coping capacities and have a toxic impact. They argue that if childhood toxic stress in general affects health, then studying violence exposure provides a reasonable test of this hypothesis. It would be a considerable advantage if it could be concluded how much of the disease burden in the population could be reduced, if all violence-exposed children were successfully treated. However this is more difficult to ascertain.

Childhood violence, exposure and inflammatory outcome

Inflammatory outcomes occur as a result of microbial factors, allergens, irritants and toxic compounds. Endogenous inducers include biological signals produced by stressed, damaged or otherwise malfunctioning tissues. An immune system response occurs and a successful inflammatory response eliminates the signals that originated the response and the repair of damaged tissues. If inducers become chronic, the protective acute inflammatory response can become a detrimental, chronic inflammatory state. Chronic inflammatory states can lead to significant tissue damage leading to age-related diseases. Being exposed to victimisation has been linked to abnormal immune system functioning with elevated inflammation levels (Danese *et al.* 2007, 2011). In the Dunedin study, children who had been exposed to maternal rejection, harsh parenting and disruptive caregiver changes, physical or sexual abuse were almost twice as likely as non-maltreated children to show elevated levels of multiple-clinically relevant inflammation biomarkers (Danese *et al.* 2007). These findings were independent of other co-occurring early life adversities.

In the UK environmental risk longitudinal twin study (Danese *et al.* 2011) physically maltreated children experiencing current depression exhibited elevated inflammation levels. The inflammatory alterations of victims of child maltreatment also showed similar alterations in adult life. The link with depression appears to be the strongest. It is argued that reversing the effects of victimisation on inflammation could potentially reduce a health burden.

Childhood violence exposure and telomere–chromosome erosion

Telomeres are the repeated sequences which cap and protect the ends of chromosomes. They play a major role in regulating cellular replication. Moffitt and the Klaus-Grawe Think Tank (2013) state that this plays a major role in regulating cellular replication and that a lack of protection progressively shortens the process of cellular replication. Cells enter a state of reduplicative arrest called senescence. Shorter telomere length and increased erosion rates are associated with a higher risk of morbidity and mortality (Cawthon *et al.* 2003). It is reported that studies now provide initial support for an association between childhood stress and telomere length. It is reported that these findings occur regardless of key potential confounding factors. Institutional care has been significantly associated with short telomere length in middle childhood (Drury *et al.* 2011). Children who experience two or more kinds of violent exposure showed significantly more telomere erosion (Shalev *et al.* 2012). This is a controversial area and it is asserted that more research is needed to clarify the mechanisms which govern telomere length dynamics.

Childhood violence exposure and epigenetic outcome

The epigenome is a second layer of information which regulates genomic functions, including when and where genes are actively expressed. Epigenetics refers to the reversible regulation of various genomic functions, occurring independently of the DNA sequence, mediated through biochemical changes in DNA methylation and chromatin structure. A growing body of evidence shows that epigenome changes over the life course are correlated with age, an important observation given the prevalence of many chronic diseases increasing with advancing age. There are also interference factors in the environment. Changes in DNA methylation following early life stress have been associated with long-term changes in gene expression and behaviour. Although there has been extensive research in rats and monkeys demonstrating a causal relationship between maternal care and epigenetic differences, this work needs replication. Moffitt and the Klaus-Grawe Think Tank

(2013) indicate that there have been some interesting reports linking immune function and inflammation in post-traumatic stress disorder with differential DNA methylation. This is an important area of future research which is yet to be developed.

Childhood violence exposure and gene expression outcomes

There have been a small number of studies which examine biological systems and stress, the hypothalamic-pituitary-adrenocorticol (HPA) access and the inflammatory system. There is some evidence that gene expression may mediate the effects of stress exposure on the immune system and sympathetic nervous system. This is related to maltreated children showing higher basal levels of the stress hormone cortisol, and blunted cortisol responses to psychological stress when pharmacological challenges are made (Danese and McEwan 2012). This may have a relationship with states of arousal, and extreme responses to 'reminders' of an individual's traumatic experiences which results in extensive anxiety of re-experiencing, or the triggering of behavioural responses to such reminders, which can include an 'identification with the aggressor'.

Child violence exposure and mental health outcomes

Moffitt and the Klaus-Grawe Think Tank (2013) argue that although mental health outcomes are not a direct measure of stress, such responses should be included because they regard mental health as an indicator of the health status of the brain (Lupien et al. 2009). There is mounting evidence that mental disorders involve physiological changes, such as elevated inflammation. Health studies indicate that the disability caused by psychiatric disorders is growing, particularly in high income nations where the burden of communicable disease is now reduced. Mental health conditions account for over 40 per cent of all years lived with disability (World Health Organization 2001). Childhood victimisation has now been demonstrated to be a risk for many different kinds of mental health disorders, for co-morbidity of different mental health problems, an unfavourable course of illness and poor responses to treatment. In the Dunedin study, child maltreatment significantly predicted a more recurrent course of major depressive disorders, anxiety disorders, alcohol dependence disorders and drug dependency. We have already referred to the link to schizophrenia, psychosis and psychotic-like symptoms and some recent new work confirms the link (Arseneault *et al.* 2011; Toth *et al.* 2011; Varese *et al.* 2012).

Childhood violence, exposure and neuropsychological health outcomes

It is argued that an aggregate of an individual's neuropsychological abilities, the IQ, is a proven, reliable predictor of life-long health, or cause of morbidity, late life frailty and early mortality (Deary *et al.* 2004). The theory linking toxic childhood stress to brain health includes the sequential chain in which early life chronic stress disrupts the homeostasis of stress biology systems including inflammation and HPA access hormones – cortisol – which in turn disrupts normal development of brain structure, in turn producing observable deficits in stress-exposed individuals' tested memory, memory and attention capacities. Moffitt and the Klaus-Grawe Think Tank (2013) review the research which tests these linked factors. In the Dunedin follow-up carried out for this review, it was noted that formerly maltreated children had deficits in working memory, visuo-spatial perceptual reasoning and verbal comprehension as late as 38 years of age. It is argued that re-establishing homeostasis in stress hormone and inflammatory systems at an early stage can enhance mental abilities.

Child violence exposure and neuro-imaging outcomes

A considerable number of neuro-imaging studies using a variety of current technologies has investigated the associations with maltreatment. The majority of studies have examined adult patients with trauma-related conditions, or adults who retrospectively report maltreatment. Two excellent and comprehensive reviews (Hart and Rubia 2012; McCrory, De Brito and Viding 2010) have concluded that structural and functional findings have consistently appeared in the circuitry of the frontal and limbic regions of the brain, which includes structures such as the hippocampus, amygdala, striatum, prefrontal cortex, auto frontal cortex and anterior cingulate. Various areas of the brain have been studied in detail, particularly the amygdala, because it is involved in fear conditioning and negative emotionality and stress can affect its size.

Another brain structure of interest is the prefrontal cortex, because it matures late and may be especially vulnerable to early stress, and because it is involved in emotional regulation with its link to impulsiveness and lack of empathy noted in young people responsible for disruptive behaviour. Such biological abnormalities are consistent with a pattern of adaptation to environmental threat and heightened hypervigilance. However, such adaptations incur longer-term costs, with increasing vulnerability to mental health difficulties. Moffitt and the Klaus-Grawe Think Tank (2013) state that the issue of causality is not fully addressed and there is a lack of before and after studies. In examining the issue of intervention the view is put forward that the preventative intervention approaches can impact on the stress biological processes described as mediating exposure to violence and the later manifestation of serious impacts on health.

Implications for intervention

The effectiveness of intervention is generally demonstrated by changes in psychological functioning, changes in attachment, in relationships, in capacities to show more appropriate degrees of mindfulness, mentalisation and evidence of enduring change in functioning. Moffitt and the Klaus-Grawe Think Tank (2013) drew attention to the early research demonstrating change in biomarkers tracking improvement in functioning. MacMillan *et al.* (2009) have extensively reviewed both primary prevention approaches and those that aim to prevent the recurrence of maltreatment and the associated impairment of children's health and development. In later chapters we will demonstrate how our appreciation of this research can help to develop primary, universal and targeted, secondary and tertiary approaches – preventing the recurrence of abusive parenting and the associated impairment of children: interventions which can be made widely available to front-line practitioners to prevent the occurrence or reverse the impact of violence and maltreatment.

How effective are the policy and practice in different countries?

Recognition and response to child maltreatment has been a significant feature of the high income countries reviewed by Gilbert and her colleagues (2009b). The question is has the work and intervention of child protection systems in countries across the world made a difference? Gilbert and her colleagues (2012) attempted to answer this question by reviewing the impact of policy and practice in a number of high income countries. It has already been pointed out that a limited number of children who are referred and investigated by child protection services.

Gilbert *et al.* established that a significant number of children and young people who had been maltreated but were not referred to child protection services were in contact with many different professional organisations. This emphasises the fact that professionals do not refer to child protection services, and only refer a minority, perhaps because of lack of certainty about the diagnosis, or concerns about whether there will be an adequate response. Interviews with children and young people who are old enough to be able to report indicate that there is a decrease in physical and sexual abuse in the UK, the USA and other countries. Despite some general evidence for a reduction in physically and sexually abusive actions, there is a continuing and persistent problem of neglect – the neglect of neglect, the absence of an awareness of children's needs. Neglect is universal in many parts of the world and is the most commonly recognised form of maltreatment, for example in the USA.

Gilbert *et al.* (2012), in their comparison of six countries, were interested to see whether there were consistent trends in indices within each of the countries they studied. They were then able to compare from country to country, as well as within the countries themselves. They noted that the trends for violent deaths were stable over time, and there were increasing trends of placement in out-of-home care. Although rates of deaths were stable or decreasing, out-of-home care placements were increasing, indicating that there has not been a significant decrease in the most severe forms of maltreatment. In all developed countries injury-related deaths are going down, perhaps a reflection of better healthcare, or that severely injured children are more effectively treated. The consistent increase in out-of-home care, particularly in infancy, perhaps suggests that this response may be being utilised as a form of early intervention rather than the last resort. There was no evidence for a consistent decrease or increase across all child maltreatment indices in the six countries, indicating that progress has been limited despite some of the findings of less physical and sexual abuse in childhood.

The lowest absolute rates of maltreatment were noted in Sweden, far lower than in the USA. Gilbert *et al.* (2012) observed that Sweden spent more on child protection and has implemented more universal prevention initiatives over the last 20 years than other countries. As a result there is less emphasis on child protection or out-of-home care intervention. The reverse is true for the USA, other countries being somewhere in between, with initiatives towards universal prevention, others emphasising protection and intervention of removing children from care. Gilbert *et al.* (2012) concluded that policy can make a significant impact, particularly when focused on increasing universal prevention initiatives.

The overall conclusion is that, with the exception of Sweden, a country able to invest extensively in universal prevention, the indices for child maltreatment remain stable, giving an indication of the challenge to eradicate child maltreatment.

The evidence suggests that a preventative approach that emphasises primary, universal and targeted intervention, as well as secondary and tertiary interventions, to prevent the recurrence of maltreatment and the associated impairments will need to be applied intensively. This is justified by evidence from a number of countries and a number of specific research interventions. We will discuss the notion of a blended prevention approach in Chapter 5 (Prinz) and the way that this contrasts with primary prevention approaches, as in Chapter 4 (Barlow), and interventions to prevent the recurrence of maltreatment and the associated impairment of children's health and development (Chapters 7 and 8, Bentovim).

The case for prevention

Mikton and Butchart (2009) carried out an analysis of child maltreatment prevention, systematically reviewing reviews to synthesise recent evidence on the effectiveness of universal and selective child maltreatment preventative interventions. They argue that child treatment prevention is posed to become a global health priority due to four main factors:

▲ First, that retrospective and prospective studies have established that child maltreatment has strong, long-lasting functions on brain architecture, psychological functioning, mental health, health risk behaviours and social functioning, life expectancy and healthcare costs.

▲ Second, the full implication of these effects on human capital formation, the workforce and ultimately social and economic development is now becoming better understood.

▲ Third, epidemiological studies have clearly established that child maltreatment is not peculiar to the west but is a truly global phenomenon that occurs in lower middle income countries at higher rates than in wealthier countries.

⅄ Fourth, evidence strongly suggests that treating and later trying to remedy the effects of child maltreatment are both less effective and more costly than preventing it in the first place.

Mikton and Butchart reviewed over 3000 studies through their search strategies. They included 26 reviews summarising 298 publications. Seven main types of interventions were included:

⅄ Early childhood home visitation (Olds *et al.* 2000) – Trained personnel visited parents and children in their homes, providing support, education and information to prevent child maltreatment. They also seek to improve child health and parental caregiving abilities.

⅄ Parent education programmes (Lundahl, Nimer and Parsons 2006) – These interventions are usually centre-based, delivered in groups, aiming to prevent child maltreatment by improving parents' childrearing skills, increasing parental knowledge of child development and encouraging positive child management strategies.

⅄ Child sexual abuse prevention programmes (Finkelhor, Asdigian and Dziuba-Leatheman 1995) – Universal programmes often delivered in schools teaching children about body ownership, differences between good and bad touch and how to recognise abusive situations.

⅄ Programmes to modify abusive head trauma (Dias *et al.* 2005).

⅄ Multi-component interventions (Kees and Bonner 2005) including services such as family support, pre-school education, parenting skills and childcare.

⅄ Media-based interventions – These are media campaigns to raise public awareness, often regarded as a critical part of any child maltreatment strategy.

⅄ Support and mutual aid groups – Aiming to strengthen parents' social network.

Extensive review of the evidence indicated that four of the seven types of universal and selective interventions are promising for preventing actual child maltreatment: home visiting, parent education, abusive head trauma prevention and multi-component programmes. Evidence for others is mixed, for example, sexual abuse prevention programmes give children information but whether they actually prevent a child being harmed is more questionable.

Mikton and Butchart's review of child maltreatment prevention has been reinforced by the MacMillan *et al.* (2009) review published in the *Lancet*. They reviewed some additional studies which were not available in the Mikton and Butchart review. Barlow updates issues concerning primary prevention in Chapter 4, and Prinz the use of a 'blended' approach in Chapter 5 – combining Triple P parenting and a media-based intervention, which had a significant impact on the incidence of child abuse registration on a population base.

The use of specific preventative interventions needs to be looked at in the total context of an approach described earlier which emphasised that a focus on the welfare of children and their families and the community can have a significant impact on the rate of child maltreatment, versus an approach which puts more emphasis on protection and identification. These approaches may well provide a clear direction for eradication of child maltreatment. In later chapters we will explore the value of these preventative approaches in more detail (Barlow, Prinz, Bentovim and Findlater).

References

Arseneault, L., Cannon, M., Fisher, H.L., Polanczyk, G., Moffitt, T.E. and Caspi, A. (2011) 'Childhood trauma and children's emerging psychotic symptoms: A genetically sensitive longitudinal cohort study.' *American Journal of Psychiatry 168*, 65–72.

Bentovim, A. (1995) *Trauma Organised Systems: Physical and Sexual Abuse in Families.* London: Karnac.

Bentovim, A., Cox, A., Bingley-Miller, L. and Pizzey, S. (2009) *Safeguarding Children Living with Trauma and Family Violence: A Guide to Evidence Based Assessment, Analysis, Planning and Intervention.* London: Jessica Kingsley Publishers.

Boden, J.M., Horwood, L.J., Fergusson, D.M. (2007) 'Exposure to childhood sexual and physical abuse and subsequent educational achievement outcomes.' *Child Abuse and Neglect 31*, 1101–1114.

Brewerton, T.D. (2007) 'Eating disorders, trauma and comorbidity – focus on PTSD eating.' *Eating Disorders 15*, 4, 285–304.

Cawthon, R.M., Smith, K.R., O'Brien, E., Sivatchenko, A. and Kerber, R.A. (2003) 'Association between telomere length in blood and mortality in people aged 60 years or older.' *Lancet 361*, 393–395.

Center on the Developing Child (Harvard University) (2012) 'The persistent absence of responsive care disrupts the developing brain: Working paper 12.' Available at www.developingchild.harvard.edu, accessed on 15 April 2014.

Danese, A., Pariante, C.M., Caspi, A., Taylor A. and Poulton R. (2007) 'Childhood maltreatment predicts adult inflammation in a life-course study.' *Proceedings of the National Academy of Sciences 104*, 1319–1324.

Danese, A., Caspi, A., Williams, B., Ambler, A. *et al.* (2011) 'Biological embedding of stress through inflammation processes in childhood.' *Molecular Psychiatry 16*, 244–246.

Danese, A. and McEwen, B.S. (2012) 'Adverse childhood experiences, allostasis, allostatic load, and age-related disease.' *Physiology and Behaviour 106*, 29–39.

Deary, I.J, Whiteman, M.C., Starr, J.M., Whalley L.J. and Fox, H.C. (2004) 'The impact of childhood intelligence on later life: Following up the Scottish mental surveys of 1932 and 1947.' *Journal of Personality and Social Psychology 86*, 130–147.

Dias, M.S., Smith, K., de Gueagry, K., Mazur, P., Li, F. and Shaffer, M.L. (2005) 'Preventing abusive head trauma in infants and young people: A hospital based parent education programme.' *Paediatrics 115*, 470–477.

Dixon, L., Brown, K. and Hamilton Jiacritis, C. (2005) 'Risk factors of parents abused as children.' *Journal of Psychology and Psychiatry 45*, 47–57.

Drury, S.S., Theall, K., Gleason, M.M., Smyke, A.T. *et al.* (2011) 'Telomere length and early severe social deprivation: Linking early adversity and cellular aging.' *Molecular Psychiatry 17*, 719–727.

Evans, E., Hawton, K. and Rodham, K. (2005) 'Suicidal phenomena and abuse in adolescents: A review of epidemiological studies.' *Child Abuse and Neglect 29*, 45–58.

Fang, X., Brown, D.S., Florence, C.S. and Mercy, J.A. (2012) 'The economic burden of child maltreatment in the United States and implications for prevention.' *Child Abuse and Neglect 36*, 156–165.

Felitti, V.J., Anda, R.F., Nordenberg, D., Williamson, D.F. *et al.* (1998) 'Relationship of childhood abuse and household dysfunction to many of the leading causes of death in adults. The Adverse Childhood Experiences (ACE) Study.' *American Journal of Preventive Medicine 14*, 245–258.

Finkelhor, D. (2008) *Childhood Victimisation: Violence, Crime and Abuse in the Lives of Young People.* Oxford: Oxford University Press.

Finkelhor, D., Asdigian, N. and Dziuba-Leatheman, J. (1995) 'The effectiveness of victimisation prevention instruction: An evaluation of children's responses to actual threats and assault.' *Child Abuse and Neglect 19*, 141–153.

Fluck, J., Merkel-Holguin, L., Harn, A. and Runyan, D. (2013) 'Differential response: Looking at this child welfare reform from an evidence and rights based perspective.' Presentation at ISPCAN European Regional Conference, 16 September.

Fox, J.A. and Zawitz, J.A. (2007) *Homicide Trends in the United States.* Washington DC: US Department of Justice.

Gilbert, R., Fluke, J., O'Donnell, M., Gonzalez-Izquirdo, A.G. *et al.* (2012) 'Child maltreatment: Variation in transient policies in six developed countries.' *Lancet 379*, 758–772.

Gilbert, R., Kemp, A., Thoburn, J., Sidebotham, P. *et al.* (2009b) 'Recognising and responding to child maltreatment.' *Lancet 373*, 167–180.

Gilbert, R., Spatz Widom, C., Browne, K., Fergusson, D., Webb, E. and Janson, S. (2009a) 'Burden and consequences of child maltreatment in high income countries.' *Lancet 373*, 68–81.

Gill, D. (1975) 'Unravelling child abuse.' *American Journal of Orthopsychiatry 45*, 346–356.

Glaser, D. and Bentovim, A. (1979) 'The abuse of children with disability.' *Child Abuse and Neglect 3*, 565–575.

Hart, H. and Rubia, K. (2012) 'Neuroimaging of child abuse: A critical review.' *Frontiers in Human Neuroscience 6*, 1–24.

Jaffee, S.R., Caspi, A., Moffitt, T.E., Polo-Tomas, M. and Taylor, A. (2007) 'Individual, family, and neighbourhood factors distinguish resilient from non-resilient maltreated children: A cumulative stressors model.' *Child Abuse and Neglect 31*, 231–253.

Kees, M.R. and Bonner, B.L. (2005) *Child Abuse Prevention and Intervention Services.* New York: Kluwer Academic Plenum.

Lundahl, B.W., Nimer, J. and Parsons, B. (2006) 'Preventing child abuse, a meta analysis of parent training programmes.' *Research in Social Work Practice 16*, 251–263.

Lupien, S.J., Paulozzi, L., Melanson, C., Simon, T. and Arias C. (2009) 'Effects of stress throughout the lifespan on the brain, behaviour and cognition.' *Nature Reviews Neuroscience 10*, 434–445.

MacMillan, H., Wathen, C.N., Barlow, J., Fergusson, D.M., Leventhal, J.M. and Taussig H.N. (2009) 'Interventions to prevent child maltreatment and associated impairment.' *Lancet 373*, 250–266.

McCrory, E., De Brito, S.A. and Viding E. (2010) 'Research review: The neurobiology and genetics of maltreatment and adversity.' *Journal of Child Psychology and Psychiatry 51*, 1079–1095.

McHolm, A.E., MacMillan, H.L. and Jamieson, E. (2003) 'The relationship between childhood physical abuse and suicidality among depressed women: Results from a community sample.' *American Journal of Psychiatry 160*, 933–938.

Mikton, C. and Butchart, A. (2009) 'Child maltreatment prevention: A systematic review of reviews.' *Bulletin of the WHO 87*, 353–361.

Miller, G.E., Chen, E. and Parker, K.J. (2011) 'Psychological stress in childhood and susceptibility to the chronic diseases of aging: Moving toward a model of behavioural and biological mechanisms.' *Psychological Bulletin 137*, 959–997.

Moffitt, T.E. and the Klaus-Grawe Think Tank (2013) 'Childhood exposure to violence and long and life-long health: Clinical Intervention Science and Stress Biology Research joined forces.' *Development and Psychopathology 25*, 1619–1634.

Munro, E. (2011) *The Munro Review of Child Protection, Final Report: A Child Centred System.* London: Stationery Office.

Noll, J.G., Zeller, M.H., Trickett, P.K. and Putnam, F.W. (2007) 'Obesity risk for female victims of childhood sexual abuse: A prospective study.' *Paediatrics 120,* 361–367.

Olds, D., Hill, P., Robinson, J. and Song, N.C. (2000) 'Update on home visiting for pregnant women and parents of young children.' *Current Problems of Paediatrics 30,* 109–241.

Pinheiro, P.S. (2006) *World Report on Violence against Children.* Geneva: United Nations.

Reading, R., Bissell, S., Goldhagen, J., Harwin, J. *et al.* (2009) 'Child maltreatment is a violation of children's human rights. How do we address this more effectively?' *Lancet 373,* 332–343.

Rutter, M., Beckett, C., Castle, J., Kreppner, J., Stevens, S. and Sonuga-Burke, E. (2009) *Policy and Practice Implications from the English and Romanian Adoption Study.* London: BAAF.

Salter, D., McMillan, D., Richards, M., Talbert, T. *et al.* (2003) 'Development of sexually abusive behaviour in sexualised victimised males: A longitudinal study.' *Lancet 9,* 356, 471–46.

Shalev, I., Moffitt, T.E., Sugden, K., Williams, B. *et al.* (2012) 'Exposure to violence during childhood is associated with telomere erosion from 5 to 10 years of age: A longitudinal study.' *Molecular Psychiatry 18,* 5, 576–581.

Simpson, T.L. and Miller, W.R. (2002) 'Concomitance between childhood sexual and physical abuse and substance use problems. A review.' *Clinical Psychology Review 22,* 27–77.

Skuse, D., Bentovim, A., Hodges, J., Stephenson, J. *et al.* (1998) 'Risk factors for development of sexually abusive behaviour in sexualised victimised adolescent boys: cross sectional study.' *British Medical Journal 18,* 317, 175–179.

Sternberg, K.J., Lamb, M.E., Guterman, E. and Abbott, C.B. (2006) 'Effects of early and later family violence on children's behaviour problems and depression: A longitudinal, multi-informant perspective.' *Child Abuse and Neglect 30,* 283–306.

Sullivan, P.M. and Knutson, J.F. (2000) 'Maltreatment and disabilities: A population-based epidemiological study.' *Child Abuse and Neglect 24,* 1257–1273.

Svedin, C.G. and Priebe, G. (2007) 'The Baltic Sea Study on adolescent sexuality.' *Novo Report,* 159–177.

Thomas, C., Hyponnen, E. and Power, C. (2008) 'Obesity and type 2 diabetes risk in mid-adult life: The role of childhood adversity.' *Paediatrics 121,* 1240–1249.

Tianari, P., Wynne, L., Sarri, A., Lahti L. *et al.* (2004) 'Genotype environmental interaction in schizophrenia spectrum disorders.' *British Journal of Psychiatry 184,* 216–222.

Toth, S.L., Pickering Stronach, E., Rogosch, F.A., Caplan, R. and Cicchetti, D. (2011) 'Illogical thinking and thought disorder in maltreated children.' *Journal of the American Academy of Child and Adolescent Psychiatry 50,* 659–668.

UNICEF (2013) *Championing Human Rights – A Global Study of Individual Human Rights Centres for Children.* Geneva: UNICEF.

Varese, F., Smeets, F., Drukker, M., Lieverse R. *et al.* (2012) 'Childhood adversities increase the risk of psychosis: A meta-analysis of patient-control, prospective- and cross-sectional cohort studies.' *Schizophrenia Bulletin 38,* 661–671.

Widom, C.S. (1999) 'Posttraumatic stress disorder in abused and neglected children grown up.' *American Journal of Psychiatry 156,* 1223–1229.

Widom, C.S., Marmostein, N.R. and White, H.R. (2006) 'Childhood victimization and illicit drug use in middle adulthood.' *Psychology of Addictive Behaviours 20,* 394–403.

World Health Organization (2001) *The World Health Report 2001 – Mental Health: New Understanding, New Hope.* Geneva: WHO.

WHO Regional Office for Europe (2008) *Health for All Database (HFA-DB).* Copenhagen: WHO Regional Office for Europe.

Yates, T.M., Carlson, E.A. and Egeland, B. (2008) 'A prospective study of child maltreatment and self-injurious behaviour in a community sample.' *Development Psychopathology 20,* 651–671.

Chapter 3

THE ROLE OF HEALTH SERVICES IN RESPONDING TO CHILD MALTREATMENT

Jenny Woodman and Ruth Gilbert

Introduction

In this chapter we show how the evidence base challenges the conventional view of the role that healthcare providers should play in tackling child maltreatment. In Section 1 we first highlight widespread calls for a public health approach to child maltreatment and describe what this means in terms of a response from healthcare services. We go on to describe the child welfare system in the UK as the context within which health professionals are working and explain why we have coined the term 'maltreatment-related concerns'. In the second section of the chapter, we outline what is known about the recognition of child maltreatment in primary and secondary care.

In the third section we turn our attention to how health professionals respond to children who have prompted concerns about maltreatment. We demonstrate how the evidence base points to the need for wider contribution from healthcare services, including a direct response to children and families. Although policy and research have not fully defined this contentious, wider role, we outline the evidence which suggests that it is being adopted in some form in current practice, particularly in primary care services. This direct response to children and families is based on noticing and responding to parental risk factors for child maltreatment and harmful parent–child interaction, which we argue is consistent with a preventive public health approach. Based on literature about current practice, we show how these front-line responses are a way of facilitating a diversity of subsequent pathways for a heterogenous population of patients who prompt concerns about child maltreatment in primary and secondary healthcare settings.

In the fourth section of the chapter we outline recent research on the effectiveness of direct responses by front-line health professionals to children and families across the spectrum of poor treatment of children through to maltreatment. Our discussion is grounded in the UK policy and service context but we draw on international research literature and the key concepts and arguments are applicable to other industrialised countries. Although the contribution of nurses and other healthcare staff is important, our focus is on the contribution of doctors in primary and secondary care.[1]

Section I: A public health approach to maltreatment

What is a public health approach to maltreatment?

Over the last two decades there has been increasing recognition that child maltreatment includes a range of severity that extends into the 'normal' population (Barlow and Calam 2011; Daniel, Taylor and Scott 2011; Gilbert, Woodman and Logan 2012; O'Donnell, Scott and Stanley 2008; Slep and Heyman 2008; Waldfogel 2009; Wolfe and McIsaac 2011). From this 'continuum' perspective (Wolfe and McIsaac 2011), behaviour towards and interaction with children ranges from the optimal to the severely abusive (Figure 3.1) and there is a continuum of child welfare. Conceptualising maltreatment as one end of this continuum makes it clear that there is no natural or obvious cut-off where poor treatment or poor parenting of children becomes 'maltreatment'. Unsurprisingly, the grey area between poor treatment and maltreatment can cause conceptual difficulty for both experts and members of the public when considering the types of acts, interactions or situations which might constitute maltreatment (Frameworks Institute 2013). Children in this grey area can be thought of as 'the marginally maltreated'; they might be experiencing mild maltreatment and/or not yet be seen to be suffering serious consequences from maltreatment (Waldfogel 2009).

The acceptance of the continuum model of child welfare has led to calls for a public health approach to responding to child maltreatment (Barlow and Calam 2011; Daniel *et al.* 2011; Gilbert *et al.* 2012;

---

1 Primary care services are the first point of contact for all patients within the healthcare system. In an English context this includes GPs, practice nurses and health visitors. Secondary care services are specialist services which are not usually the first point of contact within the healthcare system. In an English context this includes specialists such as paediatricians or cardiologists.

O'Donnell *et al.* 2008). A public health approach takes a population-based perspective which emphasises the importance of responding to need along the whole of the child welfare continuum. Fundamentally, a public health approach prioritises prevention and early intervention. As shown in Figure 3.1 such an approach focuses on risk factors across the population: it attempts to reduce maltreatment by 'shifting the curve' in order to improve outcomes for all children across the whole continuum. This approach is based on assumptions that the population in the middle and to the left of the curve (Figure 3.1) have some degree of risk and scope for improvement and that there are interventions that work across the distribution of child welfare.

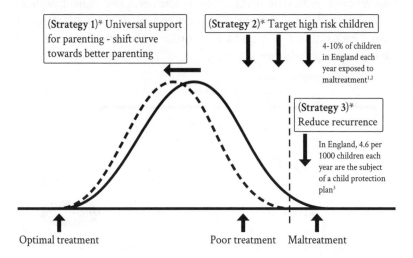

Figure 3.1 A public health approach to child maltreatment invests in universal support for parents (strategy 1) as well as targeting high risk children (strategy 2) and attempting to reduce recurrence where maltreatment has already occurred (strategy 3)

Source: Radford *et al.* (2011); Gilbert *et al.* (2012) and Department for Education (2012–13). Reproduced with permission from Gilbert *et al.* (2012).

A preventive public health approach makes sense if the line between poor treatment and maltreatment is viewed as unclear and if small benefits for the high numbers of children in the middle of the curve can lead to great benefit for the population as a whole. As described in Chapter 2, a public health approach is also strengthened by its compatibility with an approach that prioritises the rights of the child and evidence suggesting early intervention is the most effective approach in terms of outcome and costs.

In a public health approach, attempts to shift the parenting curve rely on universal and upstream interventions to address the major risk factors for harmful parent–child interaction which are rooted in parents' own life course and capacity, neighbourhood risk factors (such as deprivation, violence and lack of access to good schools and other services) and societal risk factors (for example, poverty and socio-economic inequalities; Barlow and Stewart-Brown 2003; Marmot 2010; Social Exclusion Task Force 2007). Alongside upstream and universal interventions, a public health approach can deliver targeted interventions to prevent maltreatment where need, risk of maltreatment and/or propensity to benefit is highest and to children and families where maltreatment is occurring in order to reduce recurrence and adverse consequences (see Figure 3.1).

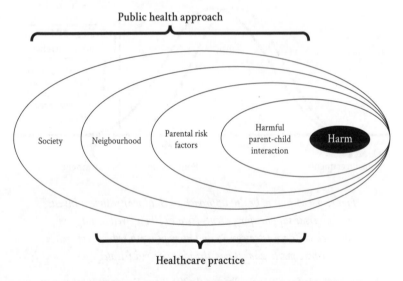

Figure 3.2 The contribution of healthcare services

From the perspective of healthcare services, opportunities for early intervention and prevention are located in the contact between health professionals and children or their parents or carers. As Figure 3.2 shows, addressing societal and neighbour risk factors for child maltreatment through upstream and universal interventions is usually beyond the scope of healthcare services. Instead, a preventive public health approach to maltreatment within healthcare services is likely to be characterised by efforts to recognise and respond to parental risk factors for maltreatment and harmful parent–child interaction (see Figure 3.2).

HEALTHCARE RESPONSES IN THE CONTEXT OF THE CHILD WELFARE SYSTEM

Responses to child maltreatment within healthcare services are shaped by the wider context of the child welfare system. In a UK context healthcare professionals should be able to use referrals to children's social care to help families access a range of interventions, including preventive and early interventions which are designed to support families at many stages of the child welfare continuum. However, provision of early intervention and support services by children's social care is not a right. Local authority decisions about offering family support services under Section 17 of the Children Act 1989 to an individual child in need and their family can take account of the resources available. As a result children and families who may benefit from services provided by children's social care might not always receive them. In the following section we describe policy aspirations to a public health approach within children's social care and outline what we know about the challenges of implementing this type of response in practice. As we will see in Sections 2 and 3, this is an important context for understanding how healthcare services might be able to implement preventive responses when professionals have concerns about child maltreatment.

The theory: a public health response

Similar to many other industrialised countries (Gilbert, Fluke *et al.* 2012; Trocme *et al.* 2013), the UK child welfare system is one of differential response (Children Act 1989). As the name suggests, the system includes multiple pathways to child welfare services. The multiple pathways were enshrined in primary legislation in response to arguments put forward in the late 1980s when the then Children Bill was being debated in Parliament. Later in the 1990s they were explicitly set out in statutory guidance following a national debate that the traditionally narrow focus on child protection, which required establishing evidence of harm and culpability, ignored the broader spectrum of child welfare need, caused delays and barriers to helping families and was directed towards coercive, and sometimes punitive, interventions (Child Welfare Information Gateway 2014; Department of Health 1995; Department of Health, Home Office and Department for Employment 1999; Parton

2011). The differential response system was designed to provide help at an earlier stage as well as preventing unnecessary statutory child protection investigations which could have serious adverse effects on a child and family and be costly.

Since the enactment of the Children Act 1989 there have been multiple pathways into child welfare services in the UK. Professional decisions about which pathway it is most appropriate to follow once a referral has been accepted by children's social care hinge on the concepts of 'children in need' and 'significant harm' which underpin the Children Act 1989. For children judged to be in need of services in order to achieve or maintain a 'reasonable standard of health and development' or because they are disabled, but who are not suffering or likely to suffer significant harm, there is a pathway to services, as a 'child in need' under Section 17 of the Children Act 1989. Child in need services are voluntary: families can choose whether or not to accept state intervention.

Reaching the threshold of 'significant harm' justifies compulsory state intervention in family life in accordance with Section 31 of the Children Act 1989. There is no absolute definition of significant harm: statutory guidance for professionals states that judgements should take into account the nature and severity of abuse, premeditation, impact on the child's health and development, parental capacity to meet the child's needs and the child's wider social environment (HM Government 2013). If a child is judged to be suffering or likely to suffer significant harm, statutory 'child protection' action should be initiated in accordance with *Working Together to Safeguard Children* (HM Government 2013).

Assessments and interventions can be coercive: if parents or caregivers do not comply or insufficient progress is made, legal action can be initiated to remove the child and place him or her in local authority care. Local Authority children's social care may provide services to safeguard and promote the child's welfare (under Part 111 of the Children Act 1989 which relates to Local Authority support for children and families) while Section 47 enquiries are being carried out or after protective action has been taken and an application is being made for a care or supervision order (Department of Health, Deparment of Education and Home Office 2000, paragraph 1.27). In England, in 2012–13, approximately seven times as many children received child in need services (3.6% of the child population) than were the subject of a child protection plan (0.46%, see Figure 3.3; Department for Education 2013).

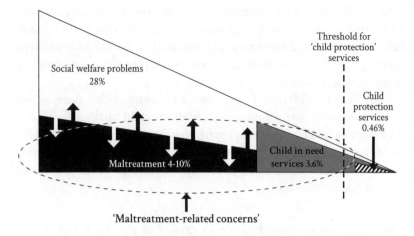

Figure 3.3 Maltreatment-related concerns

Social welfare problems: Twenty-eight per cent of 12,583 families with very young children were experiencing two or more hardships (for example: parental depression or alcohol or substance abuse, financial stress or overcrowding; Sabates and Dex 2012). Two per cent of 7,657 families were experiencing five or more indicators of disadvantage in 2005: no parent in the family is in work; family lives in poor quality or overcrowded housing; no parent has any qualifications; mother has mental health problems; at least one parent has a longstanding limiting illness, disability, or infirmity; family has low income (below 60 per cent of the median); or family cannot afford a number of clothing or food items), based on a cross-sectional survey of a representative sample in 2005 (Social Exclusion Task Force, 2007).

Maltreatment: At least four per cent (and as many as ten per cent) of children experience abuse or neglect each year in developed countries, based on self-reporting studies of children and parents (Finkelhor *et al.* 2009; Gilbert *et al.* 2009b; Gilbert *et al.* 2012b; Radford *et al.* 2011, Woodman and Gilbert 2013).

Child protection services: 0.466 per cent of children in England were made the subject of a child protection plan in 2012–13. (Department for Education 2013; Gilbert *et al.* 2012b; Woodman and Gilbert 2013).

Child in need services: 3.6 per cent of children in England were made the subject of a child in need plan in 2012–13 (Department for Education 2013).

For children who might benefit from early help but who do not meet thresholds of child in need (including children suffering or likely to suffer significant harm), early help assessments should be undertaken using, for example, the Common Assessment Framework (HM Government 2013). In such cases, non-social work professionals (including healthcare professionals) can undertake the assessment with support from children's social care and can act as the lead professional where a multi-agency response is required. *Working Together to Safeguard*

Children defines a lead professional role as one of advocacy, support and service coordination (HM Government 2013). This route to early help assessment and services is not intended to be used for children meeting thresholds of children in need (including significant harm or likely significant harm; HM Government 2013).

In theory, differential response and early help systems are compatible with the continuum model of child maltreatment and a preventive public health approach (Drake 2013). The alternative pathways are designed to allow professionals to access appropriately therapeutic and/or compulsory services for children across the whole child welfare continuum.

The reality: an overstretched service skewed to the sharp end

However, it is widely acknowledged that it has been difficult to sustain Parliament's vision for a broad focus on child welfare in practice (Parton 2011; Tunstill, Aldgate and Thoburn 2010). The child welfare system is pulled in two directions and, in the context of scarce resources, responses for those at the sharp end of the continuum (depicted in Figure 3.1) are prioritised over preventive services for those in the middle of the continuum (Parton 2011; Tunstill *et al.* 2010). Public and media outcry over failure of services to prevent child deaths has been identified as a key driver of the prioritisation of child protection responses (Parton 2011).

Although a far higher proportion of children in England receive child in need services than are the subject of child protection plan each year (see Figure 3.3), there is evidence that the need for supportive services outstrips provision in children known to children's social care and that the threshold of 'significant harm' is used as a rationing device in an overstretched service (Brandon, Lewis and Thoburn 1996; Broadhurst *et al.* 2010; Holmes *et al.* 2010). In interview studies in England (Canvin *et al.* 2007; Dale 2004; Davies and Ward 2012) and Ireland (Buckley, Carr and Whelan 2011), participating families and professionals stated that it was very difficult to access services before child protection thresholds for intervention were met (Buckley *et al.* 2011; Canvin *et al.* 2007; Dale 2004; Davies and Ward 2012). When scarcity of resources increases, either due to cuts in funding, increases in workload or both, child protection thresholds tend to go up (Mansell 2006). In a survey of 600 social workers and managers in England in 2013, 88 per cent said that recent austerity measures had resulted in increased thresholds for statutory child protection intervention (Community Care 2013).

There is a particular tendency for cases of serious neglect and emotional abuse to be 'downgraded' to child in need cases (Community Care 2012; Community Care 2013), where delayed and inadequate service provison can have disastrous consequences (Brandon *et al.* 2008). Insufficient service provision for children classified as 'in need' in the UK is likely to be exacerbated by ongoing cuts to funding which disproportionally affect services below the child protection threshold (correct at the time of writing in February 2014; Hopwood, Pharoah and Hannon 2012).

Referral to children's social care is necessarily an important part of the responses by other professionals and, indeed, referral to children's social care is a duty for professionals when they consider a child to be suffering or at risk of suffering significant harm (HM Government 2013). However, we have a picture of a child welfare system that is already operating at full capacity and in which thresholds are extremely high, even for acceptance of a referral. In this context it does not make sense for referral to social care and participation in social care procedures to be the only available response or the end point for other professionals when responding to concerns about abuse and neglect, particularly for children in the middle of the welfare continuum. Despite the emphasis in UK policy on interagency working beyond referral to children's social care (in assessment, planning and intervention) (HM Government 2013), responses by non-social work professionals have traditionally been conceptualised as referral to social care and, sometimes, participation in social care procedures (Daniel, Taylor and Scott 2010) and there are reports that many practitioners still see referrals as a way of handing over responsibility to children's social care (Davies and Ward 2012). However, in Section 3 we report some examples of how healthcare professionals in some settings are enacting direct responses to children and families who prompt concerns about abuse and neglect. These direct responses do not involve a mentality of transferring responsibility via onward referral to another agency.

Uncertainty about the balance of benefit and harm

Although it has been argued that the majority of clients and professionals experience child protection services positively (Drake 2013; Drake and Jonson-Reid 2007) studies from England (Cossar, Brandon and Jordan 2011; Dale 2004), Ireland (Buckley *et al.* 2011) and America (Drake and Jonson-Reid 2007) have reported that a substantial minority of clients were dissatisfied with the service and some experienced assessments and reviews as 'traumatic', 'stressful' and 'intimidating', saw child protection plans as stigmatising and as empty promises for services which were never delivered and felt as if they were living under the constant threat of having children removed. Although it is difficult to generalise from qualitative studies which have small numbers and are often unrepresentative due to differences in those who participate and those who do not, we can conclude that at least some clients experience intervention by children's social care as punitive and aggressive. This is in direct contrast to the stated aims of UK children's social services which were designed to be largely therapeutic and to support children and families to stay together wherever possible. Interview studies with professionals and opinion pieces suggest that some healthcare professionals (Gilbert *et al.* 2009a) and even social workers (Jones 2001; Wrennall 2010) share service users' misgivings about the net benefits of the child protection system, at least in some cases.

These views and experiences exist in the context of a very weak evidence base about the balance of harms and benefits of the child protection system for children and their families, either in the UK or elsewhere (Drake 2013). Two case-series of children who had experienced significant harm (Brandon and Thoburn 2008) or reunification following out-of-home care for neglect (Farmer and Lutman 2010; Lutman and Farmer 2013) reported that 40–60 per cent of children had good or satisfactory outcomes. However, in the same two studies a very substantial minority had poor outcomes with ongoing and serious concerns and/or a downward trajectory. Because there is no comparator group in case series, these studies can only provide extremely weak evidence: there is no way of separating the effect of the intervention from what would have happened in the absence of the intervention (Guyatt *et al.* 2011).

Cohort studies, which provide a comparator group, have been conducted on the effectiveness of out-of-home care for maltreated children in terms of well-being and development in three countries, namely England, USA and Sweden (Forrester and Harwin 2008; Wade *et al.* 2010, 2011; World Health Organization 2013). The studies in Sweden and the USA compared out-of-home care to in-home care (World Health Organization 2013) and the Wade *et al.* study compared outcomes for maltreated children who remained in care with those who returned home. The strength of this evidence and what can be inferred is contentious. One view, as articulated by Davies and Ward (2012) is that 'all three empirical studies in this Research Initiative [i.e., Lutman and Farmer 2013; Wade *et al.* 2011 and Ward, Brown and Westlake 2012], as well as an increasing body of other research [Forrester and Harwin 2008; Skuse and Ward 2003; Ward, Skuse and Munro 2005] demonstrate that the majority of children who become looked after in the UK today benefit from care' (pp.146–147).

Another view, which the authors of this chapter share, maintains that the evidence base is too weak to draw conclusions about whether or not out-of-home care works to improve outcomes across the population of maltreated children. We argue that selection bias in the cohort studies prevents reliable inferences being drawn about whether out-of-home care is beneficial or harmful. Because cohort studies include a comparison group, they are far more informative than case series, but they cannot fully measure and account for the child and family characteristics that influence the decision to remove a child (or reunify a child – as in the study by Wade *et al.* 2011). These same characteristics also influence the child's outcomes, resulting in confounding and biased results. A recent systematic review concluded that there was no clear evidence of benefit or harm of out-of-home-care for maltreated children in terms of developmental outcomes (World Health Organization 2013, Chapter 4). The systematic review included only comparative studies that had taken into account confounding due to child or family characteristics. Only studies from Sweden and the USA were sufficiently robust to meet the inclusion criteria for the review, which provides the best available evidence on the effectiveness of placement into out-of-home care in developed country settings (Post, de Beer and Guyatt 2013).

As the equivocal nature of the evidence is driven largely by methodological weaknesses in the observational study designs (we do not know that the intervention works, rather than we know it does not work), researchers have called for randomised controlled trials of child protection interventions, including out-of-home care (Drake 2013; World Health Organisation 2013). We also advocate using randomised controlled trials to evaluate reunification and placement into care where there is uncertainty among practitioners and to evaluate other standard child protection interventions including child protection plans and/or referral to children's social care. Ethically, randomised trials can only occur where there is genuine uncertainty about whether or not to offer the intervention to the child (Davies and Ward 2012; Drake 2013; World Health Organization 2013). Results from robust randomised controlled trials are the surest way to settle the debate about the impact of out-of-home care (and other interventions) for maltreated children.

Summary

First, despite its aims, the child welfare system faces significant barriers in responding effectively to children across the child welfare continuum and thresholds for acceptance of referrals are high and thresholds for service provision higher still. This is recognised in mixed accounts of children's social care from parents, some of whom will have had children removed or been under scrutiny, and professionals. There is a lack of evidence about the balance of benefit and harm of out-of-home care across the population of maltreated children. As we shall see later, in Section 3, high thresholds and professional ambivalence about the child welfare system have been identified as key drivers of sub-optimal identification and response to child maltreatment by healthcare professionals, especially when professionals do not think children meet the thresholds for intervention by children's social care. In Section 3, we argue that 'direct' responses might be one way that healthcare professionals can respond to children whether or not they meet thresholds for responses by children's social care.

Defining the spectrum as 'maltreatment-related concerns'

In line with a public health perspective, the scope of our discussion here includes the role of healthcare services for children who are judged to be on the borders of maltreatment within the grey area of the child welfare continuum as well as for children who are clearly suffering maltreatment. Our broad approach to defining child maltreatment makes sense given the difficulties in accurate assessments of whether children are suffering harm and in the context of a child welfare system which encourages 'downgrading' of risk of harm as a response to limited resources. We use the term 'maltreatment-related concern' to capture the full range of professional concerns about child maltreatment and 'maltreatment-related problem' to refer to the full range of child and family problems that prompt professional concern. The term 'maltreatment-related concern' includes concerns about parental risk factors for maltreatment and sub-optimal parenting or parent–child interaction which is judged to have the *potential* to become harmful. It also includes concerns that are absolutely and definitively about child maltreatment and are labelled as such.

As Figure 3.3 shows, the numbers of children experiencing maltreatment-related problems each year in England will be high. The group includes the 4–10 per cent of children who are estimated to be maltreated each year, as well as an unknown proportion of the large swathe of children (up to 28%) with social welfare problems who are judged by professionals to be in the grey area of the continuum, between poor treatment and maltreatment.

Section 2: Recognition of maltreatment-related problems by healthcare professionals

The first step in responding to child maltreatment is to notice that there is a problem. All professionals in the UK, including healthcare professionals, have a statutory responsibility to identify children in need, including those children suffering, or likely to suffer, significant harm (HM Government 2013). In other words, healthcare professionals have a responsibility to identify the full range of maltreatment-related problems in families, including parental risk factors such as substance abuse and problematic parent–child interaction, regardless of whether they currently meet local thresholds for receiving services from Local Authority children's social care. In recent years there has been a shift in UK policy towards emphasising what was previously implicit: health professionals, including those working within adult services, have a responsibility to enquire about children and consider the impact of the problems they are treating on their capacity to parent and on the child. This message was embodied in the 'Think Family' policy agenda of the government (Social Exclusion Task Force 2007) and has since been written into multiple pieces of guidance by national healthcare bodies in the UK (Intercollegiate Committee for Standards for Children and Young People in Emergency Care Settings 2012; National Institute for Health and Clinical Excellence 2008; National Institute for Health and Clinical Excellence 2009a; National Institute for Health and Clinical Excellence 2012; National Society for the Prevention of Cruelty to Children and Royal College of General Practitioners 2011; Royal College of Psychiatrists 2011).

Although reviews of child deaths have highlighted that general practitioners (GPs) could be better at assessing the impact of parental risk factors such as maternal alcohol use on parenting capacity (Brandon *et al.* 2011), qualitative studies with GPs in England and Denmark and with Dutch paediatric primary care doctors consistently report that problems in adults who have children are the most common prompt for maltreatment-related concerns in general practice (Hølge-Hazelton and Tulinius 2010; Lykke, Christensen and Reventlow 2008, 2011; Schols, De Ruiter and Ory 2013; Tompsett *et al.* 2010; Woodman *et al.* 2013). The concerns discussed by GP participants in these studies were commonly about children in the grey area between children in need and child protection thresholds (Lykke *et al.* 2008, 2011; Woodman *et al.* 2013). Other important prompts for concern were consultations with the child (often for problems not directly related to maltreatment), knowledge about the child's wider environment and information from other professionals (Schols *et al.* 2013; Woodman *et al.* 2013).

The limited evidence that is available about hospital settings tells a similar story. In an audit of 681 maltreatment-related notifications to children's social care in 2011–12 from all departments of one acute general hospital in England, a substantial proportion (40%) was initiated in response to presentations by parents, of which 60 per cent were at the Emergency Department (Gonzalez-Izquierdo *et al.* in press). Like some other hospital departments (Hoytema van Konijnenburg *et al.* 2013; Kaye *et al.* 2009), this hospital had a policy of asking specific adult patients (for example, with domestic violence, substance abuse or attempted suicide) whether they have a child at home (Gonzalez-Izquierdo *et al.* in press). We do not know how common it is to have a policy of asking about children at home in hospitals across the UK. A smaller audit of three months of concerns within a paediatric department in a different English hospital reported that almost 40 per cent of the concerns in 64 children were triggered by observed parental behaviour (for example, disregard of a child's needs or aggression towards family members) or concerns about parenting capacity (for example, due to mental health problems) (Kugler *et al.* 2012). Both these audits and an early audit of a similar policy in an Emergency Department indicated that healthcare professionals were recognising maltreatment-related concerns along the whole spectrum of the child welfare continuum, including but not limited to cases with high levels of certainty and/or severity (Gonzalez-Izquierdo *et al.* in press; Kaye *et al.* 2009; Kugler *et al.* 2012).

The international research literature suggests that the burden of maltreatment-related problems in acute hospital and general practice settings occurs among children in the borders between poor treatment and maltreatment rather than among children with serious non-accidental injury, even in hospital settings. It is well established that the probability of abuse is high in young children with certain types of serious injury such as thoracic fractures or retinal haemorrhages (in the absence of confirmed accidental trauma or medical explanation) (National Institute for Health and Clinical Excellence 2009b). However, because these highly predictive injuries are rare, they account for only a small proportion of all maltreatment-related problems in children admitted to hospital (Lee, Gonzalez-Izquierdo and Gilbert 2012). The largest burden of maltreatment (i.e., most cases) occurs among children who, based on their presenting signs and symptoms, might be deemed to be at low risk because they have common presentations. Focusing on the few high-risk presentations improves specificity but reduces sensitivity of recognition (Lee *et al.* 2012; Woodman *et al.* 2008).

As an illustration of this point, an Australian cohort study which used a large and representative sample of linked data from hospital admissions and child protective services reported that 30 per cent of children admitted with *accidental* injury were known to child protective services and could therefore be considered high risk for maltreatment-related problems (McKenzie *et al.* 2012). Another Australian study, also linking representative hospital and social care data, but this time using a case-control design found an approximately tenfold increased risk of maltreatment allegations among children admitted for injury/poisoning *and* among those admitted for 'external causes of morbidity' and mental/behavioural problems (O'Donnell *et al.* 2010). Because acute injury admissions account for only a small proportion of all paediatric admissions (less than 12 per cent in children under five years old) (Gonzalez-Izquierdo *et al.* 2010), the absolute numbers of maltreatment-related problems in non-injured children will be far greater than in injured children. It is a clinician's job to identify maltreatment-related problems in children who present for reasons which are either not related or only indirectly (not obviously) related to the maltreatment. Not only does maltreatment result in multiple and long-term health problems for children (as described in Chapter 2) but there are higher than average rates of chronic conditions and disabilities among maltreated children. For these reasons healthcare professionals should expect to see maltreated children for illness as well as injury and for symptoms not (obviously) attributable to maltreatment (Jaudes and Mackey-Bilaver 2008; Stein *et al.* 2013; Sullivan and Knutson 2000).

A narrow focus on children with highly predictive injuries may provide false reassurance about children without these injuries and divert clinician attention away from the majority of maltreatment-related problems (Lee *et al.* 2012). A further problem can be caused when less predictive markers are used as screening tools for child maltreatment, as can be seen in the significant body of research evaluating checklists for use in Emergency Departments. These checklists include markers such as repeat attendance, injuries in infants, delayed presentation, inconsistent history or inconsistency between history and physical examination and inappropriate parent–child interaction (Louwers *et al.* 2013; Woodman 2009; Woodman *et al.* 2008, 2010). Due to the relatively low incidence of maltreatment in this population and the high incidence of these markers in the non-maltreated population, the predictive value is consistently reported to be low. If used as a screening tool, not only are these markers likely to divert attention away from many maltreated children without the markers, they also risk overwhelming the system by prompting concern in an unfeasibly high number of non-maltreated children (Louwers *et al.* 2013; Woodman 2009; Woodman *et al.* 2008, 2010).

The small amount of evidence we have indicates that clinicians are not confining their attention to the small numbers of children presenting with injury. Findings of two small audits in English hospitals suggest that physical abuse and/or injury were only present in very few cases which prompted maltreatment-related concern (Kugler *et al.* 2012; Rachamim *et al.* 2011) and qualitative studies suggest that GPs spend more time and energy responding to (possible) neglect and emotional abuse than physical and sexual abuse (Tompsett *et al.* 2010; Woodman *et al.* 2013). This is not surprising when we consider that neglect and emotional abuse are consistently reported to be the most common types of child maltreatment in the community (Gilbert *et al.* 2009b; Radford *et al.* 2011; Stoltenborgh in press) and it is only a minority of cases in which there is injury and harm which is both visible and attributable to maltreatment, even among children suffering physical abuse (Glaser 2011; National Scientific Council on the Developing Child 2012; Radford *et al.* 2011; Ruiz-Casares, Trocme and Fallon 2012).

Overall there is some, albeit limited, evidence to suggest that health professionals are recognising maltreatment in a way that is consistent with a public health approach, at least in some settings. They seem to be identifying problems across the child welfare continuum and using parental risk factors and parent–child interaction as triggers for concern. There is some evidence that these concerns frequently pertain to non-injured children and include problems related to neglect and emotional abuse.

Although health professionals undoubtedly under-recognise maltreatment-related problems, it is almost impossible to quantify the extent to which this is the case. A study using a large and nationally representative sample reported that maltreatment-related codes were recorded at a rate of 52 per 100,000 paediatric injury admissions in England between 2000 and 2008 and that, once deprivation had been taken into account, this rate was similar in Western Australia for all but the youngest of children (Gonzalez-Izquierdo et al. 2013). An analysis of a representative sample of 20 hospitals in Queensland, Australia reported that 0.3 per cent of all paediatric admissions (including non-injuries) had a maltreatment-related code in one year between 2005 and 2006 (McKenzie and Scott 2011). These estimates are very much lower than the 4–10 per cent of children who are estimated to be maltreated each year (Gonzalez-Izquierdo et al. 2013; McKenzie and Scott 2011).

However, we cannot assume that the gap represents 'missed' maltreatment-related problems. We do not know whether or how frequently children with maltreatment-related problems are admitted to hospital (Woodman 2009) and, because there are substantial barriers to recording, professional concern will not always result in a maltreatment-related code in the admission record. Disincentives for doctors to record maltreatment-related concerns include uncertainty of diagnosis in combination with stigma attached to the label and the imperative to involve children's social care (about which there is high ambivalence (Gilbert et al. 2009a) once the problem is named. When relying on routine hospital data, there is the complication of a 'coder' who interprets the doctor's notes and enters codes in accordance with national coding guidance (Gonzalez-Izquierdo et al. 2013). A validation of maltreatment-related codes in hospital discharge records against clinical records and notifications to children's social care found the codes to be highly specific but they were relatively insensitive (i.e., injured children with a maltreatment-related code had genuinely prompted a maltreatment-related concern for doctors but many children who had prompted concern did not have a code in their record) (Gonzalez-Izquierdo et al. in press).

Rates of maltreatment-related codes in primary care data are higher than in hospital data, though still far below estimates of maltreatment in the community. A UK study reported that there were 9.5 maltreatment-related codes per 1000 child years of GP registration, which was equivalent to a code for 0.8 per cent of all children registered with a GP (Woodman *et al.* 2012b). For the same reasons outlined for hospital data, we cannot assume all maltreated children without codes have been 'missed' by doctors. Additionally, for GPs (who, in the UK, enter the codes themselves) there is an additional worry that a family will see the code (Royal College of General Practitioners 2010), and the doctor–patient relationship will suffer as a result (Gilbert *et al.* 2009a; Gonzalez-Izquierdo *et al.* 2013; Woodman *et al.* 2012a). A very small validation exercise with nine GPs in England (discussing 25 children) suggested that maltreatment-related codes in primary care records are, as with hospital data, specific but not sensitive (Woodman *et al.* 2012a). For both hospital and GP data, it is likely that there is greater under-coding for children perceived to be in the grey area of the child welfare continuum and, consequently (as described in Section 1), for concerns about neglect and emotional abuse (McKenzie *et al.* 2011; Woodman *et al.* 2013).

Due to the limitations of maltreatment-related codes, we cannot use the results from these large database studies as accurate estimates of the incidence of either maltreatment-related problems in children presenting to healthcare services nor of recognised concerns in healthcare settings. However, studies based on maltreatment-related codes can be used as a *minimum* estimate of concerns and problems. They tell us that identification is unquestionably sub-optimal but that, in absolute terms, there is a substantial number of children who have maltreatment-related problems already known to health professionals in primary and secondary care. This prompts the question: how are health professionals responding to these children? And could responses be improved?

Section 3: Responses by healthcare professionals

Policy and research have conceived of health professionals as primarily playing the role of a 'sentinel' (Tompsett *et al.* 2010) identifying maltreatment and referring cases on to children's social care (Daniel *et al.* 2011; Woodman *et al.* in press). Although the UK does not have mandated reporting of child maltreatment as do Canada, New Zealand, the USA and Australia (Gilbert *et al.* 2012), the sentinel role is enshrined in statutory guidance: healthcare professionals in the UK have a responsibility to make appropriate referrals to children's social care (HM Government 2013). Statutory duties for health professionals also include elements of a 'multi-agency team player' role (Tompsett *et al.* 2010) (there is a responsibility to support social care processes) and a 'gate-keeper' role (they must share relevant information with other agencies) (HM Government 2008, 2013).

Historically, efforts to improve service coverage for the large group of children with maltreatment-related problems who are not receiving services have concentrated on improving identification of maltreatment by non-social care professionals, including healthcare professionals. However, it is increasingly being recognised that children's social care thresholds for intervention would simply rise as a response to increased referrals in the absence of extra resources, as described in Section 1 (Davies and Ward 2012; Mansell 2006). High thresholds for service provision deter referrals because the (perceived) harm to the patient-clinician relationship or to the family is not outweighed by any (perceived) benefit, and service overload can itself undermine service provision as attention is diverted to assessments away from interventions, especially where there is mandated reporting (Mansell 2006).

As with under-recording of concerns, the issue of under-referring is likely to be most acute for concerns about emotional abuse and neglect which are (perceived as) less likely to meet thresholds for service provision than concerns about physical and sexual abuse, as described in Section 1 (Daniel *et al.* 2011; Trocme *et al.* 2011). For these reasons, academics have begun to persuasively argue that poor coverage of services for maltreated children is driven as much by currently available responses as by sub-optimal identification of relevant problems (Daniel *et al.* 2011; Gilbert *et al.* 2009a). With this shift in thinking, policy and research attention has turned to responses with healthcare services which can occur before or alongside referral to children's social care: we shall refer to these as 'direct responses'. Although there have been calls for universal services to be able to 'respond directly' to children hovering around or below thresholds of 'significant harm' (Daniel *et al.* 2011), there is little clarity about what these 'direct responses' might look like in practice. In the following section, we draw on guidance for healthcare professionals and evidence about current practice to describe some examples of 'direct responses' in healthcare settings.

Guidance on direct responses by healthcare professionals

Guidance from national healthcare bodies in the UK recommends some direct responses by healthcare professionals: record concerns, discuss concern with colleagues, gather further information and review the child (General Medical Council 2012; National Institute for Health and Clinical Excellence 2009b). These direct responses are conceptualised as a way of monitoring problems and conducting continued risk assessments to inform decisions about whether the children should be referred to children's social care. Statutory guidance in England states that GPs can take a 'lead professional' role for children who are below the threshold for referral to children's social care, which consists of 'supporting the family, acting as an advocate and coordinating support services' (HM Government 2013).

Guidance for recording concerns is by far the most detailed: health professionals should record all concerns about maltreatment in the parent *and* child's record (if they have access to both) including 'minor concerns' which do not reach thresholds for referral to children's social care (General Medical Council 2012; National Institute for Health and Clinical Excellence 2009b). Records should contain relevant clinical findings, decisions, actions, any information-sharing with other professionals and conversations with the child or family and should be made as soon as possible following the concern (General Medical Council 2012; National Institute for Health and Clinical Excellence 2009b).

Recommendations developed using empirical data and professional consensus and which are supported by the Royal College of GPs encourage GPs to 'flag' concerns with (as a minimum) a single 'cause for concern' code (Woodman *et al.* 2012a). This approach was designed to make children 'findable' on the system and minimise GPs being 'put off' by complex recording requirements (Woodman *et al.* 2012a). Although we have considerable evidence from studies of routine data that healthcare professionals are recording maltreatment-related concerns, to date there is no evidence available on the impact of recording. On its own recording is unlikely to improve things for the child or family and indeed may even cause harm through stigma, disruption of the doctor–patient relationship and/or discouraging families from using services (Canvin *et al.* 2007; Woodman *et al.* 2012a, 2013). We need studies investigating whether (and how) recording changes clinician behaviour and whether (and how) it results in benefit or harm to the child and family.

Policy and guidance is much less clear how a role of monitoring, support, coordination and advocacy might work in practice for doctors. However, qualitative research with primary care doctors in England and the Netherlands suggest that this role is already accepted and enacted in some form, at least by some of these professionals in some settings (Schols *et al.* 2013; Tompsett *et al.* 2010; Woodman *et al.* 2013).

The earliest of the three relevant studies about primary care (Tompsett *et al.* 2010) surveyed 96 GPs and conducted in-depth interviews with 14 GPs and 19 strategic level staff from two Primary Care Trusts and Local Safeguarding Children Boards, three focus groups with young people, young mothers and a minority ethnic group; and a Delphi consensus about the guiding principles of GPs in safeguarding children (with 25 experts)[2]. Data were collected between 2006 and 2007 in England. The study identified four (not mutually exclusive) roles that GPs could adopt in responding to maltreated children: the 'case-holder', the 'sentinel', the 'gatekeeper' and the 'multi-agency team player' (Tompsett *et al.* 2010).

1. *The case-holder:* GP has ongoing relationship with family before, during and after referral to children's social care. This role builds on voluntary disclosure and establishing trust over time with the parents.

2. *The sentinel:* GP identifies child maltreatment and refers the concern to children's social care or other health services.

3. *The gatekeeper:* GP provides information to other agencies so that those agencies can make decisions about access to services.

4. *Multi-agency team player:* GP has continued engagement with other professionals outside the practice. This role is fulfilled when GP contributes actively to children's social care child protection processes.

Of these four roles, the 'case-holder' is the only one which involved direct responses to children and there is little further detail in the study about the nature of the 'ongoing' involvement with families. In keeping with the absence of the 'case-holder' role for health professionals in UK policy, this was a role that was recognised by the majority of GPs but not by other professionals in the study (Tompsett *et al.* 2010). This may have been because the data were collected before implementation of the Common Assessment Framework (Children's Workforce Development Council 2009), although early assessment and help services led by

---

2 Delphi consensus is a group communication process which aims to achieve a convergence of opinion on a specific real-world issue using a series of questionnaires delivered using multiple iterations to collect data from a panel of experts.

non-social work professionals are not intended to be used for children meeting thresholds of child in need (HM Government 2013).

The second study, by Woodman *et al.*, was based on interviews in 2010–11 with GPs (N=14), practice nurses (N=2) and health visitors (N=2) from four 'expert' practices in England. The study identified four direct responses to maltreatment-related concerns in current practice (monitoring, advocating, coaching and opportune healthcare) as well as the practices of recording and referral to and joint working with other agencies (Woodman *et al.* 2013):

1. *Monitoring:* keeping a 'watchful eye' on families and being 'a bit more vigilant'.

2. *Advocating:* 'you've got to stand up and shout for people' (making a case to other agencies on the patient's behalf).

3. *Coaching:* activating parents by attempting to shift mind-set, take responsibility for their problems and, eventually, change behaviours.

4. *Opportune healthcare:* providing (missed) routine and preventive healthcare for children during consultations for other reasons.

There is remarkable consistency between the results of these two studies (Tompsett *et al.* 2010; Woodman *et al.* 2013) as well as those from a Dutch study which was based on three focus groups with public child healthcare nurses (N= 11) and public child healthcare physicians (N= 6) in 2009–10 (Schols *et al.* 2013). The four direct responses reported by Woodman *et al.* can be seen as components of the 'case-holder' role as described by Tompsett *et al.* and there is overlap between the strategies that Woodman *et al.* and Schols *et al.* identified for enacting this role, which include: home-visits, inviting the family back to clinic, discussion with colleagues (Schols *et al.* 2013; Woodman *et al.* 2013) including at multidisciplinary team meetings, building relationships and links with other health professionals (monitoring and opportune healthcare) and investing in relationships with families (advocating and coaching) (Woodman *et al.* 2013). In these three studies doctors described how they relied on relationships with parents to keep families engaged with primary care and create a situation where parents were likely to accept support or advice (Schols *et al.* 2013; Tompsett *et al.* 2010; Woodman *et al.* 2013). They were also aware that they relied on relationships with parents, wider family members and other professionals (especially health visitors in the UK) to keep themselves apprised of information that was necessary for accurate risk assessment (Schols *et al.* 2013; Tompsett *et al.* 2010; Woodman *et al.* 2013).

With regard to secondary care settings, there is some evidence that multidisciplinary team meetings are being used to enact a 'case-holder' role which facilitates direct responses to maltreatment-related concerns. In Emergency Departments in Amsterdam, there is a policy to offer family support from a multidisciplinary team (including a paediatrician, a social worker, a child psychologist and/or a nurse) to parents who present with substance misuse, domestic violence or attempted suicide (Hoytema van Konijnenburg *et al.* 2013). In a study of the first two years of this policy (2010–12), the majority of parents (73%) who were referred to the multidisciplinary hospital team engaged with these voluntary services. Parents received counselling on the consequences of their behaviour for their children and therapy was offered to the parent, child or both alongside interventions to improve parent–child interaction and/or requests for enhancement of existing intervention by children's social care (Hoytema van Konijnenburg *et al.* 2013).

In at least some paediatric inpatient departments in the UK, similar multidisciplinary teams that include a hospital social worker meet regularly to discuss children who prompt maltreatment-related and other wider welfare concerns (Kugler *et al.* 2012). The purpose of the team meetings has been described as information sharing and decision making (Kugler *et al.* 2012), however it is also likely that, as in the Dutch example, the professionals support families and intervene by, for example, facilitating access to hospital mental health services and/or acting as patient advocates for housing or immigration services (Kugler *et al.* 2012). Additionally, the social worker would carry statutory responsibilities.

In summary, there is evidence that direct responses to maltreatment-related concerns are already a part of current practice in some primary care and hospital settings. It has been suggested that, at least for primary care clinicians, these direct responses draw on core clinical skills and are therefore likely to be commonly employed for a range of patients, including those who prompt maltreatment-related concerns (Hoytema van Konijnenburg *et al.* 2013; Tompsett *et al.* 2010; Woodman *et al.* 2013). Based on what we know about current practice within healthcare services in the context of the child welfare system, we suggest that direct responses are characterised by offering doctors a diversity of action which may include building parental esteem or parenting capacity, advocating for other welfare services such as improved housing or continuing to support and monitor the family using a strong doctor–patient relationship. In studies about current practice, direct responses have been applied to a heterogeneous population, including families with parental risk factors or harmful interaction through to families with child maltreatment.

As shown in Figure 3.4, we envisage that direct responses can occur before a referral to children's social care for lower risk cases (hopefully averting the need for a referral) or in tandem with referral to children's social care and alongside services provided by this agency. A partnership approach between children's social care and other agencies, including health, is consistent with a public health approach in its potential to address current barriers to proactive responses for children in the middle of the child welfare continuum. However, in the context of disjoint between health and social care services, it is probable that partnership responses from GPs and children's social care would require system and/or attitude changes (Tompsett *et al.* 2010; Woodman *et al.* 2013).

'Direct' (first-line pluripotential) responses from healthcare professionals might be a way of minimising the potential harms of the current systems, which may thrust families onto a judicial pathway towards coercive interventions or which do not provide follow-up or services for those beneath the threshold (as explained in Section 1). Direct responses might also contribute to improved outcomes through changing parental attitude/behaviour (for example, in terms of alcohol use) and/or improving parent–child interaction. On the other hand, it is imperative that direct responses by healthcare professionals do not cause net harm to a child or family. It has been argued that healthcare professionals do not have sufficient expertise or resources, including time and inclination, to safely take on a case-holding role for families who prompt maltreatment-related concerns (Fitzpatrick 2011; Masters 2012) and that such a role may deter families from using healthcare services (Canvin *et al.* 2007; Woodman *et al.* 2013). We need to know that direct responses, which are already occurring in some healthcare settings, do not cause harm. We also need to assess whether direct responses may improve outcomes for children and families who prompt maltreatment-related concerns.

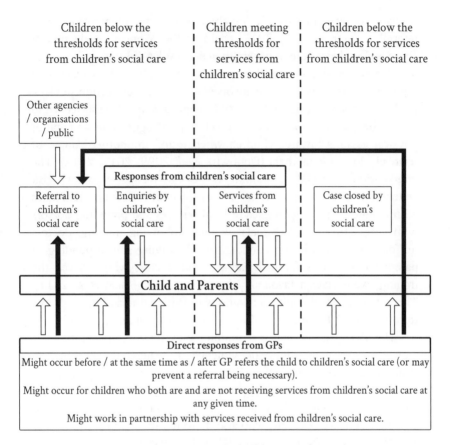

Figure 3.4 Direct responses by healthcare professionals in relation to services from children's social care

Section 4: The evidence base for direct responses by healthcare professionals

There is extremely limited evidence to help us assess the balance of harm and benefit of direct responses to maltreatment-related concerns in primary and secondary healthcare. We know of only three relevant interventions that have been evaluated using randomised controlled trials (RCTs). One RCT aimed to improve recognition and response to child maltreatment in high- and low-risk families in paediatric primary care settings in the USA: the 'Safe Environment for Every Kid' (SEEK) trial. Two further RCTs related to primary care intervention for women suffering domestic violence but include 'direct' approaches that are relevant to responses to child maltreatment: the 'Identification and referral to improve safety (IRIS)' trial and the 'Women's evaluation of abuse and violence care in general practice' (WEAVE) trial.

The SEEK trial reported a reduction in child maltreatment in a high-risk sample (measured as involvement in child protection services, medical problems relating to possible neglect and self-reported child assault by parents) and lowered psychological aggression and minor physical assaults towards children when tested in another sample of relatively low-risk mothers (Dubowitz *et al.* 2009, 2011, 2012). The intervention consisted of: training doctors to recognise parental risk factors for maltreatment, using motivational interviewing techniques with families, directing families to local services and providing doctors with access to an on-site social worker. Following training, doctors felt more comfortable and confident in identifying and responding to parental risk factors for maltreatment and doctors who received the training were viewed favourably by patients (Feigelman *et al.* 2011). There were methodological limitations to this trial including high loss to follow-up (20%) and lack of an intention-to-treat analysis.

The IRIS trial evaluated a training plus support intervention for women experiencing domestic violence in general practice in two Primary Care Trusts (PCTs) in England. The intervention programme included practice-based training sessions, a prompt within the medical record to ask about domestic abuse, and a referral pathway to a named domestic violence advocate, who also delivered the training and further consultancy for GPs (Feder *et al.* 2011). The IRIS trial used referrals as its main outcome measure and reported a much increased referral rate in the intervention practices to the specialist advocacy service (incidence rate ratio: 22.1 (95% CI 11.5, 42.5)) and two other specialist domestic violence agencies (incidence rate ratio: 6.4 (95% CI 4.2, 10.0)) (Feder *et al.* 2011). However, in absolute terms, the increase in referrals was so small that it was unlikely to be of any clinical significance (increased from 0.03% to 0.04% of all women) and other researchers question whether an increase in referrals indicates an improvement in services and/or outcomes for women (Hegarty and Glasziou 2011). The cost effectiveness analysis of the trial was very uncertain: the confidence intervals (CI) indicate that there could be a societal cost of as much as £136 per woman or a societal saving of up to £178 per woman over one year (Devine *et al.* 2012). There is no mention of children or safeguarding them in any of the publications relating to the IRIS study.

A similar trial in Australia, WEAVE, evaluated training of GPs to identify domestic violence and offer/deliver several 30-minute counselling sessions on emotions and relationships to women with identified domestic violence. This trial did not find any difference between the intervention and control groups in quality of life, safety planning and behaviour, or mental health 12 months after the intervention. GP inquiry about the safety of children was higher in the intervention group at six months post-intervention (odds ratio: 5.1 (95% CI 1.9, 14.0)) but we do not know whether this had any impact on women or their children (Hegarty *et al.* 2010, 2012).

The 'coaching' and 'advocacy' elements of the case-holder role as described by Woodman *et al.* (2013) share characteristics with the motivational interviewing and advocacy component of the SEEK, IRIS and WEAVE trials. Although it is not at all clear from these trials whether motivational interviewing improves (or negatively impacts upon) outcomes for children and families, the results from the SEEK trial are promising. Taken together, the three trials suggest that motivational interviewing may be a feasible 'direct response' in primary care. It may be that any positive impact is greatest for a subset of patients who actively seek help (Feder *et al.* 2009; Hoytema van Konijnenburg *et al.* 2013; Woodman *et al.* 2013). However, achieving attitude or behaviour change in patients through coaching is highly skilled work and has been described by GPs as 'one of the most difficult aspects of practice' (Blakeman *et al.* 2010). GPs recognise that coaching can trigger patient disengagement and/or avoidance of services if attempted in the absence of a strong doctor–patient relationship or with insufficient skill (Blakeman *et al.* 2010; Schols *et al.* 2013; Woodman *et al.* 2013). Likewise, evidence about packages of clinician training in hospitals and co-location of social workers in hospitals is far from conclusive but does warrant further evaluation.

Summary

Current UK policy and guidance about the recognition of maltreatment-related concerns by healthcare professionals is consistent with a preventive public health approach and there is evidence of this approach in current practice, at least in some primary and secondary care settings. Although the recognition of maltreatment-related concerns could undoubtedly be improved, there are already a substantial number of children who prompt maltreatment-related concerns in primary and secondary care. In the context of large numbers of maltreated children who prompt concerns but are below the threshold for children's social care assessment or intervention, it does not make sense for referral to children's social care to be the *only* response available to healthcare professionals.

There is evidence that some healthcare professionals in some settings are taking a more preventive public health approach by enacting direct responses to children and families. These include monitoring, coaching (motivational interviewing), advocacy and providing opportune healthcare which rely on robust relationships with multidisciplinary colleagues and a strong doctor–patient relationship. Information is lacking on the benefits or harms of these direct responses but they are promising avenues for further exploration. It might be that direct responses are best suited to specific groups such as help-seeking families, children where there are concerns about neglect or emotional abuse or children who are 'marginally maltreated'. To avoid the potential for direct responses to reinforce dangerous 'silo' working, ways of partnership (inter-agency) working need to be developed which can include direct responses from healthcare professionals. Research is needed into how direct responses in healthcare settings might work symbiotically with the Common Assessment Framework (Children's Workforce Development Council 2009) which is designed to facilitate inter-agency working and access to services for children who do not meet thresholds of children in need, including those suffering significant harm (or likely significant harm). Direct responses already being used in practice need to be properly evaluated to determine whether they cause more good than harm and for whom.

Acknowledgements

This chapter includes research funded by an MRC/ESRC interdisciplinary studentship for Jenny Woodman and by the Department of Health (The Policy Research Unit in the Health of Children, Young People and Families).

Notes

Some of the core concepts and data in this chapter were originally presented in our earlier publications:

Woodman, J., Woolley, A., Gilbert, R., Rafi, I. *et al.* (in press) *Policy, Practice and Public Perspectives on the Role of GPs in Safeguarding Children: A Collaborative Study Involving UCL-Institute of Child Health, the RCGP, the University of Surrey and the NSPCC.* London: NSPCC.

Gonzalez-Izquierdo, A., Ward, A., Smith, P., Walford, C. *et al.* (in press) 'Notifications for child safeguarding from an acute hospital in response to presentations to healthcare by parents.' *Child: Care, Health and Development.*

Gonzalez-Izquierdo, A., Cortina-Borja, M., Woodman, J., Mok, J. *et al.* (under review) 'Maltreatment or violence-related injury in children and adolescents admitted to the NHS: Comparison of trends in England and Scotland between 2005 and 2011.' *BMJ Open.*

Woodman, J., Gilbert, R., Allister, J., Glaser, D. and Brandon, M. (2013) 'Responses to concerns about child maltreatment: A qualitative study of GPs in England.' *BMJ Open 3*, 12.

Gonzalez-Izquierdo, A., Ward, A., O'Donnell, M., Li, L. *et al.* (2013) 'Cross-country comparison of victimisation-related injury admission in children and adolescents in England and Western Australia.' *BMC Health Services Reserach 13*, 1, 260.

Woodman, J. and Gilbert, R. (2013) 'Child maltreatment: Moving towards a public health approach.' *Growing up in the UK II.* London: BMA.

Gilbert, R., Woodman, J. and Logan, S. (2012) 'Developing services for a public health approach to child maltreatment.' *International Journal of Children's Rights 20*, 3, 323–342.

Woodman, J., Allister, J., Rafi, I., de Lusignan, S. *et al.* (2012) 'Simple approaches to improve recording of concerns about child maltreatment in primary care records: Developing a quality improvement intervention.' *British Journal of General Practice 62*, 600, e478–e486.

Woodman, J., Freemantle, N., Allister, J., de Lusignan, S., Gilbert, R. and Petersen, I. (2012) 'Variation in recorded child maltreatment concerns in UK primary care records: A cohort study using The Health Improvement Network (THIN) database.' *PLOS ONE 7*, 11, 1–9.

Gilbert, R., Fluke, J., O'Donnell, M., Gonzalez-Izquierdo, A. *et al.* (2012) 'Child maltreatment: Variation in trends and policies in six developed countries.' *Lancet 379*, 9817, 758–772.

Lee, J.J., Gonzalez-Izquierdo, A. and Gilbert, R. (2012) 'Risk of maltreatment-related injury: A cross-sectional study of children under five years old admitted to hospital with a head or neck injury or fracture.' *PLOS ONE 7*, 10, e46522.

Kugler, B., Woodman, J., Carroll, J., Fertleman, C. and Gilbert, R. (2012) 'Child protection guidance needs to address parent behaviour.' *Child: Care, Health and Development 39*, 5, 760–761.

Rachamim, E., Hodes, D., Gilbert, R. and Jenkins, S. (2011) 'Pattern of hospital referrals of children at risk of maltreatment.' *Emergency Medicine Journal 28*, 11, 952–954.

Gonzalez-Izquierdo, A., Woodman, J., Copley, L., van der Meulen, J. *et al.* (2010) 'Variation in recording of child maltreatment in administrative records of hospital admissions for injury in England, 1997–2009.' *Archives of Disease in Childhood 95*, 11, 918–925.

Gilbert, R., Kemp, A., Thoburn, J., Sidebotham, P. *et al.* (2009) 'Recognising and responding to child maltreatment.' *Lancet 373*, 9658, 67–80.

Gilbert, R., Widom, C.S., Browne, K., Fergusson, D., Webb, E. and Janson, S. (2009) 'Burden and consequences of child maltreatment in high-income countries.' *Lancet 373*, 9657, 68–81.

References

Barlow, J. and Calam, R. (2011) 'A public health approach to safeguarding in the 21st century.' *Child Abuse Review 20*, 4, 238–255.

Barlow, J. and Stewart-Brown, S. (2003) 'Why a universal population-level approach to the prevention of child abuse is essential.' *Child Abuse Review 12*, 5, 279–281.

Blakeman, T., Bower, P., Reeves, D. and Chew-Graham, C. (2010) 'Bringing self-management into clinical view: A qualitative study of long-term condition management in primary care consultations.' *Chronic Illness 6*, 2, 136–150.

Brandon, M. and Thoburn, J. (2008) 'Safeguarding children in the UK: A longitudinal study of services to children suffering or likely to suffer significant harm.' *Child and Family Social Work 13*, 4, 365–377.

Brandon, M., Belderson, P., Warren, C., Gardner, R. *et al.* (2008) 'The preoccupation with thresholds in cases of child death or serious injury through abuse and neglect.' *Child Abuse Review 17*, 5, 313–330.

Brandon, M., Lewis, A. and Thoburn, J. (1996) 'The Children Act definition of 'significant harm' – interpretations in practice.' *Health & Social Care in the Community 4*, 1, 11–20.

Brandon, M., Sidebotham, P., Bailey, S. and Belderson, P. (2011) *A Study of Recommendations Arising from Serious Case Reviews 2009–2010.* London: Department for Education.

Broadhurst, K., Wastell, D., White, S., Hall, C. *et al.* (2010) 'Performing 'initial assessment': Identifying the latent conditions for error at the front-door of local authority children's services.' *British Journal of Social Work 40*, 2, 352–370.

Buckley, H., Carr, N. and Whelan, S. (2011) '"Like walking on eggshells": Service user views and expectations of the child protection system.' *Child and Family Social Work 16*, 1, 101–110.

Canvin, K., Jones, C., Marttila, A., Burstrom, B. and Whitehead, M. (2007) 'Can I risk using public services? Perceived consequences of seeking help and health care among households living in poverty: Qualitative study.' *Journal of Epidemiology & Community Health 61*, 11, 984–989.

Child Welfare Information Gateway (2014) *Differential Response to Reports of Child Abuse and Neglect.* Washington DC: Child Welfare Information Gateway. Available at www.childwelfare.gov/pubs/issue_briefs/differential_response/differential_responsea.cfm, accessed on 17 April 2014.

Children Act 1989. London: Stationery Office.

Children Act 2004. London: Stationery Office.

Children's Workforce Development Council (CWDC) (2009) *The Common Assessment Framework for Children and Young People: A Guide for Practitioners: Early Identification, Assessment of Needs and Intervention.* Available at www.plymouth.gov. uk/caf_for_practitioners_national_guidance.pdf, accessed on 17 April 2014.

Community Care (2012) 'Social workers unlikely to act quickly on neglect cases.' Sutton: Community Care. Available at www.communitycare.co.uk/ articles/27/09/2012/118548/social-workers-unlikely-to-act-quickly-on-neglect-cases.htm, accessed on 17 April 2014.

Community Care (2013) 'Community Care survey exposes how rising thresholds are leaving children in danger.' Sutton: Community Care. Available at www. communitycare.co.uk/2013/11/19/community-care-survey-exposes-rising-thresholds-leaving-children-danger/#.UqL4-fRdXA0, accessed on 17 April 2014.

Cossar, J., Brandon, M. and Jordan, P. (2011) *Don't Make Assumptions: Children's and Young People's Views of the Child Protection System and Messages for Change.* London: Office of the Children's Commissioner.

Dale, P. (2004) '"Like a fish in a bowl": Parents' perceptions of child protection services.' *Child Abuse Review 13,* 2, 137–157.

Daniel, B., Taylor, J. and Scott, J. (2010) 'Recognition of neglect and early response: Overview of a systematic review of the literature.' *Child and Family Social Work 15,* 2, 248–257.

Daniel, B., Taylor, J. and Scott, J. (2011) *Recognizing and Helping the Neglected Child: Evidence-Based Practice for Assessment and Intervention.* London: Jessica Kingsley Publishers.

Davies, C. and Ward, H. (2012) *Safeguarding Children across Services: Messages from Research on Identifying and Responding to Child Maltreatment.* London: Jessica Kingsley Publishers.

Department for Education (2013) *Characteristics of Children in Need in England 2012–13.* London: Department for Education. Available at www.gov.uk/government/collections/statistics-children-in-need, accessed on 17 April 2014.

Department of Health (1995) *Child Protection: Messages from Research.* London: HMSO.

Department of Health, Department for Education and Employment and Home Office (2000) *The Framework for the Assessment of Children in Need and their Families.* London: Stationery Office. Available at http://webarchive.nationalarchives. gov.uk/20130107105354/http:/www.dh.gov.uk/prod_consum_dh/ groups/dh_digitalassets/@dh/@en/documents/digitalasset/dh_4014430. pdf, accessed on 17 April 2014.

Department of Health, Home Office and Department for Education and Employment (1999) *Working Together to Safeguard Children.* London: Stationery Office.

Devine, A., Spencer, A., Eldridge, S., Norman, R. and Feder, G. (2012) 'Cost-effectiveness of Identification and Referral to Improve Safety (IRIS), a domestic violence training and support programme for primary care: A modelling study based on a randomised controlled trial.' *BMJ Open 2,* 3 e001008.

Drake, B. (2013) 'Differential response: What to make of the existing research? A response to Hughes *et al.*' *Research on Social Work Practice 23*, 5, 539–544.

Drake, B. and Jonson-Reid, M. (2007) 'A response to Melton based on the best available data.' *Child Abuse and Neglect 31*, 4, 343–360.

Dubowitz, H., Feigelman, S., Lane, W. and Kim, J. (2009) 'Pediatric primary care to help prevent child maltreatment: The Safe Environment for Every Kid (SEEK) Model.' *Pediatrics 123*, 3, 858–864.

Dubowitz, H., Lane, W.G., Semiatin, J.N. and Magder, L.S. (2012) 'The SEEK model of pediatric primary care: Can child maltreatment be prevented in a low-risk population?' *Academic Pediatrics 12*, 4, 259–268.

Dubowitz, H., Lane, W.G., Semiatin, J.N., Magder, L.S., Venepally, M. and Jans, M. (2011) 'The Safe Environment for Every Kid model: Impact on pediatric primary care professionals.' *Pediatrics 127*, 4, e962–970.

Farmer, E. and Lutman, E. (2010) *Case Management and Outcomes for Neglected Children Returned to Their Parents: A Five Year Follow-Up Study.* London: Department for Children, Schools and Families.

Feder, G., Davies, R.A., Baird, K., Dunne, D. *et al.* (2011) 'Identification and Referral to Improve Safety (IRIS) of women experiencing domestic violence with a primary care training and support programme: A cluster randomised controlled trial.' *Lancet 378*, 9805, 1788–1795.

Feder, G., Ramsay, J., Dunne, D., Rose, M. *et al.* (2009) 'How far does screening women for domestic (partner) violence in different health-care settings meet criteria for a screening programme? Systematic reviews of nine UK National Screening Committee criteria.' *Health Technology Assessment 13*, iii–iv, xi–xiii, 1–113, 137–347.

Feigelman, S., Dubowitz, H., Lane, W., Grube, L. and Kim, J. (2011) 'Training pediatric residents in a primary care clinic to help address psychosocial problems and prevent child maltreatment.' *Academic Pediatrics 11*, 6, 474–480.

Finkelhor, D., Turner, H., Ormrod, R. and Hamby, S.L. (2009) 'Violence, abuse, and crime exposure in a national sample of children and youth.' *Pediatrics 124*, 5, 1411–1423.

Fitzpatrick, M. (2011) 'How to protect general practice from child protection.' *British Journal of General Practice 61*, 588, 436.

Forrester, D. and Harwin J. (2008) 'Parental substance misuse and child welfare: Outcomes for children two years after referral.' *British Journal of Social Work 38*, 8, 1518–1535.

Frameworks Institute (2013) *Mapping the gaps betwen expert and public understandings of child maltreatment.* Washington D.C.: Frameworks Institute. Available at http://frameworksinstitute.org/pubs/mtg/childmaltreatment, accessed on 11 November 2013.

General Medical Council (2012) *Protecting Children and Young People: The Responsibilities of All Doctors.* London: GMC.

Gilbert, R., Fluke, J., O'Donnell, M., Gonzalez-Izquierdo, A. *et al.* (2012) 'Child maltreatment: Variation in trends and policies in six developed countries.' *Lancet 379*, 9817, 758–772.

Gilbert, R., Kemp, A., Thoburn, J., Sidebotham, P. *et al.* (2009a) 'Recognising and responding to child maltreatment.' *Lancet 373*, 9658, 167–180.

Gilbert, R., Widom, C.S., Browne, K., Fergusson, D., Webb, E. and Janson, S. (2009b) 'Burden and consequences of child maltreatment in high-income countries.' *Lancet 373*, 9657, 68–81.

Gilbert, R., Woodman, J. and Logan, S. (2012) 'Developing services for a public health approach to child maltreatment.' *International Journal of Children's Rights 20*, 3, 323–342.

Glaser, D. (2011) 'How to deal with emotional abuse and neglect: Further development of a conceptual framework (FRAMEA).' *Child Abuse and Neglect 35*, 10, 866–875.

Gonzalez-Izquierdo, A., Ward, A., O'Donnell, M., Li, L. *et al.* (2013) 'Cross-country comparison of victimisation-related injury admission in children and adolescents in England and Western Australia.' *BMC Health Services Research 13*, 1, 260.

Gonzalez-Izquierdo, A., Ward, A., Smith, P., Walford, C. *et al.* (in press) 'Notifications for child safeguarding from an acute hospital in response to presentations to healthcare by parents.' *Child: Care, Health & Development.*

Gonzalez-Izquierdo, A., Woodman, J., Copley, L., Van Der Meulen, J. *et al.* (2010) 'Variation in recording of child maltreatment in administrative records of hospital admissions for injury in England, 1997–2009.' *Archives of Disease in Childhood 95*, 11, 918–925.

Guyatt, G.H., Oxman, A.D., Vist, G., Kunz, R. *et al.* (2011) 'GRADE guidelines: 4. Rating the quality of evidence—study limitations (risk of bias).' *Journal of Clinical Epidemiology 64*, 4, 407–415.

Hegarty, K. and Glasziou, P. (2011) 'Tackling domestic violence: Is increasing referral enough?' *Lancet 378*, 9805, 1760–1762.

Hegarty, K.L., Gunn, J.M., O'Doherty, L.J., Taft, A. *et al.* (2010) 'Women's evaluation of abuse and violence care in general practice: A cluster randomised controlled trial (WEAVE).' *BMC Public Health 10*, 1, 2.

Hegarty, K.L., O'Doherty, L.J., Chondros, P., Valpied, J. *et al.* (2012) 'Effect of type and severity of intimate partner violence on women's health and service use: Findings from a primary care trial of women afraid of their partners.' *Journal of Interpersonal Violence 28*, 2, 273–294.

HM Government (2008) *Information Sharing: Guidance for Practitioners and Managers.* London: Department of Children, Schools and Families.

HM Government (2013) *Working Together to Safeguard Children: A Guide to Inter-Agency Working to Safeguarding and Promoting the Welfare of Children.* London: Department for Education.

Hølge-Hazelton, B. and Tulinius, C. (2010) 'Beyond the specific child: What is "a child's case" in general practice?' *British Journal of General Practice 60*, 570, e4–9.

Holmes, L., McDermid, S., Soper, J., Sempik, J. and Ward, H. (2010) *Extension of the Cost Calculator to Include Cost Calculations for All Children in Need.* A Report to the Department for Education. Loughborough: University of Loughborough.

Hopwood, O., Pharoah, R. and Hannon, C. (2012) *Families on the Front Line? Local Spending on Children's Services in Austerity.* London: Family and Parenting Institute.

Hoytema van Konijnenburg, E.M., Sieswerda-Hoogendoorn, T., Brilleslijper-Kater, S.N., Van der Lee, J.H. and Teeuw, A.H. (2013) 'New hospital-based policy for children whose parents present at the ER due to domestic violence, substance abuse and/or a suicide attempt.' *European Journal of Pediatrics 172*, 2, 207–214.

Intercollegiate Committee for Standards for Children and Young People in Emergency Care Settings (2012) *Standards for Children and Young People in Emergency Care Settings.* London: RCPCH.

Jaudes, P.K. and Mackey-Bilaver, L. (2008) 'Do chronic conditions increase young children's risk of being maltreated?' *Child Abuse and Neglect 32*, 7, 671–681.

Jones, C. (2001) 'Voices from the front line: State social workers and New Labour.' *British Journal of Social Work 31*, 4, 547–562.

Kaye, P., Taylor, C., Barley, K. and Powell-Chandler, A. (2009) 'An emergency department intervention to protect an overlooked group of children at risk of significant harm.' *Journal of Emergency Medicine 26*, 6, 415–417.

Kugler, B., Woodman, J., Carroll, J., Fertleman, C. and Gilbert, R. (2012) 'Child protection guidance needs to address parent behaviour.' *Child: Care, Health and Development 39*, 5, 760–761.

Lee, J.J., Gonzalez-Izquierdo, A. and Gilbert, R. (2012) 'Risk of maltreatment-related injury: A cross-sectional study of children under five years old admitted to hospital with a head or neck injury or fracture.' *PLOS ONE 7*, 10, e46522.

Louwers, E.C., Korfage, I.J., Affourtit, M.J., Ruige, M. *et al.* (2013) 'Accuracy of a screening instrument to identify potential child abuse in emergency departments.' *Child Abuse and Neglect 37*, 110–117.

Lutman, E. and Farmer, E. (2013) 'What contributes to outcomes for neglected children who are reunified with their parents? Findings from a five-year follow-up study.' *British Journal of Social Work 43*, 3, 559–578.

Lykke, K., Christensen, P. and Reventlow, S. (2008) '"This is not normal…" – signs that make the GP question the child's well-being.' *Family Practice 25*, 3, 146–153.

Lykke, K., Christensen, P. and Reventlow, S. (2011) 'The consultation as an interpretive dialogue about the child's health needs.' *Family Practice 28*, 4, 430–436.

Mansell, J. (2006) 'The underlying instability in statutory child protection: Understanding the system dynamics driving risk assurance levels.' *Social Policy Journal of NZ 28*, 97–132.

Marmot, M. (2010) 'Fair society, healthy lives: Strategic review of health inequalities in England post 2010 (The Marmot Review).' London: UCL.

Masters, N.J. (2012) 'What is the role of GPs in safeguarding children?' *BMJ 344*, e4123.

Mckenzie, K. and Scott, D.A. (2011) 'Using routinely collected hospital data for child maltreatment surveillance: Issues, methods and patterns.' *BMC Public Health 11*, 7.

McKenzie, K., Scott, D., Fraser, J.A. and Dunne, M.P. (2012) 'Assessing the concordance of health and child protection data for 'maltreated' and 'unintentionally injured' children.' *Injury Prevention 18*, 1, 50–57.

McKenzie, K., Scott, D.A., Waller, G.S. and Campbell, M. (2011) 'Reliability of routinely collected hospital data for child maltreatment surveillance.' *BMC Public Health 11*, 8.

National Institute for Health and Clinical Excellence (2008) *Promoting Young People's Social and Emotional Wellbeing in Primary Education.* London: NICE.

National Institute for Health and Clinical Excellence (2009a) *Promoting Young People's Social and Emotional Wellbeing in Secondary Education.* London: NICE.

National Institute for Health and Clinical Excellence (2009b) *When to Suspect Child Maltreatment.* London: NICE.

National Institute for Health and Clinical Excellence (2012) *Social and Emotional Wellbeing: Early Years.* London: NICE.

National Scientific Council on the Developing Child (2012) *The Science of Neglect: The Persistent Absence of Responsive Care Disrupts the Developing Brain: Working Paper 12.* Available at www.developingchild.harvard.edu, accessed on 18 April 2014.

National Society for the Prevention of Cruelty to Children and Royal College of General Practitioners (2011) *Safeguarding Children and Young People: A Toolkit for General Practice.* London: RCGP.

O'Donnell, M., Nassar, N., Leonard, H., Jacoby, P. at al. (2010) 'Rates and types of hospitalisations for children who have subsequent contact with the child protection system: A population based case-control study.' *Journal of Epidemiology and Community Health 64*, 9, 784–788.

O'Donnell, M., Scott, D. and Stanley, F. (2008) 'Child abuse and neglect – is it time for a public health approach?' *Aust NZ Journal of Public Health 32*, 4, 325–330.

Parton, N. (2011) 'Child protection and safeguarding in England: Changing and competing conceptions of risk and their implications for social work.' *British Journal of Social Work 41*, 5, 854–875.

Post, P.N., de Beer, H. and Guyatt, G.H.(2013) 'How to generalize efficacy results of randomized trials: recommendations based on a systematic review of possible approaches.' *Journal of Evaluation in Clinical Practice 19*, 4, 638–643.

Rachamim, E., Hodes, D., Gilbert, R. and Jenkins, S. (2011) 'Pattern of hospital referrals of children at risk of maltreatment.' *Journal of Emergency Medicine 28*, 11, 952–954.

Radford, L., Corral, S., Bradley, C., Fisher, H. *et al.* (2011) *Child Abuse and Neglect in the UK Today.* London: NSPCC.

Royal College of General Practitioners (2010) *Enabling Patients to Access Electronic Health Records: Guidance for Health Professionals.* London: RCGP.

Royal College of Psychiatrists (2010) *Parents as Patients: Supporting the Needs of Patients Who Are Parents and Their Children.* London: RCPsych.

Ruiz-Casares, M., Trocme, N. and Fallon, B. (2012) 'Supervisory neglect and risk of harm. Evidence from the Canadian Child Welfare System.' *Child Abuse and Neglect 36*, 6, 471–480.

Sabates, R. and Dex, S. (2012) *Multiple Risk Factors in Young Children's Development.* London: Centre for Longitudinal Studies, Institute of Education.

Schols, M.W., De Ruiter, C. and Ory, F.G. (2013) 'How do public child healthcare professionals and primary school teachers identify and handle child abuse cases? A qualitative study.' *BMC Public Health* 13.

Skuse, T. and Ward, H. (2003) *Outcomes for Looked After Children: Children's Views, the Importance of Listening. An Interim Report to the Department of Health.* Loughborough: Centre for Child and Family Research, Loughborough University.

Slep, A.M. and Heyman, R.E. (2008) 'Public health approaches to family maltreatment prevention: Resetting family psychology's sights from the home to the community.' *Journal of Family Psychology 22*, 4, 518–528.

Social Exclusion Task Force (2007) *Reaching Out: Think Family: Analysis and Themes from the Families at Risk Review.* London: Cabinet Office.

Stein, R.E., Hurlburt, M.S., Heneghan, A.M., Zhang, J. *et al.* (2013) 'Chronic conditions among children investigated by child welfare: A national sample.' *Pediatrics 131*, 3, 455–462.

Stoltenborgh, M. (in press) 'The prevalence of child maltreatment across the globe: Review of a series of meta-analyses.' *Child Abuse Review.*

Sullivan, P.M. and Knutson, J.F. (2000) 'Maltreatment and disabilities: A population-based epidemiological study.' *Child Abuse and Neglect 24*, 10, 1257–1273.

Tompsett, H., Ashworth, M., Atkins, C., Bell, L. *et al.* (2010) *The Child, the Family and the GP: Tensions and Conflicts of Interest for GPs in Safeguarding Children May 2006–October 2008.* Final Report February 2010. London: Kingston University.

Trocme, N., Fallon, B., Maclaurin, B., Chamberland, C., Chabot, M. and Esposito, T. (2011) 'Shifting definitions of emotional maltreatment: An analysis of child welfare investigation laws and practices in Canada.' *Child Abuse and Neglect 35*, 10, 831–840.

Trocme, N., Fallon, B., Sinha, V., Van Wert, M., Kozlowski, A. and Maclaurin, B. (2013) 'Differentiating between child protection and family support in the Canadian child welfare system's response to intimate partner violence, corporal punishment, and child neglect.' *International Journal of Psychology 48*, 2, 128–140.

Tunstill, J., Aldgate, J. and Thoburn, J. (2010) 'Promoting and safeguarding the welfare of children: A bridge too far?' *Journal of Child Services 5*, 3, 14–24.

Wade, J., Biehal, N., Farrelly, N. and Sinclair, I. (2010) *Maltreated Children in the Looked After System: A Comparison of Outcomes for Those Who Go Home and Those Who Do Not.* London: Department for Children, Schools and Families.

Wade, J., Biehal, N., Farrelly, N. and Sinclair, I. (2011) *Caring for Abused and Neglected Children: Making the Right Decisions for Reunification or Long-Term Care.* London: Jessica Kingsley Publishers.

Waldfogel, J. (2009) 'Prevention and the child protection system.' *Future Child 19*, 2, 195–210.

Ward, H., Brown, R. and Westlake, D. (2012) *Safeguarding Babies and Very Young Children from Abuse and Neglect.* London: Jessica Kingsley Publishers.

Ward, H., Skuse, T. and Munro, E.R. (2005) 'The best of times, the worst of times: Young people's views of care and accommodation.' *Adoption and Fostering 29*, 1, 8–17.

Wolfe, D.A. and McIsaac, C. (2011) 'Distinguishing between poor/dysfunctional parenting and child emotional maltreatment.' *Child Abuse and Neglect 35*, 10, 802–813.

Woodman, J. (2009) 'Do patterns of healthcare use predict child maltreatment?' London: London School of Hygiene and Tropical Medicine. Available at www.lshtm.ac.uk/library/MSc_PH/2008-09/490407.pdf, accessed on 18 April 2014.

Woodman, J. and Gilbert, R. (2013) *Child Maltreatment: Moving Towards a Public Health Approach. Growing Up in the UK II.* London: BMA.

Woodman, J., Allister, J., Rafi, I., De Lusignan, S. *et al.* (2012a) 'Simple approaches to improve recording of concerns about child maltreatment in primary care records: Developing a quality improvement intervention.' *British Journal of General Practice 62*, 600, e478–e486.

Woodman, J., Freemantle, N., Allister, J., De Lusignan, S., Gilbert, R. and Petersen, I. (2012b) 'Variation in recorded child maltreatment concerns in UK primary care records: A cohort study using The Health Improvement Network (THIN) database.' *PLOS ONE 7*, 11, 1–9.

Woodman, J., Gilbert, R., Allister, J., Glaser, D. and Brandon, M. (2013) 'Responses to concerns about child maltreatment: A qualitative study of GPs in England.' *BMJ Open 3*, 12, e003894.

Woodman, J., Lecky, F., Hodes, D., Pitt, M., Taylor, B. and Gilbert, R. (2010) 'Screening injured children for physical abuse or neglect in emergency departments: A systematic review.' *Child: Care, Health and Development 36*, 2, 153–164.

Woodman, J., Pitt, M., Wentz, R., Taylor, B., Hodes, D. and Gilbert, R.E. (2008) 'Performance of screening tests for child physical abuse in accident and emergency departments.' *Health Technology Assessment 12*, iii, xi–xiii, 1–95.

Woodman, J., Woolley, A., Gilbert, R., Rafi, I. *et al.* (in press) *Policy, Practice and Public Perspectives on the Role of GPs in Safeguarding Children: A Collaborative Study Involving UCL–Institute of Child Health, the RCGP, the University of Surrey and the NSPCC.* London: NSPCC.

World Health Organization (2013) *European Report on Preventing Maltreatment.* Copenhagen: WHO.

Wrennall, L. (2010) 'Surveillance and child protection: De-mystifying the Trojan Horse.' *Surveillance and Society 7*, 3/4, 304–324.

Chapter 4

PREVENTING ABUSE

Getting it Right from the Start

Jane Barlow

Introduction

A number of high profile cases have drawn attention to the need for more effective working in terms of the safeguarding of very young children (for example, Haringey Local Safeguarding Children Board 2010a, b). Infants are over-represented in terms of the overall numbers of maltreated children and have a considerably higher than average risk of being the victims of homicide (Smith *et al.* 2012). Recent research found that infants identified as being at significant risk of maltreatment were not given adequate protection within a timeframe that was consistent with their developmental needs (Ward *et al.* 2010, 2012).

The focus of this chapter is on maltreatment that occurs during the first two years of a child's life. The evidence suggests that this is a significant period in terms of the child's rapidly developing nervous system and their ability for affect regulation, and that parent–infant interaction and the attachment relationship play a key role in facilitating these aspects of development. The first part of this chapter examines the specific aspects of the parent–infant interaction that facilitate normal infant development, and describes the characteristics of severely compromised interaction. It examines the evidence about the factors that compromise a parent's ability to provide sensitive attuned interaction, and the long-term impact on the child of such 'atypical' or anomalous parent–infant interaction.

The second part of the chapter examines a new care pathway aimed at the early identification and support of women who are at high risk of severely compromised parent–infant interaction. It is suggested that such perinatal models should involve the provision of intensive assessment and support beginning in pregnancy and continuing throughout the first year, and the early removal of infants (i.e., by 6–8 months of age) where there is insufficient evidence of improved parent–infant interaction (Barlow and Schrader-MacMillan, 2010).

Definition

Maltreatment refers not only to acts toward the child that 'have a high probability of causing harm to their health or to any aspect of their development (physical, emotional or social etc)', but also, according to the World Health Organization, 'the failure to provide a developmentally appropriate and supportive environment in which the child can develop the full range of emotional and social competencies commensurate with her or his personal potential' (WHO 1999).

The failure to provide a developmentally appropriate and supportive environment is particularly significant when it occurs during the first and second year of life because infants in most western countries are highly dependent on a limited number of caregivers, and because their interaction with these primary caregivers plays a significant role in their later development (see below for a detailed discussion). It is suggested that a key aspect of a developmentally appropriate environment in the first year of life is sensitive parent–infant interaction and adequate levels of stimulation, and that severely compromised interaction and stimulation therefore constitute emotional maltreatment and neglect.

The prevalence of early abuse

Recent estimates show that severely suboptimal parenting of infants is a major public health problem. Infants under one account for up to 11.3 per cent of children who are the subject of a child protection plan in England (Department for Education 2013). Neglect (49%) and emotional abuse (25%) account for nearly three-quarters of these, but infants also face four times the average risk of child homicide (see Bunting 2011 for an overview), the risk being greatest in the first three months and the perpetrators being the parents in most cases. Non-accidental head injuries are also high in this age group and result in up to 30 per cent mortality and significant neurological impairment in around half of the survivors (Dias *et al.* 2005). Rates of abuse of very young children in the general population may be up to 25 per cent higher than indicated by official estimates (Sidebotham 2000).

Concern about possible abuse of infants has increased over the past few years, and recent estimates by the Association of Directors of Children's Services of a large sample of Local Authorities found a 63.3 per cent increase in children under the age of one with a child protection plan (Brooks 2010).

The Department for Education (2013) child death statistics found that 16 per cent of deaths of babies aged 0–27 days and 29 per cent of deaths of infants aged 28–374 days had modifiable factors.

Parent–infant interaction

The impact of the environment

The first two years of a child's life are particularly important in terms of later development, primarily because of the impact of the early environment on the infant's developing neurological system. Research from a range of disciplines (for example, neuroscience, developmental psychology, infant mental health, and genetics) has converged in terms of a recognition that the child's neurodevelopment is highly dependent on and influenced by the child's environment, and that 'ontogenesis' (i.e., the development of the self) 'proceeds in the context of the nature–nurture interaction' (Glaser 2000). Perhaps most significantly, it is recognised that 'the self-organization of the developing brain occurs in the *context of a relationship with another self,* another brain', and that the infant's primary caretaker fulfils this role (Schore 1994, p.xx). There is now a significant body of research highlighting the impact of particular types of early environmental experience on the infant's developing brain (for example, the natural experiments created by the children raised in Romanian orphanages who experienced considerable sensory deprivation (Chugani *et al.* 2001)), in addition to research about the impact of early trauma, neglect and maltreatment (for example, Grassi-Oliveira, Ashy and Stein 2008; Glaser 2000).

In addition, infants are born unable to regulate their affect, and the capacity for affect regulation is a function of the parent–infant interaction and is mediated via the attachment relationship, which begins during the first year of life. The attachment system comprises a significant bio-behavioural feedback mechanism with a key role in the dyadic regulation of emotion (Schore 1994, 2001). Around two-thirds of infants have a secure attachment, with the remaining children being either insecurely attached (i.e., either 'avoidant' in which they over-regulate their emotions or 'resistant' in which they under-regulate them) or disorganised, in which no consistent pattern of behaviour is established. The precursors of a secure attachment relationship are maternal sensitivity and attunement (for example, De Wolff and Van Ijzendoorn 1997), and a number of types of compromised parent–infant interaction (see below) have been associated with disorganised attachment, which is found in around 82 per cent of children who have been abused (Carlson *et al.* 1989).

Which aspects of parent–infant interaction are important for infant development?

Infants have a range of self-organising neurobehavioral capacities, but are on the whole highly dependent on their caregiver to help them to regulate their internal states, which takes place through *reciprocal* interactions with attachment figures (Tronick 2007). Early research in the field of developmental psychology identified that mother–infant interaction was bi-directional, synchronous and coordinated, such that infants communicate to the parents their regulatory state (i.e., being distressed), and sensitive parents are able to respond to the meaning of such communication (Tronick 2007). Tronick (1989) used a range of microanalytic observations of parent–infant interaction and the still-face paradigm to demonstrate the impact on infants of perturbations to normal interactional exchanges, particularly in mothers experiencing postnatal depression. Overall, this research highlighted the importance of split-second interactions, where parents acknowledge infant cues by responding contingently, elaborating infant expressions and adjusting the timing to hold attention and affect, in supporting the infant in the key developmental task of learning to regulate their emotions and behaviour (see Tronick 2007 for a summary).

While early research in the field of attachment highlighted the importance of parenting that was 'sensitive' for infants to become securely attached to their primary caregiver (i.e., securely attached infants have learned that they can turn to their caregiver when distressed for comfort), a review of the evidence showed that such sensitivity did not explain all of the variance and that other aspects of parenting were also important (De Wolff and Ijzendoorn 1997). Recent research has highlighted the importance of two further components. The term 'reflective function' refers to a parent's capacity to treat their infant as an intentional being, and to understand their behaviours in terms of feelings, beliefs and intentions (Fonagy *et al.* 2002). Meins coined the term 'mind-minded' to similarly refer to a mother's ability to treat her infant as an individual with a mind (Meins *et al.* 2001, 2002). Mothers who are low in mind-mindedness tend to view the child more concretely in terms of need states that must be satisfied (Meins *et al.* 2001, 2002). Parental mind-minded comments during interaction with six-month-old infants have been significantly correlated with behavioural sensitivity and interactive synchrony (Lundy 2003; Meins *et al.* 2001) and are a better predictor of attachment security at one year than is maternal behavioral sensitivity (Meins *et al.* 2001).

Research has also highlighted the importance of 'midrange' interaction, which is characterised by parent interaction that is neither too intrusive nor too passive as a consequence of the parent being preoccupied with self-regulation or interactive regulation (i.e., optimally in the midrange) (Beebe and Lachman 2013; Beebe *et al.* 2010). This research showed that dyadic interaction outside the midrange was associated with insecure and disorganised attachment.

What characterises severely suboptimal parent–infant interaction?

A number of aspects of parent–infant interaction have now been identified as playing a significant role in derailing the development of children, particularly in terms of their attachment organisation. 'Fr-behaviour' refers to parent–infant interaction that is both frightened and frightening (Main and Hesse 1990). Such behaviours can be subtle (for example, periods of being dazed and unresponsive) or more overt (deliberately frightening children). Fr-behaviours are distinct from neglect and express a distorted image of the child, which is the consequence of the mother's unresolved trauma and losses (Jacobvitz, Hazen and Riggs 1997).

More recent research has suggested that such Fr-behaviours are 'embedded in a broader context of disrupted affective communication between mother and infant' (Lyons-Ruth *et al.* 2005). This research highlighted the importance of 'atypical' or 'anomalous' parenting behaviours that consist of 'parental withdrawing responses (i.e., maternal behaviours that are rejecting of the infant); negative-intrusive responses (i.e., where the mother is mocking or pulls at part of the infant's body); role-confused responses (i.e., where the mother seeks attention from their infant to meet her own emotional needs); disoriented responses (i.e., the mother adopts a frightened expression or has a sudden complete loss of affect) and affective communication errors (i.e., in which the mother might be positive while the infant is distressed).

A recent meta-analysis of 12 studies identified a strong association between such atypical or 'anomalous' parent–infant interaction at 12–18 months and disorganised attachment (Madigan *et al.* 2006), which is highly stable and associated with wide-ranging psychopathology in childhood (see next section).

Consequences of child maltreatment during the first two years of life

Recent reviews of the evidence about the impact of early abuse on the child's developing psychobiological system have highlighted the impact on the stress response, including dysregulation of the hypothalamic-pituitary-adrenal axis and parasympathetic and catecholamine responses (Grassi-Oliveira *et al.* 2008; McCrory *et al.* 2013). The most recent of these reviews found that the 'structural consequences of childhood maltreatment include disruptive development of the corpus callosum, left neocortex, hippocampus, and amygdala'; 'functional consequences include increased electrical irritability in limbic areas, frontal lobe dysfunctions and reduced functional activity of the cerebellar vermis'; and 'neurohumoral consequences included the reprogramming activity of hypothalamo-pituitary-adrenal (HPA) axis and subsequently the stress response' (McCrory *et al.* 2013).

In terms of attachment and related developmental problems, up to 80 per cent of children who are abused during the first few years of life have 'disorganised' attachment in which there is:

> *A lack of an organised strategy for using a caregiver in times of distress, revealed through odd behaviors (for example, repeated incomplete approaches to the parents, stilling, failing to seek contact when very distressed) that appear to reflect fear and confusion on the part of the infant. (Benoit et al. 2001, p.621)*

Disorganised attachment is associated with developmental psycho-pathology (Green and Goldwyn 2002), including symptoms that meet clinical criteria in older children (for example 8–12 years) (Borelli *et al.* 2010). Early emotional maltreatment is also associated with a range of problematic behaviours in childhood (for example, non-compliance; negativistic, impulsive behaviour; high dependence on teachers; nervous signs; self-abusive behaviour and other problems) (Egeland, Sroufe and Erickson 1983), and with mental illness by adolescence (a majority of these children had received at least one diagnosis of mental illness and 73 per cent were comorbid for two or more disorders) (Egeland 2009).

The most recent UK prospective longitudinal study of a group of infants identified as suffering or likely to suffer significant harm found that by three years of age over half the children without a recognised medical condition were showing evidence of significant developmental or behavioural difficulties – aggression and speech problems being the most evident (Ward *et al.* 2010).

Factors influencing parent–infant interaction

The research on early parenting that has been characterised as 'Fr-behaviour' has identified the importance of unresolved trauma and losses on the part of the parent (Jacobvitz *et al.* 1997), and suggests that parent–infant interaction may play a significant role in the intergenerational transmission of abuse and trauma. A number of other factors have also been shown to be associated with suboptimal parent–infant interactions, including parental mental health problems, substance dependency and domestic abuse (Cleaver, Unell and Aldgate 2011).

A range of mental health problems have been identified as impacting the parent–infant relationship. Postnatal depression, for example, has been shown to be associated with parental intrusiveness and/or neglect (Murray *et al.* 1996), while more severe mental illnesses (SMIs) such as schizophrenia have been associated with less sensitivity and responsivity to the baby at entry to in-patient care but not at discharge (Pawlby *et al.* 2005), with maternal responding that is more remote, insensitive, intrusive and self-absorbed (Wan *et al.* 2007, 2008a), and with speech that is less infant-directed (Wan *et al.* 2008b), although not in all studies (Pawlby *et al.* 2010). Recent research suggests that parents diagnosed with borderline personality disorder (BPD) are less sensitive and show less structuring in their interaction with their infants, and that their infants are less attentive, interested and eager for interaction with their mother (Newman *et al.* 2008). This study also found these mothers to be less satisfied with their parenting, less competent and more distressed. There is also evidence of significantly more mothers with BPD being rated as 'intrusively insensitive' to their infants at two months (Crandell, Patrick and Hobson 2003), and at 12 months (Hobson *et al.* 2005), and of increased 'disorganised' attachment (Hobson *et al.* 2005).

Children of drug-dependent parents are at high risk of maltreatment with one study showing a significantly higher risk of child protection proceedings in infants of substance misusing parents (32.4% vs. 7.1%) (Street *et al.* 2004). Many of the infants of drug-dependent parents are exposed to such substances *in utero* and researchers in the field have highlighted difficulties in knowing whether the problems that have been identified in the social interaction of, for example, opiate-addicted mothers (Bernstein and Hans 1994; Hans, Bernstein and Henson 1999) are due to the impact on the infant's neurobehavioural system, the dyadic organisation of the interaction or both (Tronick *et al.* 2005). Other complicating factors include the high exposure of such infants to other toxic substances (i.e., alcohol and tobacco) (Tronick *et al.* 2005), and the co-morbidity that is also often present. Studies nevertheless show that cocaine exposure is associated with higher levels of negative and mismatched engagement with infants (i.e., in which the mother was negatively engaged with a neutrally engaged infant) (Tronick *et al.* 2005).

Although there is currently no research that has explicitly examined the parent–infant interaction of women experiencing domestic violence, research suggests an impact of domestic violence during infancy in terms of increased distress reactions to conflict (De Jonghe *et al.* 2005), and trauma symptoms (Bogat *et al.* 2006), with evidence that the impact of such violence on infant externalising behaviour is mediated by parental mental health and parenting behaviours.

Preventing abuse: a model of early intervention

Working within the child's timeline

Recent research has identified an urgent need to provide adequate protection for infants within a timeframe that is consistent with their developmental needs (Ward *et al.* 2010, 2012). This requires the implementation of a perinatal model of assessment and intervention that is aimed explicitly at identifying and working with high-risk families during pregnancy and the immediate postnatal period, with the primary aim of supporting women to make the necessary changes that will enable them to continue to parent their baby, alongside effective assessment that will enable early removal (i.e., before six months of age), where there is sufficient evidence that a satisfactory level of change has not been achieved.

Oxfordshire Parents under Pressure (OXPuP) comprises one such model of working that has been established in a children's social care team of both social and family support workers. OXPuP involves the delivery of an intensive evidence-based intervention within the context of an assessment of the parents' *capacity to change*. The care pathway involves referral by midwives, at 18 and 28 weeks of pregnancy, of all pregnant women who meet the criteria for being vulnerable (such as severe mental health problems, substance/alcohol misuse, domestic violence, previous removal of child).

Assessment of parenting capacity aims to evaluate the parent's current ability to meet the developmental needs of their children, and typically involves a cross-sectional assessment including the collection of evidence about previous events (history) and current functioning (Harnett 2007). The assessment of *capacity to change* adds a time dimension and asks whether parents – over a specified period of time and if provided with the right support – are ready, willing and able to make the necessary changes to ensure their child's well-being and safety. It involves four key states (Harnett 2007). The first involves a cross sectional assessment, which is undertaken using a range of standardised assessment tools alongside the workers' professional judgment (known as the use of Structured Professional Judgment). Stage two involves establishing a set of short-term goals in collaboration with the family, and using goal attainment scaling, which enables the practitioner to make clear what improvement, no change and deterioration for each of the specified goals would involve. Stage three involves the delivery of a time-limited intervention or support plan aimed at helping the family to address the identified goals. The final stage involves a review of the extent to which goals have been achieved, and the re-administration of the standardised assessment instruments to ascertain if there is improved parental functioning.

The early findings suggest a correlation between the new care pathway and timely child-focused permanency planning for those babies who cannot remain within their families, and an impact in other areas, such as for example, the judicial system with potential savings of court time, and for others involved in the process such as foster carers.

Assessment tools

The evidence shows that the use of 'standardised' assessment tools can enable practitioners to provide a more accurate classification of risk of harm, compared with clinical judgment alone, which is only just better than guessing at 65 per cent (for a summary: White and Walsh 2006).

Structured Professional Judgment involves professional decision-making, which is explicitly supported by the use of standardised assessment tools (Barlow, Hall and Fisher 2012) including systems that have been explicitly designed for assessing and analysing information gathered about whether a child is suffering, or is likely to suffer significant harm (for example, Safeguarding Assessment and Analysis Framework, SAAF) (Bentovim *et al.* 2010) and the type of assessment measures recommended as part of the Assessment Framework (Department of Health, Department for Education and Employment and Home Office 2000).

The decision about which assessment tools to use as part of the OXPuP care pathway was based on the evidence about which factors are strongly associated with, or predict, latter attachment security. We therefore included a range of standardised parent–report and independent measures that are aimed at assessing parental psychological function, including the Depression, Anxiety and Stress Scale (DASS) (Lovibond and Lovibond 1995), their exposure to domestic violence (Domestic Abuse Stalking Harassment; DASH 2009), and their substance use (Alcohol Use Disorders Identification Test Audit-C). Parent–infant interaction is assessed using a three-minute videorecording of the parent and infant interacting 'as they would normally'. The interaction is coded externally using the CARE-Index, which measures three aspects of maternal behaviour (sensitivity, covert and overt hostility, unresponsiveness) and four aspects of toddler behaviour (cooperativeness, compulsive compliance, difficultness and passivity), and discriminates abusing, neglecting, problematic and adequate dyads (Crittenden 1981). The cost of coding each videotape is low (i.e., in the region of £75) and can be undertaken by a coder who has achieved court-level reliability (i.e., can produce a report that will meet the needs of a court-based assessment process) if necessary. Parenting attitudes are assessed using the Brief Child Abuse Potential Inventory (Milner 1986), and mother's feelings about the relationship with the baby in terms of her peceptions about the baby's warmth and intrusiveness are assessed using the Mother Object Relationship Scale (MORS) (Oates and Gervai 1984). Parental capacity for reflective function is assessed using an hour-long interview called the Parent Development Interview (Slade *et al.* 2005). The amount and quality of social support is assessed using the Social Support Scale (Sarason *et al.* 1983) and the home environment is assessed using the HOME Inventory which assesses a nature and quantity of the stimulation available in the home (Caldwell and Bradley 2003).

The above standardised tools are used alongside the professionals' judgement about the family's willingness to engage and the extent to which the agreed goals have been achieved to make a decision about the abilty of the parent to meet the child's developmental needs. The assessment process is undertaken within the context of the delivery of an evidence-based intervention.

An evidence-based model of intervention

The Parents under Pressure (PuP) programme is an intensive home-based intervention, which has been shown to be effective in bringing about significant reductions in child abuse potential, rigid parenting attitudes, and child behaviour problems in substance-dependent parents of children aged 2–8 years (Dawe *et al.* 2003; Dawe and Harnett 2007). It consists of 12 modules that are typically delivered over the course of 20 weeks, each session being around 1–2 hours duration, with some of the content being drawn from the Parent Workbook. The programme is delivered alongside the use of a standard case-management approach, and the selection of modules is based on individual family need. The use of a case-management framework enables the practitioner to address day-to-day issues such as housing and finances, and provides the opportunity to assess the family's ability to utilise the coping skills that are being developed. The program begins with a comprehensive assessment and individual case formulation, which is conducted collaboratively with the family, and specific targets for change are identified, which then become the focus of treatment.

The programme is underpinned by an ecological model of child development, which recognises the need to target multiple domains of family functioning, including the psychological functioning of individuals in the family, the parent–child relationship, and a range of social–contextual factors (Dawe and Harnett 2007). In terms of the parent–child relationship, the model is also underpinned by attachment theory, and focuses explicitly on enabling parents to develop a safe and nurturing relationship and to provide the type of parent–infant interaction which is strongly associated with the development of a secure attachment. For example, Module 6, *Connecting with Your Baby*, focuses on helping a parent connect with their child through a series of exercises that help the parent to reflect on their own relational experience with their baby. This module aims to support the parent to learn their baby's language, and to provide 'mindful play' in which a parent is taught to use mindfulness constructs to observe, describe and participate during play and special times. Module 7, *Mindful Child Management*, teaches non-punitive child management techniques and locates these within a developmental context to ensure that parents understand the most age-appropriate strategy to use. This also requires a sensitive understanding of the baby/child's cognitive capacity, and developmental charts supplement the Parent Workbook as a way of helping parents feel proud about their baby/child's development while also developing realistic views about their baby/child's capacity.

The parent's capacity for managing dysregulated affect and impulsive behaviour, and their ability to exercise control over their own emotional responsivity in both stressful parenting situations such as prolonged crying of an infant, and situations requiring behaviour management in order to reduce impulsive, emotion-driven punishment (Gershoff 2002) are addressed through the teaching of mindfulness techniques. These exercises involve mindfulness meditations in addition to helping a parent develop a greater awareness of being fully present in the moment with their infant during daily activities (i.e., by helping them to learn to take pleasure in watching an infant sleep, have bath times and play). The use of techniques such as 'urge surfing', and understanding craving (in relation to families where there is substance dependency), are aimed at supporting parents to manage negative mood states. As the quality of the parent–child relationship is related to the parent's capacity to provide sensitive, responsive and nurturing caregiving (Biringen and Easterbrooks 2012), the parent is helped to recognise their own areas of strengths and potential difficulties by the use of videorecording, shared discussion with the practitioner and completion of exercises using the Parent Workbook.

The use of other modules depends on the unique needs of each family. For example, the *Relationship* module is aimed at improving communication in intimate relationships, and includes sections on defining the qualities of a good and loving intimate relationship for couples with a troubled relationship history.

Mother and baby foster placements are available to support women about whom there are ongoing concerns, alongside concurrent foster care, which is aimed at preventing the 'double jeopardy' that results from a care system in which children are rescued from abusive environments and then traumatised by a series of non-permanent foster placements in which their attachment relationships are repeatedly severed (Ward *et al.* 2010, 2012).

All of the practitioners in the OXPuP team have been trained in the use of PuP, but the assessment process that is conducted alongside the delivery of this intervention is undertaken by the qualified social worker.

Early findings suggest that a significant proportion of women are able to make use of the additional support that is provided, and that for those women who are not able to make the necessary changes, decisions to remove the infant are made within a timeframe that is consistent with their longer-term developmental needs (Barlow *et al.* forthcoming).

Conclusion

Research from a range of disciplines has highlighted the first two years of life as being a critical period in terms of a number of significant aspects of development and, as such, the consequences of maltreatment that occurs during this period are both severe and protracted. The findings of a recent UK prospective longitudinal study of a group of infants at high risk of suffering significant harm found that the developmental and behavioural difficulties identified in this group occurred while infants remained living at home amidst ongoing concerns and 'whilst professionals waited fruitlessly for parents to change', or who had experienced long delays prior to being removed (Ward *et al.* 2010, 2012). This study highlights an urgent need to develop models of working to safeguard children during this period that are consistent with the child's developmental needs.

OXPuP is one example of a new care pathway that has been developed to ensure that women and couples who are at high risk of not being able to provide their infant with the type of care that is recognised to be fundamental to the infant's development, are identified early in their pregnancy and supported to achieve change. This type of intensive standardised assessment within the context of the delivery of an evidence-based method of working with parents is going to be fundamental to the eradication of child maltreatment.

References

Barlow, J. and Schrader-MacMillan, A. (2010) *Safeguarding Children from Emotional Maltreatment.* London: Jessica Kingsley Publishers.

Barlow, J., Coe, C., Dawe, S. and Harnett, P. (forthcoming) *That Sounds Like Real Social Work: A New Care Pathway for Vulnerable Pregnant Women.*

Barlow, J., Hall, D. and, Fisher, J. (2012) *Systematic Review of Models of Analysing Significant Harm.* London: Department for Education.

Beebe, B. and Lachmann, F.M. (2013) *Infant Research and Adult Treatment: Co-constructing Interactions*. London: Routledge.

Beebe, B., Jaffe, J., Markese, S., Buck, K. *et al.* (2010) 'The origins of 12-month attachment: A microanalysis of 4-month mother–infant interaction.' *Attachment and Human Development 12*, 1–2, 3–141.

Benoit, D., Madigan, S., Lecce, S., Shea, B. and Goldberg, S. (2001) 'Atypical maternal behaviour before and after intervention.' *Infant Mental Health Journal 22*, 611–626.

Bentovim, A., Cox, A., Bingley-Miller, L., Pizzey, S. and Tapp, S. (2010) *Safeguarding Assessment and Analysis Framework: Evidence Based Approaches to Assessing Harm, The Risk of Future Harm and Prospects for Intervention*. York: Child and Family Training.

Bernstein V.J. and Hans, S.L. (1994) 'Predicting the developmental outcomes of two-year-old children born exposed to methadone: Impact of social-environmental risk factors.' *Journal of Clinical Child Psychology 23*, 349–359.

Biringen, Z. and Easterbrooks, M.A. (2012) 'Emotional availability: Concept, research, and window on developmental psychopathology.' *Development and Psychopathology 24*, 1, 1–8.

Bogat, G.A., De Jonghe, E., Levendosky, A.A., von Eye, A. and Davidson, W.S. (2006) 'Trauma symptoms in infants who witness violence towards their mothers.' *Child Abuse and Neglect: The International Journal 30*, 109–125.

Borelli, J.L., David, D.H., Crowley, M.J. and Mayes, L.C (2010) 'Links between disorganised attachment classification and clinical symptoms in school-aged children.' *Journal of Child and Family Studies 19*, 3, 243–256.

Brooks, C. (2010) *Safeguarding Pressures Project: Results of Data Collection (Research Report)*. Manchester: ADCS.

Bunting, L. (2011) *The Prevalence of Infant Abuse and Maltreatment Related Deaths in the UK*. London: NSPCC.

Caldwell, B.M. and Bradley, R.H. (2003) *Home Observation for Measurement of the Environment: Administration Manual*. Tempe, AZ: Family and Human Dynamics Research Institute, Arizona State University.

Carlson, V., Cicchetti, D., Barnett, D. and Braunwald, K. (1989) 'Disorganised/disoriented attachment relationships in maltreated infants.' *Developmental Psychology 25*, 525–531.

Chugani, H.T., Behen, M.E., Muzik, O., Juhasz, C., Nagy, F. and Chugani, D.C. (2001) 'Local brain functional activity following early deprivation: A study of postinstitutionalised Romanian orphans.' *Neuroimage 14*, 1290–1301.

Cleaver, H., Unell, I and Aldgate, J. (2011) *Children's Needs – Parenting Capacity. Child Abuse: Parental Mental Illness, Learning Disability, Substance Misuse and Domestic Violence*, 2nd edn. London: Stationery Office.

Crandell, L.E., Patrick, P.H.P. and Hobson, R.P. (2003) 'Still-face interactions between mothers with borderline personality disorder and their 2-month old infants.' *British Journal of Psychiatry 183*, 3, 239–247.

Dawe, S. and Harnett, P.H. (2007) 'Reducing child abuse potential in methadone maintained parents: Results from a randomised controlled trial.' *Journal of Substance Abuse Treatment 32*, 4, 381–390.

Dawe, S., Harnett, P.H., Rendalls, V. and Staiger, P. (2003) 'Improving family functioning and child outcome in methadone maintained families: The Parents Under Pressure Program.' *Drug and Alcohol Review 22*, 3, 299–307.

De Jonghe, E.S., Bogat, G.A., Levendosky, A.A., von Eye, A. and Davidson, W.S. (2005) 'Infant exposure to domestic violence predicts heightened sensitivity to adult verbal conflict.' *Infant Mental Health Journal 26*, 3, 268–281.

Department for Education (2013) *Characteristics of Children in Need in England, 2012–13*. London: Department for Education. Available at www.gov.uk/government/uploads/system/uploads/attachment_data/file/254084/SFR45-2013_Text.pdf, accessed on 18 April 2014.

Department of Health, Department of Education and Employment and Home Office (2000) *The Framework for the Assessment of Children in Need and Their Families*. London: Stationery Office.

De Wolff, M.S. and van Ijzendoorn, M.H. (1997) 'Sensitivity and attachment: A meta-analysis on parental antecedents of infant attachment security.' *Child Development 68*, 4, 571–591.

Dias, M.S., Smith, K., de Guehery, K., Mazur, P., Li, V. and Shaffer, M.L. (2005) 'Preventing abusive head trauma among infants and young children: A hospital-based, parent education program.' *Pediatrics 115*, 4, e470–e477.

Egeland, B. (2009) 'Taking stock: Childhood emotional maltreatment and developmental psychopathology.' *Child Abuse and Neglect 33*, 1, 22–26.

Egeland, B., Sroufe, L. and Erickson, M. (1983) 'The developmental consequence of different patterns of maltreatment.' *Child Abuse and Neglect 7*, 4, 459–469.

Fonagy, P., Gergely, G., Jurist, E. and Target, M. (2002) *Affect Regulation, Mentalization and the Development of the Self*. New York: Other Press.

Gershoff, E. (2002) 'Corporal punishment by parents and associated child behaviors and experiences: A meta-analytic and theoretical review.' *Psychological Bulletin 128*, 4, 539–579.

Glaser, D. (2000) 'Child abuse and neglect and the brain: A review.' *Journal of Child Psychology and Psychiatry 41*, 1, 97–116.

Grassi-Oliveira, R., Ashy, M. and Stein, L.M. (2008) 'Psychobiology of childhood maltreatment: Effects of allostatic load?' *Revista Brasileira de Psiquiatria 30*, 1, 60–68.

Green, J. and Goldwyn, R. (2002) 'Attachment disorganisation and psychopathology: New findings in attachment research and their potential implications for developmental psychopathology in childhood.' *Journal of Child Psychology and Psychiatry 43*, 7, 835–846.

Hans, S.L., Bernstein, V.J. and Henson, L.G. (1999) 'The role of psychopathology in the parenting of drug dependent women.' *Development and Psychopathology 11*, 957–977.

Haringey Local Safeguarding Children Board (2010a) *Serious Care Review: Child A (First Review)*. London: Haringey Local Safeguarding Children Board. Available at www.gov.uk/government/uploads/system/uploads/attachment_data/file/182527/first_serious_case_review_overview_report_relating_to_peter_connelly_dated_november_2008.pdf, accessed on 1 August 2014.

Haringey Local Safeguarding Children Board (2010b) *Serious Care Review: Child A (Second Review)*. London: Haringey Local Safeguarding Children Board. Available at www.gov.uk/government/uploads/system/uploads/attachment_data/file/182538/second_serious_case_overview_report_relating_to_peter_connelly_dated_march_2009.pdf, accessed on 1 August 2014.

Harnett, P. (2007) 'A procedure for assessing parents' capacity for change in child protection cases.' *Children and Youth Services Review 29*, 9, 1179–1188.

Hobson, P., Patrick, M., Crandell, L., Garcia-Perez, R. and Lee, A. (2005) 'Personal relatedness and attachment in infants of mothers with borderline personality disorder.' *Developmental and Psychopathology 17*, 2, 329–347.

Jacobvitz, D. Hazen, N.L. and Riggs, S. (1997) 'Disorganized mental processes in mothers, frightened/frightening behavior in caregivers, and disoriented, disorganized behavior in infancy.' Paper presented at the biennial meeting of the Society for Research in Child Development, Washington, DC.

Lieberman, A.F. and Van Horn, P. (2011) *Psychotherapy with Infants and Young Children: Repairing the Effects of Stress and Trauma on Early Attachment*. New York: Guilford Press.

Lovibond, S.H. and Lovibond, P.F. (1995) *Manual for the Depression Anxiety Stress Scales*, 2nd edn. Sydney: Psychology Foundation.

Lundy, B.L. (2003) 'Father- and mother-infant face-to-face interactions: Differences in mind-related comments and infant attachment?' *Infant Behavior and Development 26*, 200–212.

Lyons-Ruth, K., Yellin, C., Melnick, S. and Atwood, G. (2005) 'Expanding the concept of unresolved mental states: Hostile/Helpless states of mind on the Adult Attachment Interview are associated with disrupted mother–infant communication and infant disorganization.' *Development and Psychopathology 17*, 1, 1–23.

Madigan, M., Bakermans-Kranenburg, M.J., van Ijzendoorn, M.H., Moran, G., Pederson, D.R. and Benoit, D. (2006) 'Unresolved states of mind, anomalous parenting behaviour, and disorganized attachment: A review and meta-analysis of a transmission gap.' *Attachment and Human Development 8*, 2, 89–111.

Main, M. and Hesse, E. (1990) 'Parents' Unresolved Traumatic Experiences Are Related to Infant Disorganized Attachment Status: Is Frightened and/or Frightening Parental Behavior the Linking Mechanism?' In M. Greenberg, D. Cicchetti and E.M. Cummings (eds) *Attachment in the Preschool Years: Theory, Research and Intervention*. Chicago: University of Chicago Press.

Main, M. and Solomon, J. (1986) 'Discovery of an Insecure Disorganized/Disoriented Attachment Pattern: Procedures, Findings and Implications for Classification of Behaviour.' In M.W. Yogman and T.B. Brazelton (eds) *Affective Development in Infancy*. Norwood, NJ: Ablex.

McCrory, E., De Brito, K.P., Bird, G., Sebastian, C. *et al.* (2013) 'Research review: The neurobiology and genetics of maltreatment and adversity.' *Journal of Child Psychology and Psychiatry 51*, 10, 1079–1095.

Meins, E.C., Fernyhough, C., Fradley, E. and Tuckey, M. (2001) 'Rethinking maternal sensitivity: Mothers' comments on infants' mental processes predict security of attachment at 12 months.' *Journal of Child Psychology and Psychiatry 42*, 5, 637–648.

Meins, E.C., Fernyhough, C., Wainwright, R., Gupta, M.D., Fradley, E. and Tuckey, M. (2002) 'Maternal mind-mindedness and attachment security as predictors of theory of mind understanding.' *Child Development 73*, 6, 1715–1726.

Murray, L., Fiori-Cowley, A., Hooper, R. and Cooper, P. (1996) 'The impact of postnatal depression and associated adversity on early mother-infant interactions and later infant outcome.' *Child Development 67*, 5, 2512–2526.

Oates, J. and Gervai, J. (1984) *Mothers Object Relations Scale: Assessing Mothers' Models of Their Infants.* Milton Keynes: Open University.

Pawlby, S., Fernyhough, C., Meins, E., Pariante, C.M., Seneviratne, G. and Bentall, R.P. (2010) 'Mind-mindedness and maternal responsiveness in infant–mother interactions in mothers with severe mental illness.' *Psychological Medicine 40*, 11, 1861–1869.

Pawlby, S., Marks, M., Clarke, R., Best, E., Weir, D. and O'Keane, V. (2005) 'Mother–infant interaction in postpartum women with severe mental illness, before and after treatment.' *Archives of Women's Metal Health 8*, 120.

Sarason, I.G, Levine, H.M., Basham, R.B. and Sarason, B.R. (1983) 'Assessing social support: The Social Support Questionnaire.' *Journal of Personality and Social Psychology 44*, 127–139.

Schore, A.N. (1994) *Affect Regulation and the Origin of the Self: The Neurobiology of Emotional Development.* Hillsdale, NJ: Erlbaum.

Schore, A.N. (2001) 'The effects of early relational trauma on right brain development, affect regulation, and infant mental health.' *Infant Mental Health Journal 22*, 1–2, 201–269.

Sidebotham, P.D. (2000) 'The ALSPAC study team. Patterns of child abuse in early childhood, a cohort study of the "Children of the Nineties."' *Child Abuse Review 9*, 311–320.

Slade, A., Bernbach, E., Grienenberger, J., Levy, D. and Locker, A. (2005) 'Addendum to Fonagy, Target, Steele, and Steele Reflective Functioning Scoring Manual for Use with the Parent Development Interview, Version 2.0.' Unpublished manuscript. New York: The City College and Graduate Center of the City University of New York.

Smith, K., Osborne, S., Lau, I. and Britton, A. (eds) (2012) 'Homicides, Firearm Offences and Intimate Violence 2010/11: Supplementary Volume 2 to Crime in England and Wales 2010/11.' London: Home Office.

Street, K., Harrington, J., Chiang, W., Cairns P. and Ellis, M. (2004) 'How great is the risk of abuse in infants born to drug using mothers?' *Child: Care, Health and Development 30*, 4, 325–330.

Tronick, E.Z. (1989) 'Emotions and emotional communication in infants.' *American Journal of Psychology 44*, 112–119.

Tronick, E.Z, (2007) *The Neurobehavioral and Social–Emotional Development of Infants and Children.* London: W.W. Norton.

Tronick, E.Z., Messenger, D.S., Weinberg, M.K., Lester, B.M. *et al.* (2005) 'Cocaine exposure is associated with subtle compromises of infants' and mothers' social–emotional behaviour and dyadic features of their interaction in the face-to-face still-face paradigm.' *Developmental Psychology 41,* 5, 711–722.

Wan, M.W., Salmon, M.P., Riordan, D., Appleby, L., Webb, R. and Abel, K.M. (2007) 'What predicts mother–infant interaction in schizophrenia?' *Psychological Medicine 37,* 537–538.

Wan, M.W., Penketh, V., Salmon, M.P. and Abel, K. (2008a) 'Content and style of speech from mothers with schizophrenia towards their infants.' *Psychiatry Research 159,* 109–114.

Wan, M.W., Warren, K., Salmon, M.P. and Abel, K. (2008b) 'Patterns of maternal responding in postpartum mothers with schizophrenia.' *Infant Behaviour and Development 31,* 532–538.

Ward, H., Brown, R., Westlake, D. and Munro, E.R. (2010) *Infants Suffering, or Likely to Suffer, Significant Harm: A Prospective Longitudinal Study.* Department for Education Research Brief. University of Loughborough: Centre for Child and Family Research.

Ward, H., Brown, R., Westlake, D. and Munro, E.R. (2012) *Safeguarding Babies and Very Young Children from Abuse and Neglect.* London: Jessica Kingsley Publishers.

WHO (1999) *Report on the Consultation on Child Abuse Prevention Geneva, March 29–31, 1999.* Geneva: WHO. Available at www.yesican.org/definitions/WHO.html, accessed on 18 April 2014.

Chapter 5

PUBLIC HEALTH APPROACH TO PARENTING AND FAMILY SUPPORT

A Blended Prevention Strategy to Reduce Child Abuse and Neglect

Ron Prinz

Successful prevention of child abuse and neglect requires a broader approach than the sole focus which historically emphasized programming for only the highest risk families. This chapter offers a framework for parenting and family support that combines prevention of child maltreatment with other prevention goals.

Public health emphasis

When we are doing prevention of any kind we should never lose sight of the fact that prevalence reduction is the primary goal. We rarely test our interventions with this goal in mind or think about how we are contributing potentially to prevalence reduction, but it is nonetheless the ultimate and overriding goal of our work. In other areas besides psychosocial problems, there have been public health strategies towards prevention applied, for example, to coronary heart disease and stroke, and these strategies in the US at least have resulted in reductions in death rates. Similarly, control of infectious diseases has been achieved through prevention strategies, including something as simple and straightforward as the posting of signs and invoking promotion in hospitals and restaurants to remind staff to wash their hands frequently and especially after using the toilet. The latter strategy draws on a principle of minimal sufficiency of general utility in public health. As a third example, public health strategies applied to motor vehicle safety have resulted in the reduction of drunk-driving and vehicle fatality rates (Centers for Disease Control and Prevention 1999).

Parenting intervention is a logical and viable domain for application of public health strategies. It has been well established that parenting has a pervasive impact on many areas of child development, behavioural health and life trajectories (Biglan *et al.* 2004; Collins *et al.* 2000; Farah *et al.* 2008; Jones and Prinz 2005; Patterson, Reid and Dishion 1992). Parenting which has gone awry in terms of child maltreatment is especially deleterious for child well-being and subsequent adjustment (Afifi *et al.* 2009; Bolger and Patterson 2003; Ialongo *et al.* 2006). Several decades of research have produced a cogent body of research on evidence-based parenting interventions that are beneficial to children and families (Barrett and Ollendick 2004; Donovan and Spence 2000; Essau 2003; Lochman and van den Steenhoven 2002; Prinz 2007; Prinz and Dumas 2004; Prinz and Jones 2003).

Prevention of child maltreatment

The area of child maltreatment prevention in the US and worldwide is actually behind when it comes to taking a public health population approach, but things are changing. The possibility of applying a public health strategy to the prevention of child maltreatment raises important questions about the rationale for such an approach, what is required, whether it is feasible, and whether it is cost prohibitive.

Rationale

EXTENT OF PROBLEMATIC PARENTING

A first aspect of the rationale involves a recognition that problematic parenting is widespread. Supported by prevalence data presented in other chapters in this volume, official cases of all types of substantiated maltreatment combined across age groups account for a prevalence rate of approximately 1 per cent of children in the US.[1] If one expands the sphere to include investigations, reports, and suspicions the rate is driven up. Nonetheless, considering that the core cases stem from the mainstays of child maltreatment, namely official substantiated cases, the rate is relatively low compared with other problems. A critical issue, though, is that official rates grossly under-estimate both child maltreatment

---

1   In the UK 0.4 per cent of children are on a 'child protection plan'.

specifically and associated problematic parenting more generally, regardless of whether the latter crosses a particular threshold for what is or is not official abuse. For the purposes of prevention, it might be more useful to think of child maltreatment as a continuum not constrained by child protective services involvement.

A telling study conducted by Des Runyan and colleagues shed light on the issue (Theodore *et al.* 2005). They conducted an anonymous random household telephone survey and found that parents reported their own parenting behaviours which met a standard definition of physical abuse at a rate 40 times greater than what the official records for those communities reflected.[2] If one takes into account that some parents might have under-reported because of social desirability demands, the actual rate of physically abusive parenting might even be higher than what was found. In other words, abusive parenting is a more common problem than official statistics reflect, but it also means the field of prevention will have to loosen up how the problem is defined.

Similarly, in my own group's work we conducted a random household telephone survey, reaching parents in 3,600 households with at least one child under age eight. Approximately half of the parents reported heavy reliance on coercive discipline strategies for child misbehaviour. This high frequency suggests that the kinds of practices which might lead to physical abuse are so common as to be almost normative, albeit that many of the coercive parenting situations do not lead to demonstrable abuse. However, in this same anonymous telephone sample, we found that 10 per cent of the parents reported they spanked using an object on a frequent or very frequent basis (i.e., not just occasionally or once in the child's lifetime).

We already know that child maltreatment is severely detrimental to child development (as noted earlier), but we also need to face the reality that problematic parenting really operates on a continuum more inclusive than official abuse and thus has a broader adverse impact on child development. The improvement of parenting in the community, which includes prevention of child maltreatment, is the important overarching goal. Decreasing the prevalence of child maltreatment ultimately contributes to the fundamental goal of raising the level of child well-being for many or all of our children, which is the basis

---

2   Woodman and Gilbert in Chapter 3 report that in developed countries 4 to 10 per cent of children self-report being subject to maltreatment.

for thinking more broadly in terms of the reach of child maltreatment prevention.

POTENTIAL FOR STIGMATISATION

The second issue is stigma and how to sidestep it. If a worker from a helping profession knocks on a parent's door and says, 'Hi, I'm here to prevent child abuse – Can I give you some assistance?' the parent is as likely as not to ask why the worker has contacted them and to say they did not ask for assistance. It is not an inviting strategy when we declare to parents, the actual consumers of our prevention services, that we are here to prevent child abuse and have selected them for such services. Undoubtedly, the general public does need to be aware of the severity and consequences of child abuse, but that is distinct from the issue of how to reach parents in a prevention capacity.

The stigma issue was addressed in a recent report by the US Institute of Medicine (IOM) focused on preventing all kinds of mental, emotional, and behavioral disorders in young people (National Research Council and Institute of Medicine 2009). To address stigma and also increase reach, the IOM task force called for a population health perspective that provides families with easy access to evidence-based preventative interventions in non-stigmatizing ways. This is a tall order but underscores the need to normalize parenting and family support, which in turn provides a less stigmatizing context for reaching families at the most severe end of the spectrum.

TOWARDS A BROADER BUT EFFICIENT APPROACH

We need to adopt intervention content that has broad appeal and avoids compartmentalizing support for parents. Along this line, there is a need to create efficiencies by addressing multiple goals through parenting family intervention, that is, drawing on the same parenting intervention system to affect several outcomes. The discussion here is restricted to the parenting intervention domain, but this same logic could be applied to other facets or influences that might affect the prevalence of child abuse (for example, extreme poverty, substance abuse, neighborhood violence). Parenting interventions are pertinent to several areas of application such as prevention of children's social, emotional, behavioral and health problems, promotion of positive transition to school, reduction of risk for subsequent adverse outcomes (for example, academic failure and dropout, substance abuse, delinquency), and of course prevention of child maltreatment. With respect to prevention, the various evidence-based parenting interventions have much in common, particularly for younger children. Instead of every sector pursuing compartmentalized parenting interventions, we need to consolidate goals and adopt a more cohesive approach to prevention.

Requirements

Several requirements are necessary for a public health approach which is applicable to the prevention of child maltreatment. First, a public health strategy by definition requires interventions with a broad reach. We need to draw on a variety of strategies to reach wide segments of the population. One strategy is to create multiple access points for parents – not just through the social services system but also the healthcare and behavioral health, education, childcare, and community support sectors. Similarly, making an intervention available via multiple format modalities can improve its reach and create greater likelihood of matching parental preference for program delivery. For parenting intervention, for example, this can take the form of individual family, small group, large group, and online programming. The inclusion of community-wide media strategies could enhance reach still further.

A second requirement for a public health approach is for the interventions to invoke flexibility and efficiency. Rather than have an intervention delivered only in its most intensive form in a one-size-fits-all approach, it is preferable to make use of a range of programming intensities. This increases the likelihood that intensity will match family need, in an efficient manner without wasting resources or services. This strategy makes use of the concept of the *minimally sufficient* effective intervention as a guiding principle to meet the needs of parents. Another facet of flexibility and efficiency is the choice of program delivery personnel. If our preventive interventions require the development of a special or elite group of professionals who are the only ones who can deliver the program, we are installing inherent limits to our strategy. An alternative is to make use of existing workforces in several different settings and service sectors, which increases the likelihood that parental preferences will be met without having to hire specialists or depend heavily on a single sector.

A third requirement is that the intervention and its components are supported by a cogent evidence base. 'Armchair'-based interventions, no matter how folksy they might sound, should not be injected into the public health domain until beneficial effects have been consistently demonstrated in controlled studies.

Feasibility

The next question posed is whether a public health approach to the prevention of child maltreatment is feasible. A few different interventions lend themselves to such an approach. One example is the Period of PURPLE Crying Program for prevention of shaken baby syndrome, which I am not going to discuss here (the reader is referred to the National Center on Shaken Baby Syndrome at www.dontshake.org). A second example is the Triple P – Positive Parenting Program, a system of parenting interventions which provides an excellent example that fits the requirements for a public health approach discussed above. The next section outlines the Triple P system and describes a study that addresses feasibility with respect to prevention of child maltreatment.

Example: the Triple P System

Triple P is not a single program but actually a system of parenting interventions as well as a broad strategy for community-wide parenting and family support (Sanders 1999, 2008, 2012). Some agencies or communities have adopted parts of the system in various ways, and there is nothing wrong with that. Ultimately, though, the overarching purpose of a system like Triple P is to optimize reach, efficiency and impact, deemed to be more likely achieved by utilization of the system. Triple P is a multi-level system with varying levels of programme intensity covering several different formats. Developed by Matthew Sanders and colleagues at the University of Queensland, Australia, Triple P has gone through over 30 years of research and development.

Blended model

From an intervention standpoint, the Triple P System involves a hybrid approach called 'blended prevention', a term not commonly found in the literature. The field has replaced primary, secondary and tertiary prevention with universal, selected, and indicated prevention.

A blended model combines universal, selected, and indicated preventive interventions. Triple P interventions also contribute beyond prevention to include early intervention and treatment. Covering the range of interventions from universal prevention to treatment at the other end of the continuum, Triple P blends all of those modes and levels of intervention into a system whereby these different strategies all serve the common good to improve reach across the population of parents (Figure 5.1).

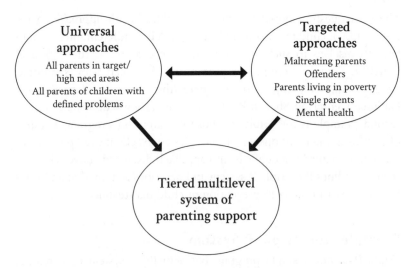

Figure 5.1 A 'blended model'

By way of an aside, Triple P is sometimes referred to as a universal parenting program. This is technically not quite accurate, and the nuance is important. 'Universal' usually means that everyone in the population ('universe') receives the intervention. An example is found in the vaccines that are administered to all young children. While the goal is population reach, Triple P uses the blended prevention strategy to provide universal *access* to parents but without the expectation that successful implementation depends on all parents partaking of every, or even any, component of Triple P.

The Triple P system itself can be depicted as a pyramid, where the pyramid represents the population of parents (see Figure 5.2).

The lowest level (Level 1 Triple P), which is a media and communication strategy implemented without requiring professional contact, forms the base of the pyramid. The base accounts for much of the population in that as much as 50–60 per cent of the population can be reached through the media and communication strategy without ever having to engage parents in actual face-to-face activities. Level 2 Triple P engages less of the population and involves brief intervention with one or two contacts.

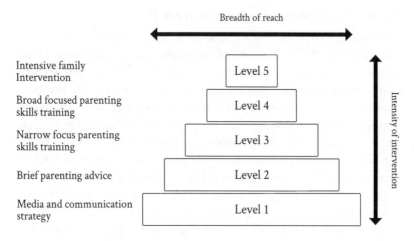

Figure 5.2 Triple P parenting triangle

Moving up the pyramid, Level 3 is also brief but involves more contact with parents. Finally at the narrower top of the pyramid, Level 4 Triple P and Level 5 Triple P involve interventions more like we see in most evidence-based parenting programs. Level 4 Triple P provides core programming to parents and families who need the more intensive level of intervention. Level 5 Triple P, which augments Level 4 programming, is intended to meet the specialized needs of families at the tip of the pyramid.

Above and beyond levels of intervention, Triple P also makes use of multiple delivery formats. Level 2 Triple P is delivered in brief consultation with individual parents, or in large parenting seminars. Level 3 Triple P is similarly delivered in brief consultation with individual parents, and also in small discussion groups. Level 4 Triple P is delivered with individual families and in groups of parents, as well as by self-directed versions via either a workbook or online.

Finally, there are the variants of Triple P. The core five-level system is intended for parents of children aged 1–12 years. Parallel streams serve parents of teenagers ages 13–16 (Teen Triple P) and parents with children who have a disability (Stepping Stones Triple P). Specialist variants of Triple P include Lifestyle Triple P (to address childhood obesity) and Family Transition Triple P (for parents going through separation or divorce).

Parenting principles and concepts in Triple P

A recurring theme in Triple P concerns self-regulation (Sanders and Mazzucchelli 2012). This theme dovetails nicely with some of the emotional regulation constructs that Barlow references (see Chapter 4). Parenting strategies that are part of Triple P emphasize children's acquisition of self-regulation in relation to language and social skills, emotions, problem-solving and independence, including for example the development of self-care skills and the modulation of distress in the face of disappointment or challenge. Another aspect of Triple P concerns a self-regulatory process whereby parents acquire or strengthen skills of personal change to enhance their own parenting and become independent problem solvers. Parental self-regulation pertains to the actual things parents do with children as well as managing their own affect and stress levels to better navigate the difficult path of parenting. Triple P also applies self-regulatory processes to the training of professionals and the management of supervisory and program-development facets of implementation and dissemination.

A core set of five principles underlie all elements of the Triple P programme, principles that are fairly robust around the world though likely expressed in various ways in different cultures. The core principles are: (1) promoting a safe and engaging environment; (2) providing a responsive learning environment; (3) utilizing assertive discipline; (4) adopting reasonable expectations; and (5) taking care of oneself as a parent. With respect to the latter principle, the assumption is that parents who take proper care of themselves are in a better position to parent more effectively.

Triple P programming draws on many parenting strategies, with 17 of these grouped into four clusters: (1) promoting a positive relationship; (2) teaching new skills and behavior; (3) encouraging desirable behavior; and (4) managing misbehavior. When parents seek out professional assistance, they often want to get help with managing child misbehavior. It turns out, though, that the key to managing and altering misbehavior is found in emphasizing the other three parenting-strategy clusters so that disciplinary episodes are not a parent's primary mode of interaction with their child. We know from the attachment literature and elsewhere the importance of building a positive parent–child relationship. We know from the literature on effective interventions with youth who have got into trouble for delinquent behavior that focusing only on sanctioning of misconduct is not sufficient and that it is necessary to build alternative behaviors that are socially acceptable. There are actually more than 17 parenting strategies in Triple P, particularly when taking into account that there are developmental variations. What a parent does with a two-year-old is very different to what they do with a ten-year-old, for example.

In practical terms, Triple P aims to help parents reduce reliance on the common practices that are counter-productive, such as yelling, spanking, humiliating, criticizing in harsh language and disregarding unsafe situations and inflicting pain and discomfort. Unfortunately, these are some of the mainstays for many parents, in part because they might not know any different or perhaps think they are doing what parents are supposed to do. Programming is intended to increase positive parenting to reduce reliance and frequency of adverse parenting practices. Some of the positive parenting targets include being clearer; making use of simple rules; recognizing and celebrating small and large day-to-day child achievements (i.e., not just every six months but many moments each day); staying calm, focused, and facilitative; making frequent use of engaging interactions and affection (but not to the point of being overbearing or smothering); and replacing criticism with constructive coaching and prompting. The idea is not to tell the parent just one way to parent but rather to expose parents to a whole range of options so that they can pick parenting strategies which suit their style but are nonetheless evidence-supported for healthy child development.

Evidence base

In terms of background about where Triple P came from and its development, before it was even officially called Triple P back in the 1980s and early 1990s, it was actually delivered exclusively in the home – a fact that is not well known. Home visitation programmes have been in vogue in the US these past several years, with Triple P being a home-visitation forerunner three decades ago. Triple P and other parenting interventions emerged as more ecologically sound departures from the more traditional practice of taking a child to a psychotherapist or mental health clinic, with a child-centered rather than a family-centered approach. The movement was towards more engagement of parents in monitoring and changing what was going on at home, in an effort to achieve greater ecological validity and impact.

Over time after several single-case experiments establishing initial efficacy and then starting to build, Triple P developers found that ideally the program could be delivered in the home, but it should not be exclusively so. Delivering services elsewhere can still permit parents to take program activities home with them and then come back and report what happened. This flexibility in terms of setting delivery is necessary to extend program reach.

Triple P has been tested in numerous studies over multiple decades. Across levels, formats, and variants of Triple P as well as child/family issues, settings, and countries, the evidence base has grown to over 140 evaluation studies including 70 randomized controlled trials. To date this research has involved 460 investigators in 14 countries, with about a quarter of the studies developer-led and a third of the studies having no developer involvement. There have been two Triple P population outcome studies to date, one in Australia directed by Sanders and his group, called the *Every Family* study (Sanders *et al.* 2008), and a second in the United States called the *U.S. Triple P System Population Trial*, described below.

Population trial

This trial employed what is called a place randomization design, which is rarely found in the evaluation of psychosocial interventions or in prevention studies of any kind. Instead of randomly assigning individuals to study conditions, as would be done in a traditional clinical trial, the unit of randomization is a place or geographic area. The place or unit of randomization in the study was a county, and there were 18 counties in total. The funding agency, the US Centers for Disease Control and Prevention, was interested in determining whether and to what extent could a preventive intervention like Triple P, which was designed for population dissemination, reduce the prevalence of child maltreatment.

The design involved randomization of 18 mid-sized counties in South Carolina, which were selected geographically but were not recruited. None of these counties had any prior exposure to Triple P. Controlling for prior child maltreatment and poverty rates as well as county size, counties were randomized to either dissemination of the Triple P system (9 counties) or usual services control (9 counties).

There were three primary outcome variables related to child maltreatment among children birth to eight years of age. The first was child out-of-home (foster care) placements, which was compiled by the state foster care system and reported monthly to a central repository.

The second was child maltreatment injuries requiring hospital treatment, which was compiled by hospitals in all counties and reported monthly along with all disease and treatment data to a central repository. The third was substantiated (founded) cases of child maltreatment compiled by the child protective services system in each county and also reported monthly to a central repository. Five years of baseline data prior to the onset of the study showed that the two sets of counties did not differ with respect to any of three variables, nor were there pre-existing trends (for example, diverging) that differentiated the two sets of counties.

In the nine Triple P counties, all five levels of the Triple P system were implemented. Over 600 service providers were trained in Triple P delivery including the existing workforces from several sectors (i.e., healthcare, public health, education including preschools, mental health, family services and non-governmental community organizations). The media and communication strategies for Level 1 Triple P were implemented by project staff. At any given moment in the 9 Triple P counties there were 85,000 families with at least one child in the birth to eight year range. Over the two years of intervention exposure, approximately 14 per cent of those families received direct services (i.e., not including the media/communication exposure), which is reasonably good coverage considering this is the first time a study of this nature had been undertaken.

In terms of outcomes, all three primary indicators related to child maltreatment showed the significant impact of Triple P (Prinz *et al.* 2009). The Triple P counties showed lower rates of child out-of-home placements compared with control counties after accounting for baseline. Similarly, the Triple P counties showed lower rates of hospital-treated child maltreatment injuries compared with control counties after accounting for baseline levels. The growth of substantiated maltreatment cases was significantly slowed in the Triple P counties compared with the control counties and accounting for baseline, but also in comparison with the other 28 counties in the state that were not part of the population trial but showed a similar trend to the control counties.

Cost consideration

The question remains whether a public health approach to child maltreatment prevention is cost prohibitive. A cost analysis was conducted by the Washington State Institute for Public Policy (WSIPP) directed by Steven Aos (Lee, Aos and Drake 2012). WSIPP examined

Triple P benefits and costs in the context of the child welfare system and found that deploying all five levels of the Triple P system yielded a return of US$6.06 for every one US dollar invested – an excellent return on investment relative to other programs and strategies. WSIPP also examined Triple P from a child mental health perspective and found that implementation of Level 4 Group Triple P produced a US$5.63 return for every one US dollar invested, which also compared favorably with other programs. These data from the WSIPP Washington State Institute for Public Policy suggest that a public health strategy like Triple P is not cost prohibitive for reducing the prevalence of child maltreatment.

Discussion and conclusion

The population approach to parenting and family support, not just for the prevention of child maltreatment but in some other domains as well, really represents a paradigm shift. The field itself is in the middle of a paradigm shift, trying to find strategies that produce greater prevention impact. If one asked people in the field 10 or 15 years ago whether it made sense to take a population approach to preventing child maltreatment, the answer might have mostly been 'No'. There was and still is scepticism about whether parenting interventions can reduce child maltreatment, and there was a fear that precious resources meant to focus on the high-risk population would be diverted. Scepticism and fears notwithstanding, the field has never managed to show that clinical and high-risk approaches actually reduce prevalence. Consequently, we have to go back to our conceptualization and ask whether we are moving towards our larger goal fast enough, and if not how we might consider expanding our thinking.

However, this newer paradigm is not meant to imply that the field should throw away what is needed within the child protection services system and within the high-risk segments of the population. A dual approach is clearly needed, and it is important to meld the two strategies (public health prevention and child protection services). Nonetheless, for both strategies we need to keep in mind that parents are the primary consumers of the associated services. If we do not look at it from their point of view, we are doomed before we start. All of the pontifications about how some parents need to change will be for naught if parents do not buy into the process. To succeed at changing prevalence rates, sticking with a destigmatized approach is critical, as is meeting the needs of parents in fundamental ways that appeal to them.

Even if there are strong parenting interventions in place, we are not off the hook for dealing with serious issues surrounding substance abuse, extreme poverty, and partner violence that provide adverse contexts for child maltreatment. With respect to substance abuse, for example, there is a dearth of treatment outcome studies with parents who have the dual problem of drug or alcohol abuse coupled with involvement with the child protective services system. There is much to learn about how to combine basic substance abuse treatment with intervention for parenting difficulties, about motivational strategies for this scenario, and about how such treatment strategies work together (or not) to produce better child outcomes. This critical area requires targeted strategies but addressing it is not incompatible with the blended prevention strategy described earlier. Rather, it is one piece that can fit into a system. A broad public health strategy can include many different elements, some of which are targeted and some of which promote universal access, but built in such a way as multiple points on the continuum are addressed in moving towards the same common goal, namely reduction in the prevalence of child maltreatment.

Notes

Research that informed aspects of this chapter was funded in part by grants from the U.S. Centers for Disease Prevention and Control (U17/CCU422317 and R18CE001340), the National Institute on Child Health and Human Development (R01HD42621) and the National Institute on Drug Abuse (R01DA031780). The findings and conclusions in this chapter are those of the author and do not necessarily represent the views of the aforementioned funding agencies.

The author is a consultant to the US Centers for Disease Control and Prevention as well as to Triple P International (the latter is the technology-transfer partner of the University of Queensland charged with the dissemination of the Triple P system).

References

Afifi, T.O., Boman, J., Fleisher, W. and Sareen, J. (2009) 'The relationship between child abuse, parental divorce, and lifetime mental disorders and suicidality in a nationally representative adult sample.' *Child Abuse and Neglect 33*, 3, 139–147.

Barrett, P.M. and Ollendick, T.H. (eds) (2004) *Handbook of Interventions that Work with Children and Adolescents: Prevention and Treatment.* London: Wiley.

Biglan, A., Brennan, P.A., Foster, S.L. and Holder, H.D. (2004) *Helping Adolescents at Risk: Prevention of Multiple Problem Behaviors.* New York: Guilford Press.

Bolger, K.E. and Patterson, C.J. (2003) 'Sequelae of Child Maltreatment: Vulnerability and Resilience.' In S.S. Luthar (ed.) *Resilience and Vulnerability: Adaptation in the Context of Childhood Adversities.* New York: Cambridge University Press.

Centers for Disease Control and Prevention (1999) 'Ten great public health achievements – United States, 1900–1999.' *Morbidity and Mortality Report 48,* 241–243.

Collins, W.A., Maccoby, E.E., Steinberg, L., Hetherington, E.M. and Bornstein, M.H. (2000) 'Contemporary research on parenting: The case for nature and nurture.' *American Psychologist 55,* 218–232.

Donovan, C.L. and Spence, S.H. (2000) 'Prevention of childhood anxiety disorders.' *Clinical Psychology Review 20,* 509–531.

Essau, C.A. (ed.) (2003) *Conduct and Oppositional Defiant Disorders: Epidemiology, Risk Factors, and Treatment.* Mahwah, NJ: Erlbaum.

Farah, M.J., Betancourt, L., Shera, D.M., Savage, J.H. *et al.* (2008) 'Environmental stimulation, parental nurturance and cognitive development in humans.' *Developmental Science 11,* 5, 793–801.

Ialongo, N.S., Rogosch, F.A., Cicchetti, D., Toth, S.L. *et al.* (2006) 'A Developmental Psychopathology Approach to the Prevention of Mental Health Disorders.' In D. Cicchetti and D.J. Cohen (eds) *Developmental Psychopathology, Vol 1: Theory and Method,* 2nd edn. Hoboken, NJ: John Wiley and Sons.

Jones, T.L. and Prinz, R.J. (2005) 'Potential roles of parental self-efficacy in parent and child adjustment: A review.' *Clinical Psychology Review 25,* 3, 341–363.

Lee, S., Aos, S. and Drake, E. (2012) *Return on Investment: Evidence-Based Options to Improve Statewide Outcomes (Document No. 12–04–1201).* Olympia: Washington State Institute for Public Policy.

Lochman, J.E. and van den Steenhoven, A. (2002) 'Family-based approaches to substance abuse prevention.' *Journal of Primary Prevention 23,* 49–114.

National Research Council and Institute of Medicine (2009) 'Preventing Mental, Emotional, and Behavioral Disorders among Young People: Progress and Possibilities.' In M.E. O'Connell, T. Boat and K.E. Warner (eds) *Board on Children, Youth, and Families, Division of Behavioral and Social Sciences and Education.* Washington, DC: Committee on Prevention of Mental Disorders and Substance Abuse Among Children, Youth, and Young Adults: Research Advances and Promising Interventions.

Patterson, G.R., Reid, J.B. and Dishion, T.J. (1992) *Antisocial Boys.* Eugene, OR: Castalia.

Prinz, R.J. (2007) 'Parenting and family-based preventive interventions: Current status and future challenges.' Commissioned technical report: Institute of Medicine and National Research Council.

Prinz, R.J. and Dumas, J.E. (2004) 'Prevention of Oppositional Defiant Disorder and Conduct Disorder in Children and Adolescents.' In P.M. Barrett and T.H. Ollendick (eds) *Handbook of Interventions That Work with Children and Adolescents.* Chichester: Wiley.

Prinz, R.J. and Jones, T.L. (2003) 'Family-based Interventions.' In C.A. Essau (ed.) *Conduct and Oppositional Defiant Disorders: Epidemiology, Risk Factors, and Treatment.* Mahwah, NJ: Erlbaum.

Prinz, R.J., Sanders, M.R., Shapiro, C.J., Whitaker, D.J. and Lutzker, J.R. (2009) 'Population-based prevention of child maltreatment: The U.S. Triple P system population trial.' *Prevention Science 10*, 1, 1–12.

Sanders, M.R. (1999) 'Triple P – Positive Parenting Program: Towards an empirically validated multilevel parenting and family support strategy for the prevention of behavior and emotional problems in children.' *Clinical Child and Family Psychology Review 2*, 2, 71–90.

Sanders, M.R. (2008) 'Triple P – Positive Parenting Program as a public health approach to strengthening parenting.' *Journal of Family Psychology 22*, 4, 506–517.

Sanders, M.R. (2012) 'Development, evaluation, and multinational dissemination of the Triple P – Positive Parenting Program.' *Annual Review of Clinical Psychology 8*, 345–379.

Sanders, M.R. and Mazzucchelli, T.G. (2012) 'The promotion of self-regulation through parenting interventions.' In V. Barkoukis (ed.) *Psychology of Self-Regulation.* Hauppauge, NY: Nova Science.

Sanders, M.R., Ralph, A., Sofronoff, K., Gardiner, P. *et al.* (2008) 'Every family: A population approach to reducing behavioral and emotional problems in children making the transition to school.' *Journal of Primary Prevention 29*, 3, 197–222.

Theodore, A.D., Chang, J.J., Runyan, D.K., Hunter, W.M., Bangdiwala, S.I. and Agans, R. (2005) 'Epidemiologic features of the physical and sexual maltreatment of children in the Carolinas.' *Pediatrics 115*, 331–337.

Chapter 6

DEVELOPMENTAL AND DYNAMIC DESIGN IN SERVICE SYSTEMS

Making the Most of What We Know

Bruce F. Chorpita, Alayna Park and Eric L. Daleiden

For the past 20 years there have been major efforts to increase the impact of science on service delivery. One rather positive note is the extent to which the evidence base has grown, with evidence-based treatments (EBTs) for children's mental health concerns numbering close to 400 in 2011 (Chorpita *et al.* 2011b) and growing steadily since then. Despite these developments, the impact of these treatments at the point of care has been less than expected or desired (Kazdin and Blase 2011; Rotheram-Borus, Swendeman and Chorpita 2012). Many of the services delivered in usual care continue to have little relation to practice supported by research (for example, Zima *et al.* 2005) and, when they do, they are not always successful at focusing on the primary therapeutic concern (for example, Garland *et al.* 2010). Not surprisingly, empirical evaluations of usual care services show that outcomes continue to lag behind research-based treatments (Weisz, Jensen-Doss and Hawley 2006). With such concerns in mind, our research team has sought to consider new ways to design service systems and their resources in order to capitalize on the knowledge afforded by this considerable literature, balancing the need to ground activity in science with the need to deal with the type of complexity not typically seen in research contexts.

A fundamental assumption underlying all of this work is that the quality of services can be improved through the application of science. Others have eloquently argued that such application is not straightforward, and often involves attempts to maximize the fit between science-based innovations and the context of the systems into which those innovations might be implemented (for example, Aarons, Hurlburt and Horowitz 2011). There are many strategies for maximizing this fit, but one particularly fruitful one that we have pursued involves the distinction between the knowledge and the products that have emanated from the past 40 years of intervention research. That is, one might consider whether to maximize the fit of the knowledge discovered in scientific trials, which is a different approach from working only with the specific products tested in those trials (for example, specific assessment protocols or treatment manuals). For example, one could inform decisions about the care of a young person experiencing traumatic stress by using the generalized knowledge that the development of a narrative can help facilitate positive emotional and cognitive changes, without fully adopting any specific interventions in which trauma narratives were tested. Obviously, there are both advantages and disadvantages to such a strategy, which will be discussed more below, but our contention is that to build effective systems one must be prepared to apply both the products and the knowledge of science.

Developmental and dynamic design

With regard to maximizing fit, two protocol design features appear to be excellent candidates for improvement. The first is that any knowledge used to guide decisions and actions in service systems should be delivered through resources that are *developmental* in nature. That is, knowledge resources (i.e., tools that facilitate informed action) should account for the fact that different providers and different families are at different places in development. The expert provider may not need a training curriculum that starts from scratch covering basic clinical and interpersonal skills and could be better served through an incremental learning opportunity that merely adds one new tool to her toolbox. Likewise, a family who has successfully completed a treatment program but has some residual concerns might not need to start an entirely new intervention program but rather could benefit from review or targeted rehearsal of specific skills. Because service systems contend with ubiquitous developmental differences among families, providers, organizations and even the knowledge base itself (Chorpita and Daleiden 2013) resources used to deliver knowledge to those systems must account for these different starting points and meet individuals where they are.

The second critical design feature is that knowledge should be delivered through resources that are *dynamic*. That is, the guides, manuals, charts, feedback systems or other resources should account for the fact that issues commonly arise in day to day service that will require adaptations or accommodations to be made. For example, a young person may experience an academic setback that becomes an immediate priority requiring strategic changes to a service plan. Likewise, a service provider participating in a training program might need to move to a new jurisdiction, or take a leave of absence for medical or family reasons, which interrupts the training plan. Ideally, such occurrences can be managed so that families, providers and organizations can continue to move forward toward their ultimate goals.

Although our work over the past 15 years has raised these issues primarily within children's mental health systems, these ideas are likely of relevance to service delivery in child welfare populations as well. Specifically, there are both direct implications – regarding managing the psychosocial and familial consequences of abuse and neglect that involved the application of indicated treatment approaches – and indirect implications – regarding general approaches to the efficient organization and application of knowledge to inform activity in service systems. Some examples are illustrated below.

Building an efficient and comprehensive service array

At the highest level, social welfare agencies must contend with a way to provide high quality services to the population of young people and families served. A widely used strategy at this point in time is to build an array of evidence-based treatment (EBT) programs. Ideally, these programs would serve a large proportion of the overall service population, and would minimally overlap – or perhaps strategically overlap – with respect to whom they serve. Thus, a child welfare system might seek to have EBTs serving families having problems with child safety, guidance and boundaries, social relationships or self-care skills. The task then becomes one of assembling a list of EBTs that targets these concerns and serves the maximum number of individuals in the population, with the minimum amount of resources. This array building is an increasingly common activity for both child welfare and child mental health systems and at the moment is largely supported through consolidated lists or registries of EBTs that serve as 'shopping lists' for system leadership.

We recently proposed that one can establish a more effective and efficient service array by structured comparison of treatment outcome research and local knowledge of the service population. Specifically, by knowing which treatments the literature has found to be effective for which clients (for example, based on treatment target, age, gender) as well as the characteristics of young people and families in the local service system (for example, prevalence of various problem types, age range), one can select treatments that are not only evidence-based, but that are also maximally relevant to the service population (for example, finding EBTs for adolescents with traumatic stress to use in a child welfare system serving large numbers of abused teens).

Chorpita, Bernstein and Daleiden (2011) recently demonstrated the application of this methodology, termed 'Relevance Mapping', with young people receiving services from the Hawaii state mental health system. Analyses involved a computer-automated comparison of 1,781 young people with intensive emotional and behavioral needs to the participant characteristics in 437 coded randomized clinical trials. From those randomized clinical trials, 98 individual treatment types (for example, cognitive behavioral therapy, contingency management, parent management training) were identified – creating over 157 billion possible EBT combinations if one were to randomly select a set of no more than eight treatments to use in the system. Thus, if one considers the full magnitude of the evidence base, selection of an appropriate array is a complex problem whose difficulty only increases as the knowledge base expands.

Based on an automated comparison of all possible service arrays, Chorpita *et al.* (2011a) found that two equally relevant arrays could be arranged for the Hawaii system, each composed of nine treatments. One treatment common to both sets was already in place in that system – *Multisystemic Therapy* (Henggeler *et al.* 1998) – and seven treatments common to both were: cognitive behavior therapy, contingency management, parent management training, cognitive behavioral therapy with parents included, intensive communication training, intensive behavioral treatment, and parent management training and problem solving. The ninth treatments differed across the two arrays, and were either self-verbalization or social skills and medication. Both arrays were built on the assumption that each treatment was matched to each young person in the service population in terms of treatment target, age and gender (for example, depressed mood in a 12-year-old girl). This arrangement partly illustrates the principle of developmental design, in that such an array is meant to match characteristics of the individuals in the system – to meet them where they are – as opposed to an array that only considers in a vacuum the strength of the evidence behind each EBT.

Unfortunately, one concern was that, irrespective of whether the best nine treatments were selected or 90 were selected, no more than 71 per cent of the young people in the Hawaii system could be matched to any EBT in the resulting service array. Thus, under all circumstances, 29 per cent of young people in the system had a combination of characteristics (problem, age, gender) matching nothing in the evidence base. When stricter standards were imposed for matching young people to treatments, such as also considering ethnicity and service setting (for example, foster care, home or community treatment, residential), 86 per cent of the young people had no EBT relevant to their characteristics. Similar results were found in an analysis of youth with intensive needs served by a large provider organization in California (Bernstein *et al.* 2013).

It should be noted that these results do not reflect negatively on the application of EBTs to community systems, but they do provide evidence against the idea of EBTs as an exclusive strategy for improving service system quality, given that some young people and families will likely be without high quality options due to the current state of the evidence base or complex individual circumstances. When one considers workforce turnover, trainability and feasibility (for example, how many EBTs can an individual provider effectively manage), geographic barriers (for example, ability to implement full arrays in remote or rural communities), and families who do not respond to their first treatment option (and thus require a second EBT), values of family choice, the need to consider alternative service quality strategies that go beyond merely selecting EBTs becomes obvious.

In light of the overall goal of service systems providing quality services to improve the lives of young people and their families, the strategy of selecting EBTs is thus both complex and insufficient, and the Hawaii example vividly illustrates the importance of the design principle of needing a dynamic architecture at the system level. That is, when a large percentage of young people in a system are 'exceptions' to the available service array, one must have a formal strategy for how to manage those exceptions. In other words, given that EBTs are not available for a substantial portion of cases, how might one ensure that quality services are delivered to those young people?

Knowledge behind the products:
another view of the evidence base

One possible strategy is informed by gaining a new view of the existing evidence base. With more than 700 randomized clinical trials in children's mental health, there is an extensive knowledge base to inform decisions about care when working outside the context of a standardized treatment protocol, as our relevance mapping analysis shows is likely to be necessary, given the current knowledge base and population diversity. Although the current tradition is to aggregate the literature within specific 'product lines', with replications of specific named protocols each building a discrete literature, one can consider ways to aggregate the knowledge more broadly, based on empirically similar characteristics among different treatments.

The distillation and matching model (Chorpita and Daleiden 2009; Chorpita, Daleiden and Weisz 2005a) was designed to provide such a strategy, using a structured methodology for identifying and categorizing common features of treatments, ultimately facilitating their aggregation and analysis. The first approach described in the model, distillation, involves coding the treatment literature at various levels of abstraction. One convenient level of abstraction we have explored for supporting knowledge to action is identifying specific practice components of treatments, known as practice elements. For example, a cognitive treatment for anxiety might include the six practice elements of cognitive training, self-monitoring, modeling, exposure to feared items, relaxation and psychoeducation. When coded at the level of elements, this protocol can then be inspected empirically to determine its similarity with other protocols among the hundreds in the evidence base. Ultimately, this analysis allows for the creation of aggregated profiles, which can illustrate which practice elements are most common among the most successful treatments. One might observe, for example, that among 16 evidence-based protocols for traumatic stress, 75 per cent include a relaxation component. One application of this fact, when working with traumatized young people outside the context of a structured protocol, might be to consider using relaxation. This inference leverages the entire knowledge base for evidence-based treatments for traumatic stress, which can involve many studies, rather than relying on a specific protocol for which only one or two supportive studies exist. Although there is no certainty that a select component common among effective protocols will itself be effective when used in isolation, the literature suggests that its use might be a promising place to start – and it presents a testable hypothesis in cases that involve monitoring and evaluation as part of the care plan.

The second process described in the model – matching – involves determining the association between practice elements and particular client or contextual characteristics, known as matching factors. Specifically, this method can be used to determine which factors (for example, problem focus, age, gender and ethnicity) yield the most dissimilar patterns of practice elements. Thus, if the frequency distribution of practice elements for treatments targeting depression is considerably different from the distribution of practice elements from those targeting disruptive behavior, those will emerge as separate 'nodes' in a problem focus factor. Ultimately, this procedure can build a distillation tree, with branches representing practice differences at various levels and sub-levels (for example, age differences within a disruptive behavior problem focus).

Aside from the ability to aggregate across otherwise distinct pockets of the treatment literature, another advantage to examining treatments at the practice element level is that it affords a level of analysis that is well matched to the routine decision schedule that characterizes clinical practice. Particularly when operating outside of a structured program, providers are often faced with the conundrum of selecting a specific technique to implement during their next session. Knowledge organized according to practice elements can point to candidate strategies to consider from those common among relevant EBTs (for example, a cognitive element is present in 72 per cent of EBTs for depressed mood). On the other hand, knowledge that is organized only according to treatment manuals as the primary unit of information provides evidence that an entire sequence of procedures (for example, one session of psychoeducation followed by five sessions of behavioral modification) are efficacious with specific populations (for example, middle-class Caucasian adolescents) in specific contexts (for example, school-based mental health center) if implemented as directed by the manual. Such information may be useful before a treatment episode begins, and can inform the selection of a specific EBT but, in other circumstances, such information becomes comparatively less efficient.

The distillation and matching model thus provides a methodology for drawing knowledge from the literature in a different format, such that one can inform new decisions, including those that drive clinical care. Although this composition provides a solid guidepost from which providers can base inferences about treatment content, the knowledge of which practice elements are relevant to which client characteristics is still insufficient, and there is a need for a framework to fully organize the selection, arrangement, delivery and evaluation of those practice elements.

Managing and Adapting Practice (MAP)

In an effort to incorporate knowledge about EBTs as well as their practice elements into a single system for designing and managing clinical service delivery, Chorpita and Daleiden (2013) proposed a model for coordinating evidence-based treatments and practices called Managing and Adapting Practice (MAP). MAP involves a set of resources and models that help providers and systems organize the implementation and adaptation of high quality mental health services across diverse populations of young people and families. The underlying principles of the MAP system expand upon the architecture of the relevance mapping (Chorpita *et al.* 2011a) and distillation and matching (Chorpita, Becker and Daleiden 2007; Chorpita and Daleiden 2009; Chorpita *et al.* 2005a) models and are based on the system design and performance improvement initiatives beginning over ten years ago in the Hawaii system of care (for example, Chorpita *et al.* 2002; Daleiden and Chorpita 2005; Daleiden *et al.* 2006).

MAP's direct service component acts more like a treatment selection, design, implementation and evaluation toolkit instead of a traditional treatment protocol. Specifically, MAP utilizes a variety of specialized tools and resources to help facilitate the decision-making process and inform key decisions in service delivery. As an example, in order to help providers develop an initial treatment plan and support ongoing decision-making, MAP employs a continually updated, comprehensive searchable database of hundreds of randomized clinical trials (PracticeWise Evidence Based Services Database (PWEBS)). Psychosocial and combined treatments and their corresponding studies tested in the context of mental health, child welfare, corrections, education and health populations are identified according to well-defined guidelines (see Chorpita *et al.* 2011b, for a detailed description of the review process), which require among other things that studies test at least one active treatment relative to a control group, report outcome data at post-treatment for a targeted population (i.e., are not universal prevention studies), and primarily involve children and adolescents, ages 18 and below. Accordingly, the PWEBS database generates psychosocial practice recommendations applicable to clinical care for young people (whether directly or via their caregivers); however, the same methodology can be applied to inform practices relevant to various other treatment targets (for example, family stability, academic performance) and within various other populations (for example, adults).

In its most common use, the PWEBS decision support tool generates a summary of all treatments meeting a user-defined strength of evidence (for example, well-established, probably efficacious, better than waitlist, no support (APA Task Force on Promotion and Dissemination of Psychological Procedures 1995)) that matches a given service population's characteristics. For example, if a treatment team wishes to know which treatments meeting a commonly used definition of 'evidence-based' are suitable for an 11-year-old girl with traumatic stress, PWEBS returns lists of all matching trials, all matching treatments, an aggregate summary showing the relative proportions of treatment types (for example, cognitive behavior therapy, cognitive behavior therapy with parents), settings (for example, clinic, school) and formats (for example, individual, group). Thus, MAP's direct service component facilitates the delivery of knowledge and guides the user to select an existing EBT if it is available in the system.

In the event that no such EBTs are available or if a standard EBT has already been implemented but the client has not met the established treatment goals, the MAP user can then design a treatment in real time, beginning with a list of procedures that are common to all relevant evidence-based treatments (in this example of the traumatized 11-year-old girl, ten evidence-based protocols tested in eight randomized trials). Based on the logic of the distillation and matching model, practices are distilled from the aggregate literature (Chorpita *et al.* 2007) and sorted according to the relative proportion of specific elements common across all of those protocols (for example, 70% of all evidence EBTs matching this 11-year-old girl used a trauma narrative procedure). Providers can then organize those elements into a plan according to common coordination rules emanating from the treatment outcome knowledge base (for example, the literature may suggest implementing a psychoeducation procedure before attempting a trauma narrative), and begin implementing the treatment components with the support of the Practitioner Guide, a 'how to' knowledge resource that spells out the important steps of each practice element in both a checklist and a detailed narrative format.

Another central aspect of the MAP system is a unifying evaluation framework used to track outcomes and practices. Specifically, this framework allows providers to more easily monitor their client's status as well as the history of therapeutic practices used. Although MAP does not require a specific measurement model, it emphasizes the importance of relevant and frequently administered measurement of progress and practices to facilitate clinical reasoning and coordinated care, with measures and the timing of their administration dictated by the nature of the decisions being made. For example, if a provider is considering modifying the treatment plan, then there must be recent outcome data indicating that another treatment focus would better suit the client. Whether the care provider has selected a standard EBT to be delivered within the larger MAP context or has designed an evidence-informed plan using practice elements from the relevant literature, the service episode is always subject to real-time evaluation and, for those treatments that allow adaptation, to self-correction.

To facilitate this strategy, MAP uses clinical dashboards as a resource to organize and deliver information from multiple evidence sources (for example, scores from standardized clinical instruments, supervisor recommendations of practices to implement during the next session), and multiple parties (for example, client, caregiver, provider) into a collaborative workspace (see Chorpita *et al.* 2008), and ultimately, present a wealth of information on case context, client progress, and practice history on a single display. In typical MAP applications, dashboards are created using a simple Excel™ spreadsheet platform that plots scores for up to five user-selected progress measures (for example, client-endorsed mood ratings, standardized total scores from the UCLA PTSD Index; Decker and Pynoos 2004) onto a progress pane that visually displays how the scores change over the course of treatment. Data on the specific practice elements implemented each session are mapped onto a separate practice pane, which is also updated during the treatment span to reflect the provider's practice history with the client. Other information that can be represented on dashboards includes treatment team practice plans or progress benchmarks for celebration or additional review, research benchmarks of clinical cutoff scores, expected rates of change (for example, Weersing 2005), expected best practice events such as session sequences from a treatment manual or practice elements retrieved from a PWEBS search, and administrative indicators for change in eligibility status, time or volume-based utilization triggers for re-authorization or intensive review, etc. Essentially, dashboards are telecommunication tools that support not only feedback, but also exploration and simulation (for example, considering various 'what ifs'). As such, dashboards can be useful not only to providers, but also to supervisors, clients, family members and other members of a treatment team.

In addition to these decision support tools, MAP's direct service model also provides a variety of coordination resources, called 'process guides', which detail the logic behind the decision making and planning regarding selected aspects of care. For example, a 'Treatment Planner' guide assists providers in coordinating an episode of care by prompting them to select a therapeutic focus, organize relevant practice elements into logical early, middle and late phases of care (referred to as 'connect', 'cultivate' and 'consolidate' phases, respectively), and construct a list of optional procedures to reference in the event that a clinical interference arises (for example, a relaxation procedure to address somatic arousal). A 'Session Planner' guide structures the planning and coordination of each treatment session or clinical encounter, and outlines important steps to consider at the beginning (for example, check in, review homework), middle (for example, advise, rehearse), and end (for example, review take-home messages, assign homework) of each meeting. Another guide, called 'The MAP', offers an overarching model for how to utilize the MAP resources to inform clinical reasoning and service review throughout the entire service episode. As an example, in order to assess a client's clinical progress, a provider can review the progress pane of the clinical dashboard, and depending on the recent scores, can choose to either continue with the current treatment plan until the goals have been met or assess whether the treatment is an appropriate fit for the client's needs. An 'Embracing Diversity' guide encourages the provider to engage in a structured consideration of possible adaptations to the plan, if indicated, across six different conceptual categories (prompting possible changes to conceptualization, communication, message, style, change agent or therapeutic procedures).

In order to help providers develop proficiency with MAP (for example, effectively coordinating both process and practice guides in an episode of clinical care), the MAP Professional Development Program was created to specify formal role descriptions and provide a structured training and credentialing process. Training for direct service providers involves at least 52 hours of training and consultation delivered over at least a six-month period, supervised clinical activity on at least two cases and the submission of a completed training portfolio for final review. Southam-Gerow et al. (2014) recently detailed the application of the

MAP Professional Development Program within Los Angeles County, California, which is currently undergoing a major system reform initiative to increase evidence-based services in the county. Over a 33-month period, 1,700 direct service providers in Los Angeles County completed their MAP training, suggesting that the MAP Professional Development Program can be scaled rapidly within a large system. In terms of specific training outcomes, the average time to completion for providers participating in a standard workshop and consultation sequence was 342 days with 86 per cent of providers passing on their first portfolio submission. Furthermore, clients and families who received MAP services showed significant improvement during the episode of care.

Promising outcome findings have also been evident in the children and adolescents receiving services through the Hawaii state system of care, which has employed an empirically based quality management system with similar principles to MAP for the past ten years. For example, Daleiden *et al.* (2006) noticed a pattern of accelerated improvement amongst young people receiving mental health services under Hawaii's evidence-based initiative, such that the median rate of improvement nearly tripled over a four-year period. As a corollary to the progressive rate of improvement, the average length of services was reduced from an average of 866 days in 2002 to 393 days in 2005. On a similar note, total service expenditures also dropped from $1,083 per point of improvement during 2002 to $648 per point of improvement during 2005.

These findings illustrate the success of the MAP system from start (i.e., provider training) to finish (i.e., treatment termination), and provide initial evidence for the potential of services that are both developmental and dynamic in nature. More importantly, MAP exemplifies a potential solution to solving a missing piece of existing service system architecture: scientifically informed, personalized treatment options for young people who would otherwise not be served by any EBTs.

The Child STEPs Effectiveness Trial

These design principles have been tested more formally in a recently completed randomized clinical trial. The Child Systems and Treatment Enhancement Projects (Child STEPs) Effectiveness Trial (Chorpita *et al.* 2013; Weisz *et al.* 2012) tested the effectiveness of different types of clinical services in ten community clinic- and school-based service organizations in Hawaii and Massachusetts for 174 young people experiencing problems with anxiety, depression or disruptive behavior. The design featured three treatment conditions, two involving different designs for EBTs and a third condition serving as a usual care control. In the 'standard' EBT-based condition, providers were trained to implement three standard EBT manuals – one for each of the three possible target areas – which featured manualized instructions and prescribed both the order and number of treatment sessions. In the modular evidence-based condition, providers were trained in the Modular Approach to Therapy for Children (MATCH) (Chorpita and Weisz 2005) which contained essentially the same clinical procedures as the standard condition, but organized procedures into individual practice elements that could be applied and adapted based on client-specific variables, such as the client's problem focus or the family's engagement with treatment. Based largely on the same underlying developmental and dynamic principles as the MAP direct service approach, MATCH utilized a series of flowcharts that mapped a default sequence of practices for each problem area (Weisz et al. 2012). For example, if the child had anxiety, the MATCH treatment pathway would suggest starting with psychoeducation and engagement procedures followed by the building of a fear hierarchy and ultimately performing repeated exposure. However, to incorporate the dynamic aspect of clinical care, MATCH also allowed the default sequence outlined in the flowcharts to be altered if interference arose in a similar fashion as suggested by many of the MAP guides, including 'The MAP' and 'Embracing Diversity'. Following the previous example, if the treatment team (for example, provider, family or supervisor) collectively determined that other aspects of a case required significant attention (for example, there were anger outbursts that were so interfering that they were preventing or disrupting the exposure therapy or homework), the provider could apply procedures from elsewhere in the MATCH library, such as a time out program or instruction for the parents in the effective use of commands or praise. Thus, MATCH represents a collaborative service architecture that encourages consideration of the developmental levels of the provider and client by allowing for more flexible implementation, but that also sets investigator-defined standards for the performance of each procedure through codified practice elements and accordingly places some limits on the degree to which providers can deviate from the logic of a traditional evidence-based treatment algorithm.

Findings from the Child STEPs Effectiveness Trial showed that young people who were treated in the MATCH condition had significantly steeper trajectories of improvement relative to young people in either the usual care or standard EBT conditions on measures of internalizing, externalizing, total symptoms and severity ratings of family-nominated problems at post-treatment. Further, young people in the MATCH condition had significantly fewer diagnoses after ending treatment than young people in the usual care control.

A second study examined client outcomes in this same sample over a two-year period (Chorpita *et al.* 2013). Results found that young people treated with MATCH improved at a significantly more rapid rate over time than young people treated with usual care, particularly within the first year of starting treatment, whereas no significant differences were found between the Modular and Standard nor the Standard and Usual Care conditions.

Findings from these two studies provide early support for treatment designs that utilize knowledge from a common library of practice elements. Although they represent specific support for the MATCH protocol, we believe that their implications for design generalize beyond this specific context. That is, the Child STEPs findings add to the mounting evidence that dynamic, developmental design that allows for structured adaptation to meet different problems and to adapt in real time may make the application of knowledge from the evidence base more robust to the types of diversity and complexity that often arise.

Specific implications and conclusions

This work so far has some specific relevance to young persons who have experienced abuse and neglect, in that all of our examples illustrate the application of efficient approaches to addressing mental health concerns, which are common in this population. More broadly, these developments speak to broader issues regarding the design of service systems for child welfare and the psychosocial treatment services available within them. Based on the relevance mapping analyses, we expect that well-constructed systems will offer a few carefully selected EBTs for common, high risk and/or high cost populations, perhaps chosen according to our methodology or a similar approach to ensure maximum impact and a specified level of redundancy. However, we do not expect that in the near future systems will be able to support a comprehensive array of EBTs such that all youth in a system will have one or more options available meeting their specific characteristics.

In light of this claim, we believe that a priority in the selection (for systems) and design (for researchers) of EBTs should be the ability of those treatments to serve a diverse and large array of individuals in the system efficiently and coordinate effectively with other operations in the system. All things being equal, fully developed programs that can flexibly address multiple different targets, such as MATCH or the Hope for Children and Families Program (see Chapter 7 of this book), represent efficient use of service resources and training time in pursuit of collective goals for youth and family functioning.

For the foreseeable future, however, we believe there will be individuals who do not benefit from existing EBTs, no matter how carefully designed or how carefully chosen. Until the literature can elaborate to encompass the many different characteristics and contexts likely to be encountered, there will remain youth and families who simply are not a clear match for any available EBTs. Further, even among those who are good candidates, some proportion will nevertheless fail to respond as expected to a given course of treatment. Thus, we believe a final consideration for service systems is to have a strategy to inform and improve the quality of usual care services, such as that illustrated by MAP, in order to continue to bring evidence and accountability to all services available to all youth in whatever manner possible.

Notes

Some of the core concepts and examples herein were originally presented in the following papers:

Chorpita, B.F. and Daleiden, E.L. (2013) 'Structuring the collaboration of science and service in pursuit of a shared vision.' *Journal of Clinical Child and Adolescent Psychology 43*, 323–338.
Chorpita, B.F., Daleiden, E.L. and Collins, K.S. (2013) 'Managing and adapting practice: A system for applying evidence in clinical care with youth and families.' *Clinical Social Work Journal 42*, 134–142.

Or as part of the following invited addresses:

Chorpita, B.F. and Daleiden, E.L. (2011) 'Finding the next frontiers.' Invited address given at the Delaware Project on Clinical Science Training: From Intervention Development to Implementation, Newark, DE, October.

Chorpita, B.F. (2012) 'Evidence based service systems for children and families: Principles of design and coordination.' Invited address given at the Conference for Eradicating Child Maltreatment: Interventions with Children and Families – Policy and Practice, London, November.

Doctors Chorpita and Daleiden are partners/owners of PracticeWise, LLC.

References

Aarons, G.A., Hurlburt, M. and Horwitz, S.M. (2011) 'Advancing a conceptual model of evidence-based practice implementation in public service sectors.' *Administration and Policy in Mental Health and Mental Health Services Research 38*, 1, 4–23.

APA Task Force on Promotion and Dissemination of Psychological Procedures (1995) Division of Clinical Psychology, American Psychological Association. 'Training in and dissemination of empirically-validated psychological treatments: Report and recommendations.' *The Clinical Psychologist 48*, 3–23.

Bernstein, A.D., Chorpita, B.F., Rosenblatt, A., Becker, K.D., Daleiden, E.L. and Ebesutani, C.K. (2013) 'Fit of evidence-based treatment components to youths served by wraparound process: A relevance mapping analysis.' *Journal of Clinical Child and Adolescent Psychology.*

Chorpita, B.F., Bernstein, A.D. and Daleiden, E.L. and the Research Network on Youth Mental Health (2008) 'Driving with roadmaps and dashboards: Using information resources to structure the decision models in service organizations.' *Administration and Policy in Mental Health and Mental Health Services Research 35*, 114–123.

Chorpita, B.F. and Daleiden, E.L. (2009) 'Mapping evidence-based treatments for children and adolescents: Application of the distillation and matching model to 615 treatments from 322 randomized trials.' *Journal of Consulting and Clinical Psychology 77*, 3, 566–579.

Chorpita, B.F. and Daleiden, E.L. (2013) 'Structuring the collaboration of science and service in pursuit of a shared vision.' *Journal of Clinical Child and Adolescent Psychology 43*, 2, 323–338.

Chorpita, B.F. and Weisz, J.R. (2005) *Modular approach to therapy for children with anxiety, depression, or conduct problems.* Honolulu and Boston: University of Hawaii at Manoa and Judge Baker Children's Center, Harvard Medical School.

Chorpita, B.F., Becker, K.D. and Daleiden, E.L. (2007) 'Understanding the common elements of evidence based practice: Misconceptions and clinical examples.' *Journal of the American Academy of Child and Adolescent Psychiatry 46*, 647–652.

Chorpita, B.F., Bernstein, A. and Daleiden, E.L. (2011a) 'Empirically guided coordination of multiple evidence-based treatments: An illustration of relevance mapping in children's mental health services.' *Journal of Consulting and Clinical Psychology 79*, 4, 470–480.

Chorpita, B.F., Daleiden, E.L., Ebesutani, C., Young, J. *et al.* (2011b) 'Evidence-based treatments for children and adolescents: An updated review of indicators of efficacy and effectiveness.' *Clinical Psychology: Science and Practice 18*, 2, 154–172.

Chorpita, B.F., Daleiden, E.L. and Weisz, J.R. (2005a) 'Identifying and selecting the common elements of evidence based interventions: A distillation and matching model.' *Mental Health Services Research 7*, 1, 5–20.

Chorpita, B.F., Daleiden, E.L. and Weisz, J.R. (2005b) 'Modularity in the design and application of therapeutic interventions.' *Applied and Preventive Psychology 11*, 141–156.

Chorpita, B.F., Weisz, J.R., Daleiden, E.L., Schoenwald, S.K. *et al.* (2013) 'Long-term outcomes for the Child STEPs randomized effectiveness trial: A comparison of modular and standard treatment designs with usual care.' *Journal of Consulting and Clinical Psychology 81*, 999–1009.

Chorpita, B.F., Yim, L.M., Donkervoet, J.C., Arensdorf, A. *et al.* (2002) 'Toward large-scale implementation of empirically supported treatments for children: A review and observations by the Hawaii empirical basis to services task force.' *Clinical Psychology: Science and Practice 9*, 2, 165–190.

Daleiden, E.L. and Chorpita, B.F. (2005) 'From data to wisdom: Quality improvement strategies supporting large-scale implementation of evidence-based services.' *Child and Adolescent Psychiatric Clinics of North America 14*, 2, 329–349.

Daleiden, E.L., Chorpita, B.F., Donkervoet, C., Arensdorf, A.M. and Brogan, M. (2006) 'Getting better at getting them better: Health outcomes and evidence-based practice within a system of care.' *Journal of the American Academy of Child and Adolescent Psychiatry 45*, 6, 749–756.

Decker, K.B. and Pynoos, R.S. (2004) 'The University of California at Los Angeles post-traumatic stress disorder reaction index.' *Current Psychiatry Reports 6*, 2, 96–100.

Garland, A.F., Brookman-Freeze, L., Hurlburt, M.S., Accurso, E.C. *et al.* (2010) 'Mental health care for children with disruptive behavior problems: A view inside therapists' offices.' *Psychiatric Services 61*, 8, 788–796.

Henggeler, S.W., Schoenwald, S.K., Borduin, C.M., Rowland, M.D. and Cunningham, P.B. (1998) *Multisystemic Treatment for Antisocial Behavior in Children and Adolescents.* New York: Guilford Press.

Kazdin, A.E. and Blase, S.L. (2011) 'Rebooting psychotherapy research and practice to reduce the burden of mental illness.' *Perspectives on Psychological Science 6*, 1, 21–37.

Rotheram-Borus, M., Swendeman, D. and Chorpita, B.F. (2012) 'Disruptive innovations for designing and diffusing evidence-based interventions.' *American Psychologist 67*, 6, 463–476.

Southam-Gerow, M.A., Daleiden, E.L., Chorpita, B.F., Bae, C. *et al.* (2014) 'MAPping Los Angeles County: Taking an evidence-informed model of mental health care to scale.' *Journal of Clinical Child and Adolescent Psychology 43*, 2, 190–200.

Weersing, V.R. (2005) 'Benchmarking the effectiveness of psychotherapy: Program evaluation as a component of evidence-base practice.' *Journal of the American Academy of Child and Adolescent Psychiatry 44*, 10, 1058–1062.

Weisz, J.R., Chorpita, B.F., Palinkas, L.A., Schoenwald, S.K. *et al.* (2012) 'Testing standard and modular designs for psychotherapy with youth depression, anxiety, and conduct problems: A randomized effectiveness trial.' *Archives of General Psychiatry 69*, 274–28.

Weisz, J.R., Jensen-Doss, A. and Hawley, K.M. (2006) 'Evidence-based youth psychotherapies versus clinical care: A meta-analysis of direct comparisons.' *American Psychologist 61*, 671–689.

Zima, B.T., Hurlburt, M.S., Knapp, P., Ladd, H. *et al.* (2005) 'Quality of publicly-funded outpatient specialty mental health care for common childhood psychiatric disorders in California.' *Journal of the American Academy of Child and Adolescent Psychiatry 44*, 130–144.

Chapter 7

HOPE FOR CHILDREN AND FAMILIES

Developing a Resource Pack Targeting Abusive Parenting
and the Associated Impairment of Children

Arnon Bentovim

Introduction

As discussed in Chapters 4 and 5 by Barlow and Prinz respectively, primary prevention is an essential approach to achieving the eradication of child maltreatment. Prinz shows that a blended approach, targeting various levels of parenting difficulties is an effective strategy to reduce the incidence of child maltreatment in a population. However, a primary prevention approach needs to be complemented by secondary and tertiary approaches to prevent the recurrence of child maltreatment through appropriate targeting of abusive and neglectful parenting, and to prevent the associated impairment of children's health and development. When maltreatment has occurred the emphasis needs to be on a process of assessment, analysis and intervention. The development of the resource pack for practitioners – *The Hope for Children and Families* (HfCF) is part of an overall approach to evidence-based assessment of parenting and family life, analysis of the impact of harm, the risks of future harm and prospects for intervention. Best evidence-based approaches need to be applied to each stage of the process of recognition, response, analysis, intervention and testing the capacity of parents to meet the needs of children. This has been the aim of the Child and Families Training approach initiated with the introduction of the Assessment Framework in 2000.

The approach adopted in the HfCF uses the methodology described by Chorpita in Chapter 6. This included the development of a practice manual based on the analysis of key components – practice elements of effective evidence-based interventions, and the integration of these into a resource pack – using a modular form of delivery. The goal is to make the resource pack widely available to a broad range of front-line practitioners to enable them to make evidence-based interventions based on the menu available in the manual, and to develop relevant skills through receiving appropriate training and supervision. Chorpita and his colleagues have demonstrated the value of a modular approach to improve practitioners' capacities to improve the mental health of children and young people. It remains to be demonstrated that a similar modular approach can prevent the recurrence of abusive and neglectful parenting, and can improve the health and development of children.

Developing front-line practice

Policy developments in the management of child maltreatment, both in the UK and elsewhere, have followed the wide reporting of child abuse tragedies in the national media. The failings of professionals and agencies to note signs of abuse and neglect, to investigate, protect, liaise or intervene effectively have been described on many occasions. A variety of responses have been advocated, including improving agency and multi-agency practice, establishing multi-disciplinary child protection teams with significant powers to investigate, making child protection reporting mandatory. A key issue has been the need to improve the skills of those professionals assessing children's needs and providing direct work to children and families. They need to be able to exercise informed professional judgements, to develop skills to analyse the often complex context they are working in and to be able to balance the rights of a child to be with their birth family, versus their right to be protected from abuse and neglect. The quality of relationships between the child, family and professionals is an essential component for effective intervention. Following the widely reported death of Baby P – Peter Connelly – Munro in a commissioned report (Munro 2011) has emphasised the need for practitioners to be knowledgeable about the latest theory and research and to achieve good outcomes for children. Social work expertise needs to be strengthened and professional training improved.

A key policy development in the UK was the introduction of the *Framework for the Assessment of Children in Need and their Families* (Department of Health, Department for Education and Employment and Home Office 2000; Figure 7.1). This is an eco-systemic evidence-based framework to describe the way children's needs are being met, the capacities of parents to provide good quality care and the influence of individual, family and environmental factors on the child and parents.

This has had a significant influence on childcare practice through the requirement for all agencies to use this framework to make assessments. A widely adopted holistic approach can improve communication and ensures a broad appreciation of the complex set of factors which are associated with different forms of child maltreatment and their perpetuation. The Assessment Framework has been adopted in a number of countries around the world.

Figure 7.1 The UK Assessment Framework for the assessment of children in need and their families

Child and Family Training were commissioned to develop a series of evidence-based tools to assist practitioners in their assessments and their analyses. Seven stages of work have been described from an initial recognition of concern that a child may be being harmed, through assessment, analysis and intervention. The stages are described in

Figure 7.2; central boxes describe the stages themselves, evidence-based tools are listed for use at the various stages on the left-hand side and the results of the assessment, analysis and action which follows are on the right-hand side.

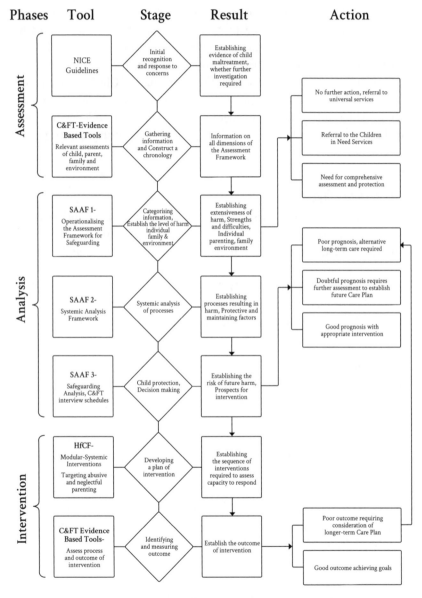

Figure 7.2 The stages of recognition, assessment, analysis and intervention of child maltreatment

The stages of recognition, assessment, analysis and intervention in child maltreatment

The first stage

The first stage is initial recognition, when a child is brought to the attention of child welfare professionals. Lead professionals responsible for the investigation of child protection in the UK are local authority social workers, working with appointed child health professionals and specialist police officers. The tools to inform this stage are provided by the guidelines issued by the UK National Institute of Clinical Excellence (NICE 2009) on the recognition and response to different forms of abuse. The result of this assessment is to establish the evidence of child maltreatment, and whether immediate protection or further investigation is required.

The second stage

The second stage of assessment is aimed at gathering information and constructing a chronology of significant events in the child and family's life. Evidence-based tools introduced by Child and Family Training are used to make relevant assessments of child, parent, family and environment (Bentovim and Bingley-Miller 2001; Cox and Walker 2002; Department of Health, Cox and Bentovim 2000). The result is to provide information in all dimensions of the Assessment Framework.

The third stage

This is the categorisation of information to establish the extensiveness of harm, and the nature of individual, family and environmental functioning. This utilises the first framework of the Safeguarding Assessment and Analysis Framework (the SAAF) (Barlow, Fisher and Jones 2012; Bentovim et al. 2009, 2012), which includes a number of evidence-based frameworks. The goal is to operationalise the Assessment Framework for Safeguarding and Protection purposes (Bentovim et al. 2009). This is based on a series of scales which describe strengths and difficulties of a child's functioning, parenting and the individual and family environment.

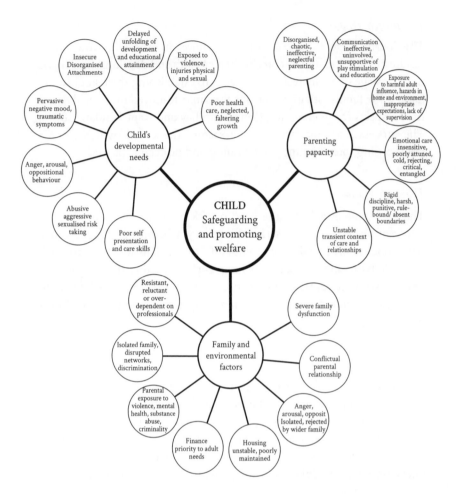

Figure 7.3 Profile of abusive and neglectful parenting and the associated impairment of children and young people's health and development

Figure 7.3 provides the descriptors of children and young people whose functioning is adversely affected by exposure to harmful parenting and individual, family and environmental factors which impact negatively on the child directly and on parenting capacity. Arranging the information under the dimension headings around the Assessment Framework triangle enables the practitioner to make an informed decision about whether referral to universal services is appropriate, or to children in need services, or whether there is sufficient concern to warrant further comprehensive assessment and protection.

The fourth stage

The fourth stage is to establish the nature of processes which have resulted in harmful impacts on children's health and development. This is the first stage of an analysis which leads to establishing the risk of future harm if the family situation remains the same, followed by an analysis of the prospects for intervention (Jones, Hindley and Ramchandani 2006). The processes are mapped using a second framework which records predisposing, precipitating, maintaining and protective factors.

The fifth stage

The fifth stage establishes the level of risk of harm, and prospects for intervention. This utilises a series of interview schedules and frameworks, with conclusions based on consensus decisions. This identifies the risk of future harm and prospects for intervention; whether the prognosis is hopeful with appropriate intervention, poor with alternative long-term care being required, or doubtful, requiring intervention to establish a future care plan.

The sixth stage

The sixth stage is to develop a plan of intervention, targeting abusive and neglectful parenting and the associated impairment of children and young people. The aim is to provide intervention to test the capacity of parents to provide adequate care. HfCF is designed to assist practitioners with these tasks, establishing goals and delivering evidence-based interventions in modular form for parents, children and young people and their families.

The seventh stage

The seventh stage is to identify and measure children's outcomes to determine whether goals have been achieved, or whether outcomes are poor, that is, parenting remaining potentially harmful and the associated impairments of children's health and development persisting unmodified. Assessments of change are measured by routine use of the range of qualitative and quantative evidence-based tools already used in the assessment process.

Developing the Hope for Children and Families Approach

Evidence-based approaches to prevent recurrence of abusive and neglectful parenting

When randomised controlled interventions (RCTs) aimed at preventing the recurrence of child maltreatment and associated impairment are examined (MacMillan *et al.* 2009) there is little consistency in approach. First, the range of effective interventions is extensive – psycho-dynamic, cognitive-behavioural, video-feed back; second, the range of foci is wide – individual, parent and family; third, different approaches incorporate effective elements of other interventions, for example, trauma-focused interventions; fourth, similar models are applied to differing forms of maltreatment successfully; and, fifth, there is inconsistent research on outcomes, some forms of abuse being studied more extensively. The practitioner has to choose between competing effective models, which require differing levels of skill and training. For a practitioner to be competent at working across the maltreatment field would require many years of complex training. Inevitably practitioners choose one approach, and this may limit the capacity of practitioners and agencies to meet the needs of families who may well have complex maltreatment patterns (Kolko, Iselin and Gully 2011).

To confront this issue Barth *et al.* (2011) based on the work of Chorpita and Daleiden (2009a) advocated the value of a Common Practice Elements Framework in the child welfare field. This conceptualises clinical practice in terms of generic components which cut across many distinct treatment protocols, identifying specific clinical procedures common to evidence-based practices (also see Garland *et al.* 2008; Wampold *et al.* 1997); Chorpita and Daleiden (2009a) distilled the Practice Elements of over 600 evidence-based interventions in the child mental health field. They developed the Managing and Adapting Practice (MAP) approach which allows practitioners to access the elements of evidence-based approaches to match the clinical need of their patients (Chorpita and Daleiden 2009b). They also developed the Modular Approach to Children with Anxiety, Depression, Trauma and Conduct (MATCH – ADTC; Chorpita and Weisz 2009) based on a number of evidence-based protocols to develop a comparable modular approach to the treatment of common mental health problems. These are key components in addressing the impairments of children and young people subjected to abusive parenting (Chorpita and Weisz 2009).

The Common Factor Framework (Duncan *et al.* 2010) is a complement to the common elements approach. This asserts that the personal and interpersonal components of intervention (for example, alliance, client motivation and therapist factors) common to all interventions are responsible for treatment outcomes to a significant extent. Such approaches are emerging as a complement to more complex specific treatment approaches.

Application of the MAP approach to the field of child maltreatment

The specific forms of neglectful and abusive parenting and associated impairments to be addressed include physical abuse, sexual abuse, neglect and emotional abuse including exposure to violence – the recognised forms of maltreatment in the UK. The approach followed was to apply the distillation approach (Chorpita and Daleiden 2009a) to RCTs which have proven effective to prevent the recurrence of the various forms of maltreatment, and which address the associated impairment of health and development. The review by Macmillan *et al.* (2009) provided the basic source of RCTs, reinforced by more recently published studies. Primary prevention interventions were excluded; outcome research which was not controlled was also excluded. Working with adult sexual offenders was also excluded as such individuals require specialist interventions by professionals, rather than by the front-line practitioners who are the goal of this approach. Working with victims of sexual abuse, children and young people responsible for harmful sexual behaviour and parents supporting children who had been abused by a family member were included. The range of studies available does not reflect the whole spectrum of maltreatment. Physical and sexual abuse 'event-focused forms of maltreatment' are the widest studied, emotional abuse and neglect 'process forms of maltreatment' the least.

Research procedure

Common Practice Elements distilled from the RCTs were available through the MAP service (PracticeWise LLC). RCTs were analysed for each form of maltreatment and the common elements which emerged were split, focused on those relating to the parent, to children, and to individuals and family. Information was analysed by frequency. This information is available through Bentovim and Elliott (2012).

Looking at each form of maltreatment individually

Physical abuse is the most extensively evaluated form of maltreatment through RCTs. This includes The Alternatives to Family Approaches (Kolko 1996; Kolko *et al.* 2009). This evaluates a broad-based cognitive behaviour therapy/family therapy approach which is delivered via a series of modules and has demonstrated its value both in the clinic and the community. Parent–child interaction therapy (Chaffin *et al.* 2004) has again been extensively researched and demonstrated to be effective, again both in the clinic and in the home and has additional effective elements, including motivational enhancement. A home visiting approach by public health nurses has proven of value (McMillan *et al.* 2005) The PCIT and Alternatives to Family Approaches are extensively manualised, and there has been effective training of these approaches to positively impact on physical abuse (also see Montgomery *et al.* 2009).

Multisystemic Therapy (MST) (Swenson *et al.* 2010) has recently been extended to include an approach to working with physical abuse and neglect as well as with adolescents with problem externalising behaviour. MST requires a team available 24 hours a day, seven days a week. The approach is intensive and now includes work with parents who have serious mental health, drug and alcohol substance abuse problems (Schaeffer *et al.* 2013). This model ensures that one team can work with the complex problems associated with abusive and neglectful parenting and associated impairments, rather than attempting to work with specialist mental health and substance abuse agencies, who may have competing priorities.

When these approaches were analysed for practice elements, over 37 were identified: 15 were targeted at parents, 7 at the family and 15 at children. Psychoeducation for the parent about the harmful impacts of abuse was a frequent practice element, other approaches included a variety of different approaches to manage oppositional behaviour. Children were helped by social skills training, communication skills, relaxation, personal safety skills and problem solving. There was a variety of approaches to help children's development, including educational support, assertiveness training and anger management. Family interventions included family therapy, motivational interview to engage family and marital and individual treatment for caregivers.

Exposure to violence and mental health difficulties has increasingly been recognised as having a harmful impact on children, leading to the impairment of their health and development. Seeing a parent being hurt and injured can have as traumatic an impact on a child as the child being hit themselves. RCTs have been developed which have included the use of child–parent psychotherapy (Ippen *et al.* 2011; Lieberman, Van Horn and Ippen 2005; Lieberman *et al.* 2006; Toth *et al.* 2002, 2006). This approach focuses on work with the child and supportive parent to help clarify the child's experiences and promote their relationship. Cohen, Mannarino and Iyengar (2011) have described the use of trauma-focused cognitive-behavioural therapy to achieve the same goals.

The majority of practice elements were targeted at children, the parent and the family. The practice elements which emerged included psychoeducation about the impact of violence or mental health difficulties, supporting parents to be able to listen supportively to their children and to improve their relationship and build rapport. Work with children included creating a trauma narrative of stressful traumatic events they had been exposed to, the development of safety skills and social skills. This area of practice has been reinforced through providing cognitive-behavioural therapy (CBT) to depressed mothers in parallel with work on protection and parenting, and the provision of interpersonal therapy in addition to parent–child psychotherapy (Toth *et al.* 2006). This is another example of a multi-disciplinary team providing intervention for the significant mental health issues of parents, and the needs of children affected by the context of abuse and neglect. The scope for multi-disciplinary teams working in the complex field of child maltreatment is proving to be an effective approach.

Victims of sexual abuse have been studied extensively. The value of trauma-focused cognitive-behavioural therapy has been well established to ameliorate the impact of sexual abuse on children (for example, Cohen *et al.* 2004; Cohen and Mannarino 1996; Deblinger *et al.* 2006; Scheringa *et al.* 2011). One study has compared individual psychodynamic treatment for children versus group treatment (Trowell *et al.* 2002) and has demonstrated the value of a more individualised approach.

The majority of practice elements were targeted at children and parents. Practice elements for children included psychoeducation about the impact of sexual abuse, cognitive behavioural skills in managing and exposing traumatic thoughts, feelings and behaviour associated with abuse, relaxation skills, problem solving skills and relationship building. Parents were provided with psychoeducation, coping and parenting skills. The approach has also been extended to working with physical abuse. Trauma-focused CBT is also employed in other effective evidence-based approaches, for example in MST and Alternatives for the Family. The model of bringing practice elements together in one resource approach is now being introduced in other effective approaches to prevent the recurrence of maltreatment and associated impairment of children and young people's health and development.

Young people responsible for harmful sexual behaviour have been worked with, including testing the efficacy of cognitive behavioural therapy for younger children (Bonner, Walker and Berliner 1999; Carpenter, Silovsky and Chaffin 2006). MST has been utilised with older children and young people (Borduin *et al.* 1990; Letourneau *et al.* 2009). Because of the limited range of interventions a consensus paper was included to reflect the views of a wide range of practitioners (Hackett, Masson and Phillips 2006).

A wide range of practice elements was targeted at children and young people and a number at parents. Practice elements included CBT to help children and young people manage harmful behaviour and develop personal safety skills; anger management, parental line of sight supervision, problem-solving and social skills were less utilised.

Neglect is probably the least studied in randomised controlled evidence-based approaches. The recent publication by Chaffin *et al.* (2012) has demonstrated significant effectiveness of a ten-year state-wide intervention study of SafeCare, an approach introduced by Lutzker and Bigelow (2002). The Safecare Approach includes interventions to improve the nature of parent interaction with young children, as well as providing better quality care of children and a safe home and environment. This has been demonstrated to have a significantly positive impact on pervasive problems of neglect, maintained over a number of years.

Brunk, Henggeler and Whelan (1987) carried out an early study demonstrating the effectiveness of MST, and Farmer and Lutman (2009) have shown that an active case management approach is an essential approach to intervention with neglect.

There has also been a growing number of approaches which have targeted a core issue in both neglect and emotional abuse, which is to intervene with disorganised and insecure attachment patterns (Bernard *et al.* 2012; Cicchetti, Rogosch and Toth 2006; Moss *et al.* 2011).

Practice elements which emerged focused on facilitating professional family relationships, engaging families and providing a proactive management approach. Parenting approaches included psychoeducation about the impact of severe neglect on children's development, managing children's behaviour, promoting positive interaction, safety and good care, and helping children with personal safety skills, nutritional and medical care. These approaches were also used in a number of studies focusing on neglect and failure to thrive (Black *et al.* 1995, 1997; Hutcheson, Black and Dubowitz 1997 and Iwaniec and Herbert 1999).

Integrating practice elements into a resource pack

The challenge was how to integrate the practice elements which emerged into a coherent and meaningful approach which could be articulated in a manual.

Practice elements overlap across different forms of interventions and different forms of maltreatment. Psychoeducation with parents and children was the most frequently utilised. The challenge was how to integrate this material to reflect the practice elements in a form which would be of value to practitioners. A consideration was whether to develop a manual for specific forms of maltreatment, or alternately to integrate practice elements across the range of abusive and neglectful parenting. Although RCTs focus on specific forms of maltreatment, in practice there are always combinations of neglectful and abusive parenting present and a wide variety of children's impairment responses. Successful interventions bring together combinations of practice elements. It seemed appropriate therefore to gather a set of practice elements into practice guidelines through developing a set of modules which could be used across the field of maltreatment and which could fit the specific needs of parents and children.

Some practice elements such as psychoeducation were used differently for different forms of maltreatment. It was recognised that guidance would need to be provided on how to apply the basic principles to different forms of maltreatment. Cognitive approaches, individual, marital and family therapy are also utilised widely with parents and children; again, guidance would need to be provided on how these approaches were to be applied in different contexts. Other approaches are more focused, for example, assertiveness training, anger management, social skills, safety skills, managing mood and anxiety, emotional processing, creating a trauma narrative. Davies and Ward (2012) advised that the original research study could provide a model to provide a comparable approach.

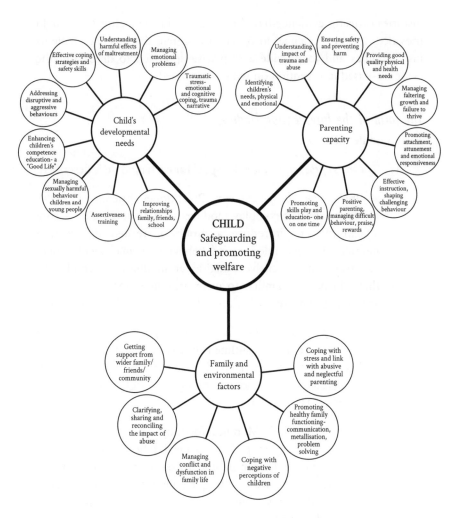

Figure 7.4 Targeting abusive and neglectful parenting and the associated impairment of children's health and development

Interventions were fitted to the descriptors of families showing abusive and neglectful parenting and the associated impairment of children and young people. Figure 7.4 describes the way in which interventions can be arranged around the Assessment Framework to modify the profile of abusive and neglectful parenting and the associated impairment of children and young people's health and development.

A group of experienced practitioners from the voluntary and statutory sector (the Writing Group – see end of chapter note) with long histories of using evidence-based approaches in the maltreatment field provided 'local experience' in order to integrate the practice elements into modules and to provide a step-wise approach to delivering the evidence-based intervention on which it is based.

The form of the Intervention Modules

Each module includes:

1. *The goals of the intervention.* The goal for each module is described.

2. *A briefing for the practitioner.* Practitioner briefing modules introduce specific complex modules such as developing secure attachments, or introduce a group of related intervention modules, for example, around behaviour management. There are also more extensive practitioner modules for conditions that will be less familiar to many frontline practitioners, such as working with sexually harmful behaviour and family work.

3. *Step by step approaches to achieve the goal of the module.* The steps of each procedure are outlined in a two-column format, with a checklist on the left-hand side and notes for practitioners and suggested scripts and activities on the right, following the MATCH–ADTC model.

4. *Location of the work.* Modules focusing on providing a safe environment and good quality care need to be undertaken in the home; other modules can be undertaken either at the home or in the practitioners' work setting. Family modules are explicitly focused on all family members and can be undertaken at home or in a work setting.

5. *Special cases.* Some modules offer special case information which explains how to adapt the material for a particular presentation, for example, in the section describing sexual abuse of a child by a parent, there is also information about when a child is abused by a close member of the family.

6. *Materials to support the development of therapeutic work.* All supplemental material is specified for each intervention: worksheets (exercises for completion by the child, parent or family members), handouts which provide information for

children, young people and their parents and carers and records which are formats used for rating of any of the measures to track progress.

7. *Tools to assess the success of the intervention for the child.* It is vital that key variables are recorded regularly and accurately.

8. *Guidance on the skills required to deliver the module* and how modules can be integrated to fit the needs of the particular child and family. In practice modules these are combined to match the particular profile of harmful processes which drive the problem areas and to build on strengths which can potentially promote better outcomes for children.

The scope of Intervention Modules

The modules focus on the following areas:

1. MODULES TO PROMOTE ENGAGEMENT AND HOPE

These initial modules introduce the approach to, and promote appropriate engagement with, the family (parents and children), separately and together. The goal is to give a message of hope, to set collaborative agreed goals, identifying targets for eradicating abusive and neglectful parenting, strengths to be built on and how children and young people's health and development are to be addressed. Criteria for success and failure need to be defined as well as the consequences of failure to achieve goals. A care, protection and intervention plan for each child needs to be established.

2. PSYCHOEDUCATION

Psychoeducation with parents and children, both separately and together, helps to convey understanding about how abusive and neglectful parenting can influence children and young people's development psychologically and neurobiologically: their capacity to learn, to develop and regulate emotions and behaviour. Parents and children are encouraged to acknowledge the nature of abuse and neglect which their children have experienced. Modules focus on helping parents understand the basic needs of children, society's expectations and what is required of parents to promote their children's development.

3. MODULES FOCUSED ON TARGETING ABUSIVE AND NEGLECTFUL PARENTING

These modules explore the way that stress in parents' lives, current and in the past, has had an impact on their capacity to meet their children's needs and to make negative attributions about children's behaviour, justifying harsh treatments. Approaches are advocated to help manage potentially harmful effects. The development of positive parenting is encouraged, promoting secure attachment attunement and positive emotional responses, problem-solving, communication and managing conflict. Neglectful parenting is countered by modules that promote good quality care, health, positive nutrition and safety through active intervention, modelling and feedback in the home. Parents are encouraged to promote development, play and skills, again through the use of modelling and active intervention. Abusive parenting is targeted by directly tackling conflict cycles, punitive responses and coercive critical parenting. Alternatives are encouraged such as enjoyable one-on-one time and the use of praise and rewards as well as effective discipline, commands and effective instruction and, where appropriate, time out.

4. MODULES SUPPORTING CHILDREN, YOUNG PEOPLE AND THEIR
CARERS TO ADDRESS ADVERSE EMOTIONAL OUTCOMES

These modules support practitioners to engage with children and young people, and to assist them to understand the way exposure to abusive and neglectful parenting that results in significant physical, emotional and sexual abuse can have an impact on emotional and behavioural functioning and can result in traumatic stress. Basic skills modules include coping with the impact on their emotional life, being able to be safe, to relax, develop helpful activities and manage traumatic symptoms and, where appropriate, anxiety and mood difficulties. Support from and sharing with a non-abusive carer is essential to targeting the range of responses associated with these impacts.

5. MODULES SUPPORTING CHILDREN, YOUNG PEOPLE AND
CARERS TO ADDRESS ADVERSE DISRUPTIVE BEHAVIOUR

A common response in older children who may have been exposed to multiple adversity is the development of disruptive responses which maintain the pattern of abuse and neglect through enactment with siblings and peers. The support of a non-abusive carer is essential to support the practitioner, delivering modules which help young people understand their response to the context of abusive care to which they have been exposed and 'live a good life', as an alternative to re-enacting abusive behaviour. Modules help address aggressive behaviour and anger and support the development of empathy, finding a substitute for anger and developing appropriate assertive skills.

Harmful sexual behaviour arises from a number of factors including exposure to abusive or neglectful parenting. Modules provide intervention for parents/carers and for children both under and over the age of 12. Steps to understand the difference between 'normal' and 'concerning' sexual behaviour are described, and steps to understand the origin of sexually harmful responses, being aware of triggers and reinforcers and developing empathic, safe relationship skills.

6. Targeting family and community relationships

Families where there has been abuse or neglect and associated impairment of children's health and development are often isolated in the community. Communication is often poor and conflict and family dysfunctional patterns are persistent and maintain a cycle of abusive and neglectful care. A series of modules addressing these concerns by promoting communication, introducing problem-solving skills and finding alternatives to conflictual and dysfunctional modes of relating, for example, when children find themselves taking on parental functions. Modules assist parents to be able to apologise and take responsibility for harmful actions, freeing children from guilt and responsibility. The practitioner is encouraged to take a key role in promoting professional and community networks of formal and informal support to strengthen the team around the family.

Integrating modules to fit the needs of the family

Modules from the Resource Pack need to be integrated to fit the needs of the particular family context. The flowchart in Figure 7.5 demonstrates an approach to integrating modules.

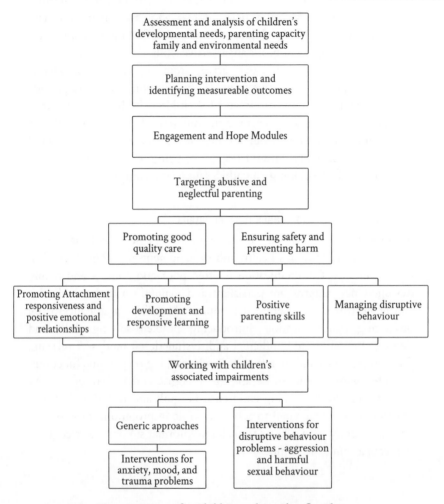

Figure 7.5 Hope for Children and Families flowchart

It illustrates the process of:

▲ The assessment and analysis of children's developmental needs, parenting capacity and family and environmental factors, and the process of planning interventions and identifying outcomes.

▲ The engagement and hope stage helps to clarify protection issues, to motivate families to work with the practitioner, to establish goals on a collaborative basis, to understand the impact of harm that their children have suffered or are likely to suffer in the family, and to establish collaborative goals and a team around the family that is also supportive of the practitioner.

▲ Key modules are then the promotion of good quality care, ensuring safety and preventing harm.

▲ Modules which need to be included to support parenting include promoting attachment and positive emotional relating, promoting developing and responsive learning, positive parenting and managing disruptive behaviour. Many of these modules work directly with children.

▲ When there are specific associated impairments, children will need to undertake work based on modules focused on their needs, as well as generic approaches which all children exposed to maltreatment would benefit from.

▲ Specific interventions for anxiety, mood and trauma.

▲ When there is significant externalising behaviour, whether it be disruptive behaviour, aggression or harmful sexual behaviour.

Figure 7.6 describes the library of modules which target the profile of abusive and neglectful parenting and the impact and associated impairment of children and young people's health and development.

Library of Modules

Initial stages of work: engagement and hope

- ☐ Engaging families, parents and children; Promoting hopefulness
- ☐ Goal setting
- ☐ How abusive and neglectful parenting affects children's development, emotional and physical; Psychoeducation

Working with parents: targeting abusive and neglectful parenting

PROMOTING GOOD QUALITY CARE

- ☐ Developing a capacity to identify and understand children's physical and emotional needs
- ☐ Providing good quality basic care
- ☐ Nutritional care: weight faltering and failure to thrive
- ☐ Supportive networking for families

ENSURING SAFETY AND PREVENTING HARM

- ☐ Ensuring safety and preventing harm
- ☐ Parents coping with stress and the link with abusive and neglectful parenting
- ☐ Helping parents cope with negative perceptions of their children
- ☐ Helpful techniques to manage conflict and dysfunction in family life
- ☐ Parenting: promoting safety for children and young people who have been harmed sexually in the family or by a trusted member of the community
- ☐ Clarifying, sharing and reconciling the impact of abusive and neglectful parenting

PROMOTING ATTACHMENT, ATTUNED RESPONSIVENESS AND POSITIVE EMOTIONAL RELATIONSHIPS

- ☐ Promoting attachment, attuned responsiveness and positive emotional relationships: younger children
- ☐ Promoting attachment, responsiveness and positive relating with older children: one-on-one time
- ☐ Promoting healthy family functioning, family communication and problem-solving skills

PROMOTING DEVELOPMENT AND RESPONSIVE LEARNING

- ☐ Promoting development, early and later

PROMOTING PARENTING SKILLS

- ☐ The use of attention and ignoring
- ☐ Giving effective instructions
- ☐ Shaping challenging behavior

MANAGING DISRUPTIVE BEHAVIOR

- ☐ Working with disruptive behavior problems
- ☐ Working with parents and carers to support work with children and young people responsible for harmful sexual behaviours

Working with children and young people's impairments: emotional and traumatic responses

GENERIC APPROACHES FOR ALL CHILDREN SUBJECT TO MALTREATMENT

- ☐ Developing a child-centred approach
- ☐ Psychoeducation intervention on the effects of maltreatment
- ☐ Safety planning
- ☐ Coping skills
- ☐ Relaxing and calming
- ☐ Describing and monitoring feelings
- ☐ Activity selection
- ☐ Problem solving
- ☐ Maintenance and building resilience

SPECIFIC INTERVENTIONS FOR IMPAIRMENTS — ANXIETY, MOOD PROBLEMS AND TRAUMA PROBLEMS

- ☐ Working with anxiety problems: helping children who experience excessive anxiety
- ☐ Working with mood problems: helping children who present with persistent low mood or with depression
- ☐ Working with trauma problems: helping children who experience traumatic responses

Working with children and young people's impairments: disruptive behavior problems

- ☐ Enhancing children's competence: education, talent and 'the good life'
- ☐ Coping with disruptive behaviour
- ☐ Assertiveness training
- ☐ Working with children under 12 who have displayed harmful sexual behaviour
- ☐ Working with adolescents (age 12+) who have displayed harmful sexual behaviour
- ☐ Developing positive relationships with family and friends

Figure 7.6 Library of Modules

A case example: the Green family

To illustrate how the Hope for Children and Families Modular Approach Resource Pack can be used in practice, a case example will be provided. This is a development of the Green family described in Bentovim *et al.* (2009), illustrating how the HfCF approach could be applied to a complex case. The Green family consists of parents Jack, aged 48, and Lesley, aged 41, and their four children Charlie, aged 13, David, aged 10, Sarah, aged 8 and John, aged 4 (Figure 7.7).

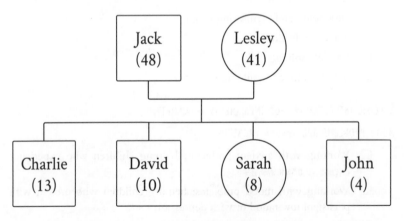

Figure 7.7 Genogram of the Green family

The presentation to professionals came about through a referral from the school who were concerned about the prolonged failure of the children's school attendance. There were also concerns about the increasingly neglected appearance of all four children, and the highly sexualised behaviour of Sarah towards other children.

An initial assessment demonstrated that both parents were emotionally and physically withdrawn; the children were like a feral group having to fend for themselves. There were expectations that Charlie would provide care for the younger children. There were poor boundaries, discipline was inconsistent and poorly sustained; family life as observed in the initial assessment was characterised by unresolved arguments and conflicts involving the parents. The children responded rather better to their father but he was absent much of the time. Each parent blamed the other for failing to care for and control the children.

Significant sexually abusive behaviour was reported involving all four children. Sarah indicated readily that Charlie and David were behaving in a sexually inappropriate ways with her and with John. Charlie was observed to be highly sexualised in his responses to the younger children. The core concern was the disorganisation of care in the home, clothing was unchanged and bedding soiled, dishes unwashed, the home dirty and chaotic. The parents were unable to get the children up in the mornings to attend school. Any attempt to discipline was met with oppositional behaviour from the older boys. John, the youngest child, showed significant developmental delay in language and skills, and he too was oppositional. Sarah was the only child who demonstrated social skills and self-care capacities.

Charlie, aged 13, was bullying his siblings and initiating intense sexual activity with Sarah involving the siblings. David, the ten-year-old, was observed to be a frozen, rigid child, strikingly immature, his language was delayed. His mother seemed to use him as a comfort object, getting him to sleep with her. The father was spending increasing amounts of time with his family. Sarah, the eight-year-old, showed evidence of highly sexualised behaviour: she described nightmares, bad dreams and described her distress at being forced into inappropriate sexual activities by Charlie and David. There were concerns at school that she was now behaving sexually inappropriately with other children. John, the four-year-old, was holding a doll continuously, an indication of his unmet needs. His attachment seemed highly disorganised, seeking closeness at one point and then intense rejection at others. He too had been involved in the sexualised behaviour.

Profile of parenting, family, individual characteristics and impact on the children

Figure 7.8 Descriptors of parenting capacity, individual and family functioning and their impact on the children

Figure 7.8 demonstrates the profile of parenting capacity, individual and family factors and impact on the children which emerged from an extensive assessment of parenting capacity, individual, child and family functioning using the Child and Family Tools described earlier.

PARENTING CAPACITY

▲ The family environment was impoverished: there was minimal interchange between the parents and between parents and the children.

▲ There was minimal play and stimulation of the children and a significant failure to support education.

▲ Management of the children was characterised by punitive, inconsistent responses to challenging behaviour. There was inappropriate boundaries and expectations, for example, Charlie taking on a parental role.

▲ The painful separation of the parents, associated with their incapacity to resolve conflicts, reinforced the poor care of the children.

▲ The parents showed minimal ability to work together, thrusting responsibility on Charlie.

▲ Care was disorganised, clothing poorly cared for, mealtimes chaotic, health issues were ignored, and there was a lack of routine and an absence of any regular activities.

▲ Parental care was therefore judged to be unresponsive, unreliable and there was inadequate supervision.

▲ Charlie and David's exploitative and abusive behaviour was unchecked: feeble attempts were made to control them and the parents denied any responsibility.

▲ There was little evidence of warmth, empathy or understanding of the children, the children's responses were clinging, rejecting, avoidant.

THE INFLUENCE OF INDIVIDUAL PARENT, FAMILY AND ENVIRONMENTAL FACTORS

▲ When the family were seen together the atmosphere was chaotic: there was a degree of over-excitement, intolerance, frustration and anger.

▲ Mother reported a protective childhood and having been sustained by family support in the early years of family life, which had meant the care of the children and the home had been more satisfactory. As the children got older and challenging, mother's parenting difficulties became evident.

▲ Father described growing up in a context of privation, loneliness and social isolation. He became increasingly critical of mother's difficulties, driving a wedge between her and her family who had played a significant, supportive role. Her depression and withdrawal increasingly frustrated his attempts to achieve some improvement in family life and he increasingly withdrew. Both parents showed evidence of significant depressed affect.

▲ The housing had been consistent, but the home was dirty, unwelcoming, uncared for and showing signs of significant neglect.

▲ The father worked consistently and there had always been just sufficient income.

▲ The family as a whole was isolated, not integrated in the community and there was a lack of community relationships and support.

▲ Support offered by professionals had been offered but there was a limited response.

THE IMPACT ON THE CHILDREN

There was an extensive impact on the children causing extensive significant harm:

▲ The children had poor self-presentation, poor self-care: they were unkempt, there was a failure of hygiene and little pride in their appearance.

▲ They had been exposed to extensive parental conflict, separation and significant neglect, and harmful sexual behaviour had emerged as an attempt to find some closeness.

⅄ There was delayed development and language skills, poor preparation for school, poor attendance at school, rejection by peers, poor social skills and an absence of a capacity to make sustaining relationships.

⅄ Attachments were disorganised, clinging, avoiding and controlling.

⅄ The children's moods were unhappy, angry, defiant, sexually aroused, withdrawn and frozen, with traumatic responses resulting.

A systemic analysis

A systemic analysis indicated that predisposing factors to the current state of affairs included the mother's dependence on the extensive support provided by her family, which had maintained early stability. Professional intervention at earlier stages had also helped maintain family organisation. The mother had not ever developed a full profile of parenting skills. The father's role was to be a traditional, consistent, supportive parent through work, not a hands on parent, although he did attempt to make a relationship with Charlie. His frustration at mother's increasing difficulties with the control of their children and management of the home led to increasing parental conflict resulting in father's absence, mother's depression and the withdrawal of her family.

Depression, withdrawal and isolation were the factors which precipitated the increasing picture of serious neglect and failure to manage the children. Charlie was being given increasing parental expectations, replacing affection and warmth with sexuality and forceful control. There were protective factors present. Sarah had a history of more secure early attachment to her mother, and she demonstrated significantly greater competency than her siblings. She was interested in education and relationships. Nutrition of the children had always been satisfactory, although there were concerns about other aspects of their development.

The mother acknowledged her failure, and that she had been aware of Charlie's abusive behaviour although she had been unable to manage or control it. The father found it difficult to accept that there had been sexually inappropriate behaviour perpetrated by Charlie and involving the younger children, and had not reinforced mother's concerns.

The analysis concluded that the overall level of harm to the children was high, and if the family situation remained unchanged the overall levels of risk of neglect and reabuse would be unacceptably high. There were poor prospects for Charlie and David being helped while living at home. They were already moving into adolescence and their defiance and oppositional behaviour against their mother, given the father's separation from the family and his lukewarm support of the assessment process meant that the mother would have to cope alone. She would be unlikely to effect the changes required, given the level of risk to the younger children from Charlie's predatory and highly aroused, inappropriately sexual behaviour. Given the degree of separation of the parents, there was some prospect of the mother being supported to be able to meet the younger children's needs with the father agreeing to live separately. Charlie was placed with a family member, a single individual, whilst David was placed in foster care. There was an agreement by the family with this proposal, and it was also sanctioned by the Court. The process of intervention is described in the next chapter.

Notes and Acknowledgements

The initial development of this work by Arnon Bentovim and Ian Elliott was made possible by a grant from the Department for Education to Child and Family Training UK, a not-for-profit organisation developing and promulgating evidence-based approaches to assessment and intervention, and the Lucy Faithfull Foundation UK, a charitable organisation which aims to protect children by targeting sexually harmful behaviour. The Department of Education funded further development to Child and Family Training UK as part of the initiative to target child neglect. This work has also been supported by the South London and Maudsley NHS Foundation Trust who supported Dr Tara Weeramanthri to provide consultative work to the project, and the contribution of Dr Andrea Danese. We gratefully acknowledge the contribution of the writing group who worked to make the manual accessible for practitioners. The approach is published in a paper in the *Journal of Clinical Child and Adolescent Psychology* (2014). We also gratefully acknowledge the support of Professor Bruce Chorpita, UCLA, Professor David Kolko, University of Pittsburgh, and Dr Lucy Berliner, Harborview Centre, Seattle.

The writing group

Child and Family Training: Dr Arnon Bentovim

The Lucy Faithfull Foundation: Hilary Eldridge, Alice Newman, Caroline Robertson

The South London and Maudsley NHS Foundation Trust: Dr Tara Weeramanthri

Kings College and the Institute of Psychiatry: Dr Andrea Danese

Swaay UK: Mette Whittaker, Nicola Gilderthorp, Samantha Richards

Child and Family Practice London: Dr Clare Gates

Southwark Safeguarding Children Board: Malcolm Ward (formerly Business Manager)

References

Barlow, J., Fisher, J.D. and Jones, D. (2012) *Systematic Review of Models of Analysing Significant Harm. Research Report RR199.* London: Department for Education.

Barth, R.P., Lee, B.R., Lindsey, M.A., Collins, K.S. *et al.* (2011) 'Evidence-based practice at a crossroads, the emergence of common elements and factors.' *Research on Social Work Practice 22,* 1, 108–119.

Bentovim, A. and Bingley Miller, L. (2001) *The Family Assessment: Assessment of Family Competence, Strengths and Difficulties.* Brighton: Pavilion.

Bentovim, A. and Elliott, I. (2012) *Application of Distillation Approach to Evidence Based Intervention with Child Maltreatment.* York: Child and Family Training.

Bentovim, A., Bingley Miller, L., Pizzey, S. and Tapp, S. (2012) *The Safeguarding Assessment and Analysis Framework.* York: Child and Family Training.

Bentovim A., Cox A., Bingley Miller, L., and Pizzey S. (2009*) Safeguarding Children Living with Trauma and Family Violence: A Guide to Evidence-Based Assessment, Analysis and Planning Interventions.* London: Jessica Kingsley Publishers.

Bernard, K., Dozier, M., Bick, J., Lewis-Moriarty, E., Lindheim, O. and Carlson, E. (2012) 'Enhancing attachment organisation among maltreated children: Results of a randomised clinical trial.' *Child Development 83,* 3, 623–636.

Black, M., Dubowitz, H., Krishnakumar, A. and Starr, R.H. (1995) 'Randomised clinical trial of home intervention for children with failure to thrive.' *Paediatrics 95,* 6, 807–814.

Black, M., Dubowitz, H., Krishnakumar, A. and Starr, R.H. (1997) Early intervention and recovery amongst children with failure to thrive – follow-up at age 8.' *Paediatrics 120,* 1, 59–69.

Bonner, B.L., Walker, C.E. and Berliner, L. (1999) *Children with Sexual Behaviour Problems: Assessment and Treatment.* Final Report. Grant number 90-CA-1469. Washington, DC: US Department of Health and Human Services National Clearing House on Child Abuse and Neglect.

Borduin, C.M., Henggeler, S., Blaske, D.M. and Stein, R.J. (1990) 'Multi-systemic treatment of adolescent sexual offenders.' *International Journal of Offender Therapy and Comparative Criminology 34,* 100–113.

Brunk, M., Henggeler, S. and Whelan, J.P. (1987) 'Comparison of multi-systemic therapy and parenting training in the treatment of child abuse and neglect.' *Journal of Consulting Clinical Psychology 55,* 171–178.

Carpenter, M., Silovsky, J.F. and Chaffin, M. (2006) 'Randomised trial of treatment for children with sexual behaviour problems: 10 year follow-up.' *Journal of Consulting and Clinical Psychology 74,* 482–488.

Chaffin, M., Hecht, D., Bard, D., Silovsky, J.F. and Beasley, W.H. (2012) 'A statewide trial of the Safe Care Home based services, model with parents in Child Protection Services.' *Pediatrics 129,* 3, 509–515.

Chaffin, M., Silovsky, J.F., Funderburk, B., Valle, L.A. *et al.* (2004) 'Parent child interaction therapy with physically abusive parents – reducing further abuse reports.' *Journal of Consulting Clinical Psychology 72,* 500–510.

Chorpita, B.F. and Daleiden, E.L. (2009a) 'Mapping evidence-based treatments for children and adolescents, application of the distillation and matching model to 650 treatments from 322 randomised trials.' *Journal of Consulting and Clinical Psychology 77,* 566–579.

Chorpita, B.F. and Daleiden, E.L. (2009b) *Managing and Adapting Practice.* Satellite Beach, FL: Practicewise.

Chorpita, B.F. and Weisz, J.R. (2009) *Modular Approach to Children with Anxiety, Depression, Trauma and Conduct Match-ADTC.* Satellite Beach, FL: Practicewise.

Cicchetti, D., Rogosch, F.A. and Toth, S.L. (2006) 'Fostering secure attachment in infants in maltreating families through preventive interventions.' *Development and Psychopathology 18,* 3, 623–649.

Cohen, J.A. and Mannarino, A.P. (1996) 'A treatment outcome study for sexually abused preschool children: Initial findings.' *Journal of the American Academy of Child and Adolescent Psychiatry 45,* 42–50.

Cohen, J.A., Deblinger, E., Mannarino, A.P. and Steer, R.A. (2004) 'A multisite, randomized controlled trial for sexually abused children with PTSD symptoms.' *Journal of American Academy of Child and Adolescent Psychiatry 43,* 393–402.

Cohen, J.A., Mannarino, A.P. and Iyengar, S. (2011) 'Community treatment for PTSD and children exposed to intimate partner violence: A randomised controlled trial.' *Archives of Paediatric and Adolescent Medicine 165,* 16–21.

Cox, A. and Walker, S. (2002) *The HOME Inventory: A Training Approach for the UK.* Brighton: Pavilion.

Davies, C. and Ward, H. (2012) *Safeguarding Children across Services: Messages from Research.* London: Jessica Kingsley Publishers.

Deblinger, E., Mannarino, A.P., Cohen, J.A. and Steer, A. (2006) 'A follow-up study of a multi-site, randomised controlled study with sexual abuse-related PTSD symptoms.' *Journal of American Academy of Child and Adolescent Psychiatry 45*, 1474–1484.

Department of Health, Cox, A. and Bentovim, A. (2000) *The Family Pack of Questionnaires and Scales*. London: Stationery Office.

Department of Health, Department for Education and Employment and Home Office (2000) *The Framework for the Assessment of Children in Need and their Families*. London: Stationery Office. Available at http://webarchive.nationalarchives.gov.uk/20130107105354/http://www.dh.gov.uk/en/Publicationsandstatistics/Publications/publicationsPolicyAndGuidance/DH_4003256, accessed on 23 April 2014.

Duncan, B.L., Miller, S.D., Wampold, B.E. and Hubble, M.A. (2010) *The Heart and Soul of Change: Delivering What Works*, 2nd edn. Washington, DC: American Psychological Association.

Farmer, E. and Lutman, E. (2009) *Case Management and Outcomes for Neglected Children Returned to Families – 5 Year Follow Up Report to the Department for Education*. Bristol: University of Bristol.

Garland, A.F., Hawley, K.M., Brookmans Frazeel, L. and Hurlburt, M.S. (2008) 'Identifying common elements of evidence-based psychological treatments for children's disruptive behaviour problems.' *Journal of the American Academy of Child and Adolescent Psychiatry 47*, 405–514.

Hackett, S., Masson, H. and Phillips, S. (2006) 'Exploring consensus in practice with youth who are sexually abusive.' *Child Maltreatment 11*, 2, 146–156.

Hutcheson, J., Black, M. and Dubowitz, H. (1997) 'Risk status and home intervention among children with failure to thrive: Follow-up at age 4.' *Journal of Paediatric Psychology 22*, 5, 651–668.

Ippen, C.G., Harris, W.W., Van Horn, P. and Liberman, A.F. (2011) 'Traumatic and stressful events in early childhood. Can treatment help those at the highest risk?' *Child Abuse and Neglect 35*, 504–513.

Iwaniec, D. and Herbert, M. (1999) 'Multidimensional approach to helping emotionally abused and neglected children and abusive parents.' *Children and Society 13*, 365.

Jones, D.P.H., Hindley, N. and Ramchandani, P. (2006) 'Making Plans: Assessment, Intervention and Evaluating Outcomes.' In J. Aldgate, D.P.H. Jones, W. Rose and C. Jeffery (eds) *The Developing World of the Child*. London: Jessica Kingsley Publishers.

Kolko, D.J. (1996) 'Individual cognitive-behavioural and family therapy for physically abused children and their offending parents: A comparison of clinical outcomes.' *Child Maltreatment 1*, 322–342.

Kolko, D.J., Dorn, L.D., Bukstein, O.G., Pardini, D., Holden, E.A. and Hart, J. (2009) 'Community vs. clinic-based modular treatment of children with early-onset ODD or CD: A clinical trial with 3-year follow-up.' *Journal of Abnormal Child Psychology 37*, 591–609.

Kolko, D.J., Iselin, A.M. and Gully, K.J. (2011) 'Evaluations of the sustainability and clinical outcome of alternatives for families: A cognitive behavioural therapy (AF-CBT) in child protection centre.' *Child Maltreatment 35*, 105–116.

Letourneau, E.J., Henggeler, S.W., Borduin, C.M., Schewe, P.A., McCart, M.R. and Chapman, J.F. (2009) 'Multisystemic therapy for juvenile sexual offenders: 1 year results from a randomised effectiveness trial.' *Journal of Family Psychology 23*, 89–102.

Lieberman, A.F., Van Horn, P.G. and Ippen, C.G. (2005) 'Towards evidence-based treatment: Child parent psychotherapy with children exposed to marital violence.' *Journal of American Academy Child and Adolescent Psychiatry 44*, 1241–1248.

Lieberman, A.F., Ghosh, M., Ippen, C. and Van Horn, P. (2006) 'Child parent psychotherapy: 6 month follow-up of a random controlled trial.' *Journal of the American Academy of Child and Adolescent Psychiatry 45*, 713–918.

Lutzker, J.R. and Bigelow, K.M. (2002) *Project 12-Ways/Safe Care. Reducing Child Maltreatment – A Guidebook for Parent Service*. New York: Guilford Press.

MacMillan, H.L., Thomas, B.H., Jamieson, E., Walsh, C.A. *et al.* (2005) 'Effectiveness of home visitation by public-health nurses in prevention of the recurrence of child physical abuse and neglect: A randomized controlled trial.' *Lancet 365*, 1786–1793.

MacMillan, H.L., Wathen, M., Barlow, J., Fergusson, D., Leventhal, J. and Taussig, H. (2009) 'Intervention to prevent child maltreatment and associated impairment.' *Lancet 373*, 9659, 250–266.

Montgomery, P., Gardner, F., Bjorstad, G. and Ramchandani, P. (2009*) Systematic Reviews of Interventions following Physical Abuse*. Research Brief DCSF-RBX-09-08A. London: Department for Children, Schools and Families.

Moss E., Dubois-Cotois, V., Tarabulsy, G.M., St-Laurent, D. and Bernier, A. (2011) 'Efficacy of a home-visiting intervention aimed at improving maternal sensitivity, child attachment and behavioural outcomes for maltreated children – a randomised control trial.' *Development and Psychopathology 21*, 195–210.

Munro, E. (2011) *The Munro Review of Child Protection, Final Report. A Child Centred System*. London: Stationery Office.

NICE (2009) *When to Suspect Child Maltreatment*. Clinical guideline 89. London: National Institute for Clinical Excellence.

Schaeffer, C.M., Swenson, C.C., Tuerck, E.H. and Henggeler, S.W. (2013) 'Comprehensive treatment for co-occuring child maltreatment and parental substance abuse: Outcomes from a 24 month pilot study of the MST building stronger families program.' *Child Abuse and Neglect 37*, 596–607.

Scheringa, M.S., Weems, C.F., Cohen, J.A., Amaya-Jackson, L. and Guthrie, D. (2011) 'Trauma-focussed cognitive behavioural therapy for post-traumatic disorder in three through six year old children – a randomised trial.' *Journal of Child Psychology and Psychiatry 52*, 8, 853–860.

Swenson, C.C., Schaeffer, C., Henggeler, S.W., Faldowski, R. and Mayhew, A.M. (2010) 'Multisystemic therapy for child abuse and neglect: A randomized effectiveness trial.' *Journal of Family Psychology 24*, 497–507.

Toth, S.L., Maughan, A., Many, J.T., Spagnola, M. and Cicchetti, D. (2002) 'The relative efficacy of two interventions in altering maltreated preschool children's representational models: Implications for attachment theory.' *Developmental Psychopathology 14*, 877–908.

Toth, S.L., Rogosch, F.A., Manley, J.T., and Cicchetti, D. (2006) 'The efficacy of toddler parent psychotherapy to reorganise attachment in the young offspring of mothers with major depressive disorders: a randomised preventative trial.' *Journal of Consulting and Clinical Psychology* 74, 1006–1016.

Trowell, J., Kolvin, I., Weeramanthri, T., Sadowski H. *et al.* (2002) 'Psychotherapy for sexually abused girls: Psychopathological outcome findings and patterns of change.' *British Journal of Psychiatry 180*, 234–247.

Wampold, B.E., Mondin, G.W., Moody, M., Stich, F., Benson, K. and Han, H. (1997) 'Meta analysis of outcome studies comparing bonafida psychotherapies: Empirically 'all must have prizes'.' *Psychological Bulletin 122*, 203–215.

Chapter 8

APPLICATION OF THE HOPE FOR CHILDREN AND FAMILIES RESOURCE PACK TO THE GREEN FAMILY

Arnon Bentovim

This chapter demonstrates how the Hope for Children and Families resource pack can be utilised to intervene with the Green family described in the previous chapter.

Initial stages of work

The initial stages of work focus on the modules of engagement and engendering hope. The aim of this phase of work is to for the practitioner(s) who plans to work with the family to meet with the parents and the Child Protection Team to clarify the nature of the task. It is helpful to link with expectations that the court would want Lesley (the mother) to demonstrate that she is able to provide better quality care for both Sarah and John, setting out the reality that there was considerable doubt because of their history. However, Lesley had recognised that she needed help to improve the quality of care for Sarah and John, and that she was willing to work with the practitioner to demonstrate she could care more satisfactorily for the children. The challenge for Lesley and for the children needed to be recognised, and the challenge for Jack (the father) living separately, having regular contact with the younger children at home, and with the children in care.

Further tasks are the establishment of the *team around the child*, that is, the practitioner, foster carers and the multi-disciplinary child-protection team; establishing a *child protection plan for each child*, to ensure there would not be contact between the younger children and Charlie, given his arousal, and Sarah's persistent traumatic symptoms and inappropriate sexualised behaviour; and an *intervention plan as part of the child protection plan*, involving regular meetings, clear expectations, and agreement to carry out the set tasks. The practitioner would be working with resource material and support from her own 'team' to achieve the agreed goals. The parents, children and practioners need to create *collaborative goals*:

- for the younger children being able to stay with their mother

- to ensure that the care and safety of the children in the home is satisfactory, and the children are safe and well cared for

- to help Sarah recover from her traumatic symptoms; for her school attendance to improve

- for John to begin to show evidence of satisfactory development, and to support his attendance at a pre-school/school facility

- to improve emotional responsiveness and relationships between mother and the younger children

- to help establish more secure attachments for both children and to address the disorganised attachment between John and his mother

- to resolve issues within the family by working with the parents together to help manage their separation and their lives as parents, not necessarily as partners

- to work with Charlie (and the family members?) to help prevent further harmful sexual behaviour, to manage inappropriate sexual impulses and to promote social skills and self-care

- to work with David to improve his emotional distress, deal with impact of involvement in harmful sexual behaviour, promote school attendance and peer relationships

- to re-establish contact between Charlie and David and the other children once therapeutic work had been completed with Sarah and John on the traumatic effects, and with Charlie and David on their inappropriate harmful sexual behaviour

- success and failure would need to be judged in terms of measured improvements in these areas.

The final stage of the *engagement and engendering hope* phase is to help the parents *understand the impact of abuse*, the way that neglect, sexual abuse, exposure to parental conflict and withdrawal can affect children. Lesley would need to be helped to identify and understand John and Sarah's needs by reviewing the *stages of child development*, identifying from the developmental chart what children achieve at different ages, the essential elements of good parenting and the basic needs of children, and to clarify the goals for each child.

In this phase practitioners need to avoid 'lecturing' parents, telling clients what to think, what they need to do. A *Socratic questioning approach* helps clients arrive at more accurate and helpful thoughts. For example in asking what a parent considers would be good parenting, to identify any thoughts they have in detail, for example Lesley might identify providing adequate nutrition. The practitioner would get her to amplify her thoughts by asking for details on good forms of nutrition. Then the practitioner might ask whether attending school would also be important, examining the basis of the parent's thoughts about this, gently challenging statements, for example about children needing to organise themselves to get to school. Through asking what their parent or friend would have to say about that, personalised alternatives can be generated, for a parent to acknowledge that maybe they would have to take more initiative in insisting that children get up and get to school on time. Parents need to own their statement rather than agreeing with a statement made by some statutory authority.

Intervention with the core parenting issues of ensuring safety, preventing harm and providing good quality basic care

Given the concerns about the state of the home, the issues of safety and the poor quality of care, it is essential to address these issues initially with Lesley. A failure to provide a context which is safe and care which is adequate would make it impossible for the children to remain in her care. In addressing the module of *ensuring safety and preventing harm* steps to providing a context of safety would include a general discussion with Leslie about safety in the home, necessary precautions given the physical agility and curiosity of children, and expectations. For example, John had been observed picking up hot saucepans from the stove, which was perhaps his idea of trying to be helpful. Specific harmful events that John or the older children had experienced would need to be discussed in detail, such as accidents in the home and the environment, trying to understand the factors which may have led to harmful events occurring. This would need to include the context where sexual abuse had occurred, the role of Lesley's depression, Jack's withdrawal, and inappropriate expectations of Charlie to take over resulted in failures of supervision and sexual abuse. Clear safety rules would need to be agreed by all family members.

Direct observation of the home would be essential: checking the home conditions using the Family Care scale. It would be tempting to have a family support worker come to improve the safety of the home. To achieve a positive outcome there needs to be an active collaboration, with the practitioner and parent agreeing goals to deal with hazards in the home and to improve the hygiene as a health issue. Problem-solving approaches are helpful, establishing the goal, thinking of many different solutions, thinking about which solution could be implemented and working together to achieve that goal.

Closely associated is the module *provision of good quality basic care*. Again it is essential to establish a clear picture of the pattern of care. The interview associated with the *Home Assessment of the Environment*, which checks care patterns over the past 24-hour period, helps to make a decision about the goals which are needed to improve the quality of care. Again a collaborative view needs to be established about what needs to be achieved, and how to ensure that clothing and bedding are clean and adequate, washing and bathing are regular and supervised, mealtimes are regular and planned, and a timetable established to ensure regular attendance at school on time. Inevitably there will be obstacles to achieving change.

Working with obstacles to achieving safety and good quality care

A decision had been made earlier that it would be most unlikely that the mother could provide safety and adequate care to the two older children. Considering obstacles to providing care and safety for the younger children, Chorpita and Daleiden (2009) have described the phenomenon of *interference*. This is defined as a process which 'interferes' with the capacity of the practitioner to be able to complete the steps of a module. This can include the effect of mental health issues – for example, Lesley's depression or the oppositional responses of the children – John is highly controlling through extensive tantrums associated with disorganised, insecure attachment. Sarah can be an ally as she has a more secure attachment with her mother. Lesley is organised by her children's responses, so is far more responsive to Sarah and far less to John, which maintains the pattern.

In parallel to working to achieve *safety and provide good care*, it would be essential to help Lesley individually, using the module *parents coping with stress and the link to abusive and neglectful parenting*. This would help Lesley understand the factors which have led her to respond with significant stress, depression and withdrawal. The introduction of relaxation and cognitive-behavioural techniques to manage stress would help her to achieve a safe context for the children and better quality care of them. There may be a need to work with a mental health practitioner to address serious levels of depression.

Addressing interference from children's oppositional responses may be met by using the modules *promoting attachment and emotional responsiveness* and *positive parenting*. The module focusing on attachment would take Lesley through a series of steps to understand the nature of attachment and its importance and identify attachment behaviour contrasting her relationships with John and Sarah, recognising that John's crying, fussing, tantrums, rejecting, controlling and distress is not manipulative or attention seeking but is a response to the negative history of their relationship. Lesley would need help to take pleasure in the delight of both her children, and begin to respond to John, despite his rejection, by learning to manage his behaviour more appropriately using strategies from the *positive parenting module*, through ignoring and differentially responding to positive aspects of his behaviour.

Positive parenting, managing difficult behaviour is an important component of improving the emotional relationship between parents and children. Lesley had considerable difficulties in managing all the children's behaviour, finding it difficult to manage their anger, oppositional responses and refusal to comply. Positive parenting modules would assist her in knowing how to take appropriate control of the children, including the older children when she sees them at contact sessions. Direct parent interaction work would be essential, using modules which provide steps to achieving positive parenting including the importance of *praise*, the use of *attention and ignoring, giving effective instructions*, the use of *rewards* and time out to manage challenging behaviour.

John's developmental delay has resulted from parental neglect, associated with his parents' withdrawal and depressed affect during essential phases of his early development. Lesley would need to be helped through the modules which provide steps to *promote early and later development.* This introduces behavioural parent interaction approaches to promote speech, language, play and encouraging educational activities, and to manage the wetting behaviour which has characterised all four children's development.

Given that there is contact between both mother and father and all the children, *positive parenting and managing difficult behaviour* modules will need to be used to help both parents manage the unruly behaviour of their children when they are together. This work would be reinforced by using the family module *promoting healthy family functioning, family communication and problem solving skills,* and the module *managing conflict and dysfunction in family life.* Parents and children are helped by a series of steps which assist them to take turns conversationally, discuss painful and difficult topics and manage conflict when it arises. This is of particular relevance to meetings with the parents to discuss their separation and the future care and contact with their children. Given the isolation of the family, using the *support networking* module would help promote engagement with both parents' families, and facilitate community support to help parents and children repair disrupted attachments and make new links with the community.

Working with children's emotional and traumatic responses

Generic approaches

Work focused on children to address the impairments of health and development is an essential component to achieving collaborative goals. Although improving parenting capacity through parent–child interaction and family work can help significantly, children's internalised experiences and responses will need direct intervention. The module *developing a child-centred approach* introduces steps which help the practitioner get to know a child like Sarah, build a relationship with her, convey a sense of interest in how she thinks, how she has been affected, being aware of her strengths as well as difficulties and helping to establish the goals that she would like to establish for herself. The steps of the module *psychoeducation on the effects of maltreatment* will help Sarah understand the impact of sexual abuse, neglect and exposure to conflict between her parents, and correct any misattributions or misperceptions that her abuse by Charlie was her fault. She will need to be helped to develop a coherent story 'narrative' of what happened and why.

Modules which address *safety planning* would be relevant for Sarah, given the vulnerability of other children to her sexual behaviour. A plan would need to be agreed both with the mother and the school to ensure that she is safe in the present and in the future and that the safety plan is followed.

The *coping skills* module will help the children recognise and manage the difficult emotions associated not only with maltreatment, but with protective action, for example, sibling separation to develop responses which are adaptive rather than maladaptive. Sarah would need to be helped to understand that sexual feelings evoked by Charlie's inappropriate sexual stimulation are 'normal' and can be managed without involving other children.

The *relaxing and calming* module introduces a way to manage uncomfortable feelings, combat bad feelings, learn to self-calm and create positive imagery. The module *describing and monitoring feelings* is an important component of this, understanding what makes Sarah feel sad, angry, happy, unhappy and how these feelings can be influenced. A feelings thermometer can help children like Sarah identify the process of thinking, feeling and doing, understanding the way that responses lead to inappropriate action and identifying how to modify her own feelings and behaviour and also those of others employing cognitive behavioural skills.

SPECIFIC MODULES TO ADDRESS ANXIETY, MOOD AND TRAUMATIC RESPONSES

Once generic modules have been completed it is essential to look at the specific needs of children, particularly those experiencing a good deal of anxiety, mood or specific trauma problems. *Trauma-focused work* with Sarah would provide psychoeducation for traumatic responses, working closely with the parent, helping both parents and children express and manage feeling states, and create a trauma narrative, processing and managing those responses. The essential element is to be aware that memories and reminders will trigger flashbacks, or re-experiences, for example, seeing somebody who looks like Charlie is what is feared rather than what actually happened, which may now be being appropriately prevented. The idea of the module is to help children like Sarah remember purposefully in a safe environment; in this way distress is lowered and put into the past rather than feeling part of the present.

Although the main therapeutic focus is on Sarah because of the extensiveness of her abusive experiences, a similar process of work would be required with John given the high level of his distress, and the nature of his challenging and oppositional behaviour.

Working with Charlie and David's disruptive behaviour

Disruptive behavioural difficulties and aggression – physical and sexual – are characteristic responses by children growing up in a context of significant adversity, neglect, physical and emotional abuse. Evidence by Cuevas *et al.* (2007) and Skuse *et al.* (1998) demonstrate that the shift from victim to perpetrator occurs as children and young people move towards adolescence, as noted through Charlie's behaviour. Once externalising disruptive behaviour occurs this can present a further challenge to parents' capacities to meet their children's needs. The impact on young people's functioning can include inappropriate drug use and involvement in the sort of intense sexualised patterns of response as noted in Charlie, which in turn had such a negative effect on all his siblings.

The approach advocated in the HfCF resource materials is to develop a module which includes the *Good Lives model.* This is a strength-based model, equipping individuals to achieve their goals in a positive way rather than through harming others. The alternative is to seek knowledge, excellence through play, work-relatedness and impacting positively on the community. Young people need considerable support to achieve these goals. It would be essential to involve Charlie's carers in this approach, ensuring that they are supportive, not undermining or critical. Despite the young person being responsible for significantly harmful behaviour, he needs support rather than criticism and positive goals need to be identified for the future, identifying his strengths and skills. Obstacles would need to be identified which prevent Charlie achieving his goals, difficulties with social skills, educational failures and non-school attendance. Together with supportive teachers, it would be essential to identify areas where help and guidance could support achieving these goals and address associated emotional and traumatic responses. Although the most immediate concern is to help a young person like Charlie manage his issues of anger and sexualised behaviour, he would need the same generic support that any child would who has grown up in a context of abusive and neglectful parenting, as described earlier.

The *managing anger and angry feelings* module is a priority, since both Charlie and David were responsible for significant bullying of the younger children, oppositional and disruptive behaviour. They would both need help to understand the way angry thoughts promote angry feelings and the actions which flow from this sequence of thoughts, feelings and actions. They would need to understand the triggers which lead to anger and are associated with sexual behaviour, learning to substitute other responses, for example, 'taming temper' with carer support.

Both Charlie and David have a significant degree of immaturity and difficulties in peer relationships. They need to learn appropriate, assertive skills, how to manage relationships and to convey their needs appropriately rather than through aggression and sexuality.

All three younger children need specific help as a result of the significantly harmful sexual behaviour perpetrated by Charlie. Modules on *managing harmful sexual behaviour* include those to help parents and carers appreciate the different categories, origins and functions of harmful sexual behaviour. Practitioners need extensive briefing, as do carers, to understand the therapeutic work that is required while recognising the nature of sexual responses at different ages in pre-adolescence and in adolescent children and young people.

The specific role of Charlie's carer, as well as parents and other family members who might have contact should be established. It is essential to understand the context in which the child or young person's behaviour occurs. Lack of supervision is key in terms of whether children and young people will continue to perpetrate sexual behaviour or whether they will be more self-contained. There is a clear distinction between harmful sexual behaviour which occurs, for example, in young children such as Sarah, which is a form of exploration and curiosity beyond the normal sexual responses of pre-adolescent children. Adolescents over the age of 12 years, such as Charlie, have the physical maturity to perpetrate more serious sexual actions. The way that carers and parents can manage and support interventions is a key aspect of achieving these goals.

There are specific modules for *working with children under the age of 12 who are responsible for harmful sexual behaviour*. The goals are to help children learn positive ways of managing sexuality, and working collaboratively to change inappropriate behaviour. This includes: learning basic simple rules about sexual behaviour and physical boundaries, receiving age-appropriate sex education, learning how to control and manage behaviour with the support of parents using positive parenting strategies and ensuring that safety skills and sexual abuse prevention are in place, as well as the social skills required to replace the use of sexual activities as a way of approaching other children.

Working with Charlie, the module *working with a child over the age of 12 responsible for harmful sexual behaviour* would requires close liaison with his carer(s) to enhance protective factors and ensure that his sexuality develops appropriately. It is essential to encourage a degree of openness and positive communication about sexual matters rather than maintain secrecy and develop age appropriate sexual knowledge (which is often strikingly limited). There would need to be specific guidance provided to help him understand what is OK and not OK in terms of touching or responses to other young people, staying safe in the future, safety planning and appropriate ways of relating. These are all essential aspects of the work.

Clarifying, sharing and reconciling the impact of abusive and neglectful parenting

At a later stage, given the extensive degree of serious neglect and failure to supervise and protect the children, an important phase of the work would be to ensure that the family members have a context to clarify what has happened, to share the impact of abusive actions and to work towards a more positive future. Charlie would need to be helped to take appropriate responsibility for harmful sexual behaviour and to acknowledge the harm that is being caused. David and Sarah would need to appreciate the power differential between Charlie and themselves so that Sarah could understand that Charlie targeted and groomed her and could satisfy herself about future safety if contact were to be re-established. Their parents would need to share responsibility for the degree of neglect which exposed the children to unresolved conflict; also their failure to be able to consider their children's needs because of a focus on their own concerns and their mental health difficulties which meant that the needs of their children were seriously neglected.

Lesley would need specific support to ensure the safety of Sarah and John who had been harmed sexually within the family context by being involved in the module *promoting safety for children and young people who have been sexually harmed by a family member*. Its steps would help her to become empowered to assist Sarah's recovery, to understand what sexual abuse is, to understand the sort of thinking which leads to sexual activities and to understand the children's perspective and promote recovery.

Assessing change

It would be essential throughout the therapy to repeat the administration of the set of measures used initially in order to assess the change and improvement within the family context. This would include:

- ▲ assessment of parenting using the Home Assessment of the Environment

- ▲ assessment of family life using the Family Assessment

- ▲ assessment of the quality of home care using the Home Conditions Scale

- ▲ using individual questionnaires and scales for parents and children to assess their sense of well-being.

The aim of the intervention is to be able to provide evidence for the Court that sufficient improvements have taken place within the family that the supervision of the Child Protective Services and the Courts are no longer necessary.

Conclusions

There is now good evidence that a Resource Pack using a manualised approach such as the HfCF can be effective in practice. However, practitioners require extensive briefing on how to use the approach effectively, how to put different modules together to meet the needs of children and families and how to develop the modules given the various practice elements being incorporated, for example aspects of CBT, systemic practice and psychoeducation. There would need to be an opportunity for regular support, supervision and feedback so that practice becomes implemented in the day to day work of the practitioner.

Because of the breadth of resource materials available within the HfCF, it can be utilised by a wide range of practitioners, working in a variety of contexts. For example, if there are concerns about parenting where a child has been assessed as being neglected or physically, sexually or emotionally abused, or where there are concerns about future attachment and good quality care by a parent with significant mental health or substance misuse problems who is expecting their first or a later child. HfCF may be utilised when an older child or young person presents through significant internalising or externalising challenging behaviour and has been subject to significant neglectful or abusive parenting. Once the approach has been established it will be essential to evaluate whether significant improvements can be achieved, and whether the HfCF can be used by a wide range of practitioners in the complex set of situations which result from when children have been maltreated.

References

Chorpita, B.F. and Daleiden, E.L. (2009) 'Mapping evidence-based treatments for children and adolescents: Application of the distillation and matching model to 615 treatments from 322 randomized trials.' *Journal of Consulting and Clinical Psychology 77*, 3, 566–579.

Skuse, D., Bentovim, A., Hodges, J., Stephenson, J. *et al.* (1998) 'Risk factors for development of sexually abusive behaviour in sexualised victimised adolescent boys: cross sectional study.' *British Medical Journal 18*, 317, 175–179.

Chapter 9

CHILD SEXUAL ABUSE

The Possibilities of Prevention

Donald Findlater

What will it take to eradicate child sexual abuse in the UK, let alone elsewhere? Guaranteed it will take a lot of effort by a lot of people, and most of those people will not be professionals in the fields of social work, child protection, law enforcement or healthcare. Whilst not diminishing the crucial role such professionals can and do play, it is important to recognise the particular complexities of child sexual abuse which mean that many 'solutions' offered regarding other forms of child maltreatment will have little direct impact on rates of child sexual abuse. It is imperative that professionals, academics, politicians, media and policy-makers acknowledge, understand and respond to this insight.

This chapter does not seek to catalogue for the reader the evidence about the adverse impacts of child sexual abuse upon its victims, whether they are male or female, child or adolescent; whether they are abused once or repeatedly, by someone they know or by a total stranger; whether they are abused in their home or at school, the sports club, the park. Surely for now it is enough to acknowledge that child sexual abuse is profoundly damaging to most of its victims, and that children and young people deserve to be protected from it.

Instead, this chapter tries simply to describe what child sexual abuse prevention does or might look like. I will use the journey I have been privileged to make over the last 30 years – from providing sex offender treatment programmes in the Probation Service to directing the development of an array of prevention services in my role with the child protection charity, the Lucy Faithfull Foundation – to challenge some thinking about sex offending and its inevitability and, hopefully, to stimulate greater interest in as well as commitment to the tangible prevention of sexual harm to children.

By child sexual abuse I mean:

The involvement of a child in sexual activity that he or she does not fully comprehend, is unable to give informed consent to, or for which the child is not developmentally prepared, or else that violates the laws or social taboos of society. Children can be sexually abused by both adults and other children who are – by virtue of their age or stage of development – in a position of responsibility, trust or power over the victim. (World Health Organization and International Society for Prevention of Child Abuse and Neglect 2006)

Based on that broad understanding, let us first return to the complexities that must inform any credible strategy, by the state and others, to prevent such abuse. Can you, the reader, consider briefly what it might take to prevent the sexual abuse of a 15-year-old female pupil by her 28-year-old male teacher on school premises? If we could roll back the clock, what circumstances might we make different to prevent the abuse from happening in the first place: different for the 15-year-old female pupil herself, or for her friends, or for her parents, or perhaps for the teacher, his colleagues and bosses, or for the very physical layout of the school where the abuse will take place. Now consider how to prevent the re-abuse of a seven-year-old male child by a 16-year-old female who regularly babysits him while his parents attend the cinema. And now the two-year-old male or female child abused and photographed on a digital camera in a nursery setting by a 38-year-old female worker. And the 13-year-old girl abused by an uncle on a family visit from abroad when he stayed overnight in the child's home. Finally, the 11-year-old twin boy and girl abused by their father while mum was attending her regular evening class? The scenarios are many and varied. The impact on the different children will likewise vary. Despite these differences, their abuse fits into the single definition above. The prevention of all of these examples of abuse requires a range of approaches involving diverse people. And for all of them there is, typically, no social or health-care professional already on the scene to 'prevent'. Their involvement will kick in later, if it does at all. Who, then, is best placed to do the preventing?

Over the past 30 years we have come to understand a great deal about sexual abuse and sexual abusers, about the 'who' and the 'how' of abuse. There is much more still to know, of course. It is right to enquire how this knowledge is used to contribute to the support and treatment of victims and their families as well as to the treatment of perpetrators. But what does this knowledge contribute to the prevention of abuse of tomorrow's children?

Across the globe I do not believe we are making the most effective use of what we know, neither in the less developed nor the more developed world, not in the global south nor the global north. Any strategies to protect children typically address part but not all of the problem, with many politicians, media commentators and members of the public seemingly believing that concentrating efforts on expensive criminal justice responses and subsequently on the management and treatment of convicted sex offenders will reap vast rewards – ignoring the evidence that only a small minority of offenders are ever convicted, that those convicted are not, typically, the most risky, and that desistance is actually the norm for this offender group. The predatory, determined, repeat offenders are in the minority, yet often policy and practice assume the opposite, with devastating consequences in terms of children being less rather than better protected.

It is an important and increasingly familiar cry – 'we need to take a public health approach to prevention of child sexual abuse'. This is, in part, in recognition of the scale of the problem both at a national and international level. However, too often *any* serious attempt at prevention is delayed, in favour of grappling with the precision of data concerning prevalence and incidence. But while that particular debate rages – and there will be no definitive, 'correct' answer – more children will experience abuse. This is not to suggest that good data on the scale of the problem, nation by nation, is not important – for how else will we ever conclude that our public health approach to prevention is working? It is simply to acknowledge that much good, preventative work can commence in advance of collecting and analysing such data.

Sex offender theory

In 1984 David Finkelhor published his 'New Theory and Research' concerning the process of child sexual abuse (Finkelhor 1984) and the world of sex offender assessment and treatment has benefited enormously from his insights. This book was published at the commencement of my own forays into the world of sex offenders with the Probation Service of England and Wales, and still today its utility is profound – in training professionals, working with offenders and their families as well as the families of victims, and in raising public awareness of risk and prevention.

Many readers will be familiar with this work about the 'four pre-conditions' to abuse (see Figure 9.1). The journey towards child sexual abuse starts with the development of a motivation to engage in sexual contact with a child – with contributory factors including sexual arousal to children, emotional congruence with children and a blockage to adult relationships. Features that might herald this motivation include childhood adversity, including experiencing child sexual abuse as a victim but also the absence of or inadequacy in the primary care-giver, whether through drugs and alcohol misuse or disempowered by domestic violence. This motivation is the start, not the end, of the process for those who abuse, clearly we cannot know the numbers who develop such a motivation but do not act on it. For those who do go on to abuse, most will grapple with their 'internal inhibitors' (the second of Finkelhor's pre-conditions) to allow themselves to progress to abuse – justifying or minimising their behaviour and its consequences; perhaps using drugs or alcohol to overcome fear or conscience or attributing the abuse to the wants and desires of the child and therefore diminishing the significance of their own role.

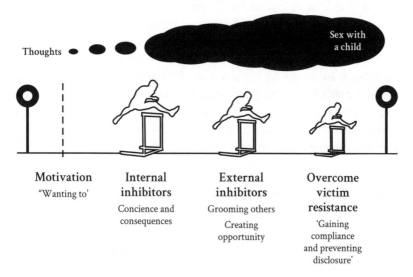

Figure 9.1 Four pre-conditions to child sexual abuse
Adapted from Finkelhor (1984)

The abuser typically recognises that other adults – erstwhile protectors of the child – would take a dim view of or react against the abusive behaviour and might intervene or report the matter to the authorities. These people are the 'external inhibitors', the third of Finkelhor's pre-conditions that need to be overcome. Herein, 'grooming' those around the child to not see or not intervene involves a range of potential tactics, including: presenting oneself in a pro-social light, generating alibis for behaviour, undermining the child's credibility through story-telling or, in a domestic setting in particular, using domestic violence and related threats to silence any observer. Of course, stereotypical representations of 'paedophiles' in the media help to blind these 'external inhibitors' from recognising the signs of abusive behaviour in those close to them who they respect, trust or love, leaving the abuser with fewer obstacles to negotiate.

Finally, the abuser needs to overcome *his* (for it is mostly males who sexually abuse, unlike with other forms of child maltreatment) 'victim's resistance', through the 'grooming' of another individual – the child who is the intended target. This is the fourth of Finkelhor's pre-conditions. Whilst physical force is an occasional strategy, more likely this grooming revolves around a child's particular vulnerability (for example, children who are bullied, friendless, lacking confidence, sexually naïve, learning disabled). We know that the vast majority of victims do not report, in part because of the grooming process but also because children are often not taught about sex and relationships in a way that clarifies expectations as well as boundaries and gives them confidence to report to a trusted adult if something troubles them, especially if that something is within the sensitive, embarrassing domain of sex. There are legion examples of grooming tactics, just as there are a multitude of reasons why abused children do not report – and this is part of the complexity we must respond to.

Criminological theory

Interestingly, in the decade prior to David Finkelhor's writing about the four pre-conditions to child sexual abuse, criminologists Cohen and Felson (1979) proposed a 'basic chemistry of a crime'. For any crime to occur, three necessary elements must converge: a likely offender, a suitable target and the absence of a capable guardian. Their essential proposition is that many people have the potential to be offenders but do not actually offend. They need the opportunity to encounter a suitable target, in the absence of a capable guardian, in order to convert their criminal potential into criminal actions. 'Routine activities theory' posits that a crucial element in the commission of a crime is the presence or otherwise of a third party. Most (potential) crime is prevented not by police but by ordinary citizens engaged in their day-to-day 'routine activities'. People routinely look out for their own children as well as those of others, just as they lock their cars, bikes and houses. Such actions make a considerable difference to rates of all crimes, including sexual abuse.

Eck (2003) further developed thinking about third parties by proposing three types of 'crime controllers'. He used the term 'guardian' to refer to persons with the responsibility, commitment and capacity to protect the potential victim.

A guardian ordinarily looks out for the potential victim – so may be a parent, a sibling, a teacher or a peer. Eck's second type of crime controller is a 'handler'. Handlers have the same kind of relationship with the potential offender as guardians have with the potential victim. These are people who can exert a positive influence over the potential offender, such as parents, teachers, friends and work colleagues. For those who have already offended, we can also include probation and (risk management) police officers as handlers. The third of Eck's crime controllers are 'place managers'. These individuals are responsible for supervising and maintaining good conduct in specific physical locations such as schools, residential homes, leisure centres, parks and so forth. Place managers can include teachers, security guards, park wardens, residential staff or the police.

According to the 'rational choice' perspective (Scott 2000), situations provide the motivated offender with criminal opportunities. But the decision to offend or not is influenced by information about the potential costs and benefits associated with the contemplated crime. Incentives for criminal behaviour are similar to those associated with non-criminal behaviour – material goods, status, excitement, sexual gratification and so on. Disincentives include the effort required to accomplish the crime, the risks of getting caught and potentially any guilt involved in violating norms or standards.

Within both sex offender and criminology literature there has long been a recognition that offenders vary in their determination to commit crimes. This has resulted in differentiating between the predisposed (and determined) sex offender, the opportunistic sex offender and the situational sex offender. The environment often plays a significant role in the commission of an offence; indeed, some (for example, Wortley and Smallbone 2006) have described how environmental features might 'provoke' offending, suggesting that without these features the crime may never have been committed. As the reader might guess, diverting a 'situational' offender from committing a crime is likely to be an easier task than preventing the same crime by a determined offender. It is good news, then, that research by Smallbone and colleagues found that only one third of their sex offender subjects were predisposed and determined (Smallbone and Wortley 2004).

For the present purposes, I must also make mention of criminological thinking about developmental crime prevention. 'Its aim is essentially to reduce criminal propensity by intervening early to forestall the negative effects of certain developmental circumstances and experiences' (Smallbone and McKillop in press). Problematic sexual outcomes have been linked to individual impulsivity and poor problem-solving, as well as to family adversity, including domestic violence and parental substance misuse (Salter et al. 2003; Skuse et al. 1998). For some boys, their experience of sexual abuse in childhood is coming to be recognised as a risk factor for sexual offending (Ogloff et al. 2012). Early interventions to ameliorate these childhood experiences would seem to offer the prospect of reducing the risk of future sexual offending as well as impacting positively on other potential problems. It is of interest that these and related features are at last becoming targets in some intervention programmes for convicted adolescent and adult offenders. What might be the outcome if we offered such interventions sooner?

The practice of prevention

My own involvement in prevention commenced with the Probation Service in 1989. The Sex Offender Treatment Programmes designed and delivered at that time had features in common with the much more intensive Wolvercote Clinic Residential Assessment and Treatment Programme that the Lucy Faithfull Foundation operated from 1995 until the clinic's closure in 2002 (Eldridge and Findlater 2009). Three hundred and five men attended this residential group-work programme, which an independent evaluation (Beech and Ford 2006) judged as being the most effective treatment programme for high risk, high deviance sex offenders available in the UK. Broadly cognitive-behavioural in approach, with an emphasis on relapse prevention and new life development, male residents were helped to accept responsibility for their abusive behaviour and to build on strengths to build an offence-free life. A positive living, learning environment supported change. Subsequent content aimed to help participants to:

➤ develop victim empathy and awareness (as a motivator for future good behaviour)

➤ recognise the role of deviant sexual fantasy in offending and develop self-management skills

➤ develop assertiveness, relationships and problem-solving skills

➤ understand links from their own childhood adversities to their offending

➤ develop relapse prevention and self-management strategies in response to the recognition of future risky situations and learn to meet their needs in positive, non-abusive ways.

Such programmes for offenders are clearly aimed at helping past offenders not to repeat their abusive behaviour – in public health terms, tertiary prevention. But in delivering the Wolvercote Clinic Programme, additional possibilities to ensure the future good behaviour of past residents arose and, alongside those possibilities, the potential to help prevent offending by unknown others.

A number of Wolvercote Clinic 'graduates' continued to have significant risk issues, in part due to an absence of appropriate family and friends (pro-social adults) in their lives beyond the Clinic. In response, the Lucy Faithfull Foundation developed 'Circles of Support and Accountability' – a model that recruits, trains and supervises volunteers to support a known, typically high-risk sex offender in their local community. The involvement of each volunteer is for a minimum of 12 months, during which time they meet up with the offender (called the Core Member) weekly for social or recreational activity, as well as meeting with the group of volunteers (the Circle) and the Core Member weekly, reducing to monthly by year-end. This model, developed by Correctional Service Canada, has demonstrated remarkable success in reducing reconviction rates by 70 per cent in Core Members (Wilson, Cortoni and McWhinnie 2009).

The possibilities of preventing individuals from offending for a first time grew out of the use of Finkelhor's pre-conditions in sex offender treatment, as well as from the involvement of adult family members and friends of the offender in treatment review meetings at the Wolvercote Clinic. Some offenders described their past struggles to avoid offending – whether at first or later – and their isolation with their uncomfortable sexual thoughts. Few could identify anywhere to turn to for help in managing such thoughts. Over time their resolve not to harm a child would weaken, perhaps at a low point in life, perhaps through use of alcohol. Having committed their first sexual crime, they felt there was no way back, nor any place to express regrets or gain support in the future management of thoughts and behaviour.

Adult family members and friends had mostly not known or recognised their loved one's sex offending at the time, but with hindsight could see indicators or patterns of behaviour that ought to have caused them concern. For example, becoming more withdrawn or secretive, creating a special relationship and opportunities for increased privacy with a particular child, increasing physical contact, taking an interest in the child's sexual development, making sexual comments about or to them. There is a host of examples that friends and family subsequently recognised as significant and that the offenders confirmed to have been indicators of their progress towards a sexual offence. Added to which, there were also signs in the behaviour and sometimes in the words of the child that could have been indicators of abuse – for example, becoming withdrawn or secretive, displaying unexplained distress or anger, expressing a reluctance to see or be left with the person, showing sexual knowledge beyond their age, experiencing soreness in genital areas – again, too often the 'external inhibitors' had not recognised the significance of these potential indicators.

From these and related insights, the Lucy Faithfull Foundation set up the *Stop it Now!* UK & Ireland campaign and its associated Helpline in 2002. It was based on a model that had been operating in the USA since 1992, the brainchild of survivor of child sexual abuse, Fran Henry. In the UK funding was secured from the Home Office and from a charitable trust for a pilot scheme. With the support of an array of children's charities and other partners – including NSPCC, Action for Children, Barnardos, Survivors UK, NAPAC (National Association of People Abused in Childhood) and NOTA (National Organisation for the Treatment of Abusers) – campaign materials were developed and distributed to inform adults of the risk of child sexual abuse, but additionally to inform them of the signs to look out for in children or those around them that might be indicators of risk or of abuse. The Helpline number was advertised via these campaign materials, but also through targeted media strategies, seeking to engage with three principal target groups:

- ⚔ adult abusers and potential abusers – to help them recognise their thoughts or behaviour as harmful or abusive and to seek help to change

- ⚔ friends and family of the above – to help them recognise the signs of abusive behaviour in those close to them and seek help about actions to take

- ⚔ parents and carers of young people with worrying sexual behaviour – to help them to recognise the signs of concerning sexual behaviour in their children and seek help about actions to take.

So, has it worked? Feedback from service users, their families and from professionals demonstrates that it is working. I believe the Helpline has become an essential feature of the child protection architecture in the UK. It will, of course, prove difficult to demonstrate a direct impact on rates of child sexual abuse. An evaluation of the Helpline and of its recently established sister helpline in Holland (funded by the Dutch Government) is due to report in May 2014, commissioned by the European Commission's Daphne Fund.

In the 11 years since the launch of the *Stop it Now!* UK & Ireland Helpline, over 38,000 calls have been taken by helpline staff, with nearly 80 per cent of these calls coming from the above target groups. One half of all calls have been from men seeking help to manage their sexual thoughts and behaviour (including those who have offended on the internet). One quarter have been from women – concerned about the sexual thoughts and behaviour of a (mostly) male relative or close friend. Parents and carers worried about the sexual behaviour of their children aged 3 to 16-years-old comprise 6 per cent of calls. Whilst concerns about male children predominate, almost 20 per cent of these calls were concerned about the sexual behaviour of a female child (Stop it Now! UK and Ireland 2013). All calls are confidential, and callers are offered support, information and advice so that they can take action to help protect one or more children. Callers with the most complex of concerns, and typically where no statutory agency is involved, are offered ongoing support as well as the opportunity of a booked phone call with a specialist worker and even a face-to-face meeting, if practicable.

Recognition of the important preventative role of the Helpline came in July 2013 when the Prime Minister, David Cameron, was speaking about child protection concerns relating to the Internet. Having first addressed the risks to children of their exposure to age-inappropriate sexual and violent content, he then urged the Internet industry to direct warning messages (subsequently referred to as 'Splash Pages') to those seeking illegal sexual images of children online. He stated that it was 'vital' that these warning messages 'should direct them to the charity *Stop it Now!* which can help people change their behaviour anonymously and in complete confidence' (politics.co.uk 2013). Unsurprisingly, call volumes have increased as a consequence, with the Helpline needing to seek additional resources to tackle the large volume of unanswered calls it currently does not have the capacity to take.

The risk posed via the internet had already prompted another service development in 2002. Following a number of high profile cases, the then Area Child Protection Committee in Surrey, where Wolvercote Clinic was based, requested help in engaging with local parents concerning the risks of online sexual grooming of teenagers and the safety measures they and their children might take. Over the past ten years this content has been developed to embrace the risks to younger children, including exposure to age-inappropriate sexual and violent content, online grooming, risks involved in the sharing of personal information, online bullying and 'sexting' (taking and sending sexually explicit images to others, typically using smartphones). In addition, delivery has extended beyond parents to now include separate sessions for children and young people themselves – to help them to be alert to online dangers, to be aware of avoidance strategies and to be familiar with people and places where they can get help and support.

So, for the Lucy Faithfull Foundation over the past 12 years, sex offender treatment work has been extended to include further tertiary prevention work with offenders, in the shape of developing Circles of Support and Accountability – an initiative now being adopted at a local level across England and Wales as well as in other parts of Europe. In addition, the *Stop it Now!* campaign helps educate the general, adult public about what risks to be alert to in order that they can prevent abuse. The *Stop it Now!* Helpline has been established to support at-risk people not to offend, but also to support adult callers to take action when they notice concerning behaviours in other adults or young people. Parents, children and young people have been targeted with information, advice and support regarding online sexual abuse risks, in order that they can enjoy the internet in greater safety.

Hopefully, the reader can see how these developments resonate with the insights of David Finkelhor described earlier. Sex offender treatment and 'Circles' serve to increase and strengthen the offender's 'internal inhibitors' but 'Circles' also creates an additional group of people who can act as effective 'external inhibitors' to any further offending by their respective Core Members. *Stop it Now!* campaign materials better educate the public, serving to increase 'external inhibitors' generally, and the *Stop it Now!* Helpline strengthens the 'internal inhibitors' of potential offender callers, just as it helps other callers be more effective 'external inhibitors' to potential offending by those they know or love. Our internet safety seminars in schools help parents be more effective 'external inhibitors' to any intended offender targeting their children online but those delivered to pupils also help increase 'victim resistance' as well as resilience.

Comprehensive framework for prevention

So, back to the cry, 'We need to take a public health approach to the prevention of child sexual abuse.' I often wonder what those uttering these words have in mind: whether this is simply a suggestion that everyone should worry more, or whether responsibility can be allocated to specific Government Departments, statutory and voluntary agencies and other individuals and organisations to take some specific steps that serve to protect children from sexual abuse.

In their seminal work combining a wealth of theoretical perspectives from criminology and sex offender theory, Smallbone and colleagues have both articulated and illustrated a comprehensive framework for the prevention of child sexual abuse. (Smallbone, Marshall and Wortley 2008). Their public health model distinguishes between primary (or universal), secondary (or selected) and tertiary (or indicated) prevention. Whilst there is not universal agreement about the precise distinctions between primary, secondary and tertiary prevention when applied to crime, the crucial insight is the possibility that interventions may be directed to preventing sexual violence before it would otherwise first occur (primary or secondary prevention) as well as after its occurrence, to prevent further offending and victimisation (tertiary prevention). In addition, the framework explicitly adopts a social ecological framework (Krug *et al.* 2002). This situates individual offenders and victims within their natural ecological context, and locates risk and protective factors at various levels of the ecological systems in which the individuals live their lives.

The resulting framework (see Table 9.1) invites us to consider targets for interventions that:

➤ prevent offending or re-offending by offenders (who, before they offend, are termed potential offenders)

➤ prevent victimisation or re-victimisation of child victims (who, before the abuse, are children and young people, plain and simple)

➤ prevent an offence or further offence within a specific family or community

➤ prevent an incident or recurrence of child sexual abuse in a specific situation or place.

Table 9.1 Twelve points of focus for preventing CSA

Targets	Primary prevention	Secondary prevention	Tertiary prevention
Offenders	• General deterrence • Developmental prevention	• Interventions with at-risk adolescent and adult males	• Early detection • Specific deterrence • Offender treatment and risk management
Victims	• 'Resistance' training • Resilience building	• Resilience building and other interventions with at-risk children	• Ameliorating harm • Preventing repeat victimisation

Situations	• Opportunity reduction • Controlling precipitators • Extended guardianship	• Situational prevention in at-risk places	• Safety plans • Organisational interventions
Ecological Systems	• Parenting education • Community capacity-building	• Responsible bystander training • Enabling guardians • Interventions with at-risk communities	• Interventions with 'problem' families, peers, schools, service agencies, and communities

The practice of prevention – again!

I have described a number of the preventative activities undertaken by the Lucy Faithfull Foundation (LFF) above. As a specialist child protection charity established in 1993, our background was in providing services to offenders, victims and families only after abuse. Alongside the Wolvercote Clinic residential assessment and treatment programme since the 1990s LFF staff have been providing assessments and intervention programmes to Family Courts in the UK and for the Youth Justice Board of England and Wales for male adult and juvenile offenders. In addition we have specialised in the assessment and treatment of female sex offenders. So LFF is an organisation that, historically, operated very much at a tertiary level of prevention. I have also described the journey towards primary and secondary prevention – into other 'boxes' on the framework above – that has been gaining momentum since 2002. I will now expand on this journey a little more.

In 2007 the Home Office published its Child Sex Offender Review. Action 1 of that review was to 'Pilot a community awareness programme, in partnership with non-governmental organisations, to provide better child protection advice and develop messages to help parents and carers safeguard children effectively' (Home Office 2007). LFF was asked to develop and deliver this piece of work, which materialised as a 90-minute seminar, with a supportive website and online learning programme called *Parents Protect* (www.parentsprotect.co.uk). Delivered as an activity of the *Stop it Now!* campaign, parents and carers were informed about the scale of the problem of child sexual abuse in order that it became a risk they took seriously. David Finkelhor's 'Four Pre-Conditions' model was described and illustrated, along with key signs of the risk of sexual abuse to look out for in adults and children. From 2011 to 2013 the Department for Education resourced the roll-out of this pilot programme across England. The Scottish and Welsh governments also resourced this work to reach out to parents in their respective nations and in both countries it continues to achieve healthy audiences. Feedback from those who attend sessions is consistently positive, with Finkelhor's pre-conditions model, the 'warning signs' of abuse and sources of support and advice being particularly valued. Post-seminar evaluations also demonstrate that parents are taking action following attendance, and are also retaining the knowledge into the longer term (Stop it Now! Wales 2013).

Two groups, however, stood out as requiring a different intervention from *Parents Protect*. Those single mothers, who either due to being very young (teenagers) or due to having experienced domestic violence, were in need of more extensive education and support, and parents from ethnic minority communities, who due to culture, religious belief or language required modified, more culturally sensitive materials, potentially delivered in a different language. For the former group, a five-session *Parents Protect Plus* was developed and is currently delivered at venues across Wales. For the latter, *Parents Protect Across Communities* materials have been developed in collaboration with community partners for Somali, Pakistani and Bengali parents, with work in progress to help the key messages become available to members of Orthodox Jewish communities. Whilst there are obstacles and frustrations to overcome, we have found a tremendous appetite to discuss the matter of child sexual abuse and its prevention within all the communities we have approached. Typically it is a matter rarely if ever acknowledged; sometimes there is flat denial of its existence within a particular community. Yet, with the respectful building of relationships alongside overt appreciation of the various strengths that a community brings to prevent abuse, especially when armed with sound information about warning signs and preventative responses, the enthusiasm and appreciation of parents has been palpable (PPAC 2013) The bigger challenge now becomes capacity to respond to demand!

In 2011 LFF staff involved in delivering internet safety seminars to children seized the opportunity to become involved in development of a primary prevention intervention aimed at ten-year-old children. *Hedgehogs* is a five-session programme of activities and education, delivered in primary schools, that builds self-esteem, provides age-appropriate sex education, engages with children about good and bad touch and develops strategies for a response should a sexually concerning situation arise. Before and after the 15-hour programme is delivered, parents are invited to an awareness-raising and feedback session.

Hedgehogs is the UK version of *Unspoken Words* – an intervention designed by Dr Alberto Pellai in Italy to help children keep themselves safe from sexual abuse (Pellai 2008). Evaluations of *Hedgehogs* by parents, teachers and children themselves were very positive, with children being described as more confident to ask questions and more respectful of each other. In addition, by the end of the programme all the children could identify two individuals they would go to if they had any concerns or felt uncomfortable about a situation or person.

The *Stop it Now!* Helpline has proved a remarkable vehicle for demonstrating the concerns of the public and the gaps in service provision when pursuing those concerns. For example, at the level of primary prevention, parents call with concerns about 'normal sexual behaviour' in children, and about resources that might help them talk to their children in age-appropriate ways about bodies, sex and boundaries. Advice and resources, such that exist, are posted on the *Stop it Now!* and *Parents Protect* websites (www.stopitnow.org.uk and www.parentsprotect. co.uk respectively) for broader access. At a secondary prevention level, men have been seeking advice and support concerning the management of their sexual thoughts involving children or young people. At a tertiary prevention level, internet offenders, their partners and other adult family members have been calling in increasing numbers for advice about actions to take now, often in the face of a visit from the police, to stay safe and legal online, protect any children within the family and make decisions about relationships going forward.

In the absence of any existing community provision to which this latter group of callers could be directed, LFF established *Inform* and *Inform+*. *Inform+* is a psychoeducational group-work programme for online child pornography offenders that helps participants accept responsibility for their online offending, recognise its links to and impact upon sexual fantasy, consider the impact of this behaviour on personal and family relationships and make plans for a future 'good life', wherein they take responsibility for managing any future risk and accept the need for being accountable to other adults within and outside of the family. For partners and adult family members, LFF established *Inform*, a psychoeducational programme that provides support, information and advice. The programme explores both the behaviour and motivations of those who offend online, the risks associated with this behaviour and the impact on participants as well as children within the family. Participants can continue in contact with programme staff or the *Stop it Now!* Helpline over the weeks, months, even years, as the impact of the online offending continues to be felt. Building on the success of these programmes, and in response to concerns expressed by police and teaching colleagues, LFF has recently developed and piloted an educational programme *Inform YP*, for young people caught up in internet-related offending and for their families.

One common concern mentioned by *Inform participants* in particular, was their anxiety about the potential for further offending as long as the internet remained available in the home. Some offenders were also concerned about this 'temptation'. As a consequence, generic accountability programmes have been brought to their attention – for example *Covenant Eyes*: internet accountability and filtering (www.covenanteyes.com). But contact with law enforcement colleagues identified the inadequacies of such products for this particular group of offenders. As a consequence, in partnership with a software company Securus, LFF designed *Securus Offender Management* – a programme that essentially installs a 'back-door' on the home computers of internet offenders that links to a remote, secure server. This server uses a catalogue of words, phrases and images associated with child pornography to identify any 'violations' to the monitoring agency (Elliott, Findlater and Hughes 2010). LFF staff now offer this home monitoring to offenders and families who want this level of accountability, and a number of police services in the UK and abroad are using it for the improved risk management of registered sex offenders.

In terms of the Smallbone framework, *Inform+* is a tertiary prevention response for offenders and *Inform* is a tertiary prevention response for families. Securus could also be seen as a tertiary intervention for offenders but it also serves as a device to manage a specific, identified situation – the use of a home computer attached to the internet by someone who has previously offended online. It would be logical to class this, then, as situational or 'place-based' prevention at a tertiary level.

Two additional situational prevention interventions deserving mention involve sports and leisure facilities where children and young people attend and schools which, by their very nature, could be viewed as 'at risk' places given the numbers of children attending and the opportunities for abuse that they afford.

Leisurewatch is a scheme designed by The Derwent Initiative, a public protection charity based in north-east England. It trains managers, staff and volunteers in leisure and recreational places to be alert to the possibilities of the risk of child sexual abuse. Alongside this awareness, they are trained in the behaviours to look out for that might be indicators of sexual abuse risk (basically through use of the Finkelhor 'Pre-conditions' model) and in the actions to take to disrupt or respond to such risky behaviours around children. Since 2003, LFF staff have provided *Leisurewatch* training, in partnership with local police personnel, in sports and leisure centres around London and the south east.

In 2002 Holly Wells and Jessica Chapman were murdered by school caretaker Ian Huntley. The resultant Bichard Inquiry (HMSO 2004) recommended that senior school staff ought to receive training on how to recruit safely – Ian Huntley's past record ought to have alerted those who recruited him as to his unsuitability. LFF has been involved in the design and delivery of this training from 2005 to the present day. *Safer Recruitment in Education* training is accredited by the Department for Education and is the expected training of those in schools across England who sit on recruitment panels. It educates heads and governors of schools about the scale of the problem of child sexual abuse, the process of abuse (using Finkelhor's pre-conditions again!), the elements of vigilance that can inform all procedural steps (from advertising and crafting person specifications to scrutinising applications, taking up references, conducting interviews, using criminal background checks), and the essentials of staff induction and training. These 'essentials' include a 'code of practice' within the job role. This code of practice serves to help staff know how *they* should behave around children, but also how they should expect *colleagues* to behave.

I have located all mentioned LFF prevention activities onto the comprehensive prevention framework (Smallbone *et al.* 2008) – see Table 9.2 on the following page.

Table 9.2 Twelve points of focus for preventative action

	Primary prevention	Secondary prevention	Tertiary prevention
Offenders and potential offenders	Hedgehogs	Stop! Helpline	Wolvercote Clinic Treatment Programme Circles of Support, and Accountability Young Offender Treatment Female Sex Offender Treatment Stop! Helpline; Inform+
Children and young people (Victims)	Hedgehogs Internet Safety Classes		
Families/ Communities	Parents Protect! Stop! Campaign materials Parents Protect Across Communities Internet Safety Seminars	Stop! Helpline Parents Protect Plus	Stop! Helpline Inform
Situations/ Places	Leisurewatch	Safer Recruitment Training Code of Practice	Securus Offender Monitoring

A child sexual abuse prevention strategy

I hope this journey towards prevention demonstrates how sex offender and criminological theories can inform and have informed the development of a number of child sexual abuse prevention activities by the Lucy Faithfull Foundation over recent years. Of course, there are many other organisations – both statutory and voluntary – which deliver services for the prevention of child sexual abuse, typically after abuse has already happened. Examples include the National Offender Management Service which provides sex offender treatment programmmes to convicted offenders in prison and in the community, Local Authority Children's Social Care Services undertaking assessments and supporting families after the suspected sexual abuse of children, other children's charities (such as NSPCC, Barnardos) providing modest numbers of therapeutic services to children following abuse. Sadly, these services and any developments towards primary and secondary prevention typically lack coordination by statutory authorities at a local or national level, just as they lack any vision for or commitment to long-term and significant funding to achieve greatest penetration, reach and impact. But they give an insight into the possibilities of prevention that will hopefully achieve support from key stakeholders in the years ahead.

Conceptually, we know there are ways to reduce the development of the motivation to abuse in young people and adults. There are also ways of increasing the internal inhibitors in potential offenders, so that their resolve not to harm others and their ability to exercise self-control are increased. Adults can be armed with information and support that enhances their abilities as 'external inhibitors' to offending. And children and young people can be helped to be more resistant and resilient in the face of possible abuse. Of course none of these aspects will be perfectly delivered or achieved, and some will be more successful in preventing particular 'types' of abuse – for example, online grooming or abuse by a member of the immediate family.

In criminological terms we can 'target-harden' children, require more effort from potential offenders, reduce the potential 'rewards' from offending and increase the risk of detection and sanction. We can put in place strategies that create more 'capable guardians', that equip relevant adults to act as effective 'handlers' of risky individuals and that provide for greater safety in 'at-risk' places.

The architect of the 'Four Pre-Conditions' model of sex offending, David Finkelhor, recently commented that 'as yet, no true evidence-based programmes or policies exist in the area of preventing child sexual abuse' (Finkelhor 2009). However, there is a growing number of studies that testify to the promise of a range of prevention endeavours, especially those involving school-based programmes for children, youth and parents as well as those that address the better management and treatment of offenders themselves. Finkelhor concludes that:

> Sexual abuse is a special challenge, different in many of its dimensions from other types of child maltreatment, crime, and child welfare problems. But enormous strides have been made to understand the problem, educate the public, and mobilize resources to address it. With additional research and program development, there is every reason to believe much more can be accomplished. (p.187)

Over the next three years, the Lucy Faithfull Foundation will be supporting some less developed nations in Eastern Europe and East Africa to utilise this knowledge and develop their own comprehensive prevention strategies in response to the particular child sexual abuse problems that they face. The ECSA (Eradicating Child Sexual Abuse) Project is developing a toolkit that catalogues the host of interventions developed across the globe to tackle and prevent child sexual abuse, and that then prompts the development of a prevention strategy that responds to local circumstances. Properly harnessed and resourced, this knowledge can help any nation to better prevent the sexual abuse of its children. The challenge is massive, with at least one in ten children experiencing sexual abuse by their eighteenth birthday (Radford et al. 2011). But given the costs to those nations and individuals as a result of such abuse, the potential rewards are immense.

I will close with the challenging words of James Mercy, Center for Disease Control, Atlanta, as relevant now as when they were spoken 15 years ago:

> Imagine a childhood disease that affects one in five girls and one in seven boys before they reach 18: a disease that can cause dramatic mood swings, erratic behaviour, and even severe conduct disorders among those exposed; a disease that breeds distrust of adults and undermines the possibility of experiencing normal sexual relationships; a disease that can have profound implications for an individual's future health by increasing the risk of problems such as substance abuse, sexually transmitted diseases, and suicidal behaviour; a disease that replicates itself by causing some of its victims to expose future generations to its debilitating effects.

Imagine what we would do as a society if such a disease existed. We would spare no expense. We would invest heavily in basic and applied research. We would devise systems to identify those affected and provide services to treat them. We would develop and broadly implement prevention campaigns to protect our children.

Wouldn't we?

Such a disease does exist. It is called child sexual abuse. (Mercy 1999)

References

Beech, A. and Ford, H. (2006) 'The relationship between risk, deviance, treatment outcome and sexual reconviction in a sample of child sexual abusers completing residential treatment for their offending.' *Psychology, Crime and Law 12*, 685–701.

Cohen, L.E. and Felson, M. (1979) 'Social change and crime rate trends: A routine activity approach.' *American Sociological Review 44*, 588–608.

Eck, J. (2003) 'Police problems: The complexity of problem theory, research and evaluation.' *Crime Prevention Studies 15*, 79–113.

Eldridge, H.J. and Findlater, D. (2009) 'A Community Residential Treatment Approach for Sexual Abusers: A Description of the Lucy Faithfull Foundation's Wolvercote Clinic and Related Projects.' In A.R. Beech, L.A. Craig and K.D. Browne (eds) *Assessment and Treatment of Sex Offenders: A Handbook.* Chichester: Wiley-Blackwell.

Elliott, I.A., Findlater, D. and Hughes T. (2010) 'Practice report: A review of e-safety remote computer monitoring for UK sex offenders.' *Journal of Sexual Aggression 16*, 2, 237–248.

Finkelhor, D. (1984) *Child Sexual Abuse: New Theory and Research.* New York: Free Press.

Finkelhor, D. (2009) 'The prevention of childhood sexual abuse.' *The Future of Children 19*, 2.

HMSO (2004) *The Bichard Inquiry Report.* London: Stationery Office.

Home Office (2007) *Review of the Protection of Children from Sex Offenders.* London: Home Office.

Krug, E.G., Dahlberg, L.L., Mercy, J.A., Zwi, A.B. and Lozano, R. (2002) *World Report on Violence and Health.* Geneva: World Health Organization.

Mercy, J.A. (1999) 'Having new eyes: Viewing child sexual abuse as a public health problem.' *Sexual Abuse: A Journal of Research and Treatment 11*, 4, 317–321.

Ogloff, J.R.P., Cutajar, M.C., Mann, E. and Mullen, P. (2012) 'Child sexual abuse and subsequent offending and victimization: A 45 year follow-up study.' *Trends and Issues in Crime and Criminal Justice, 440.* Criminology Research Council.

Pellai, A. (2008) 'Sexual abuse: Prevention is possible? The how and why of child sexual abuse primary prevention. Sexologies.' *European Journal of Sexology and Sexual Health 17/S1*, 33.

Politics.co.uk (2013) 'The internet and pornography: Prime Minster calls for action.' Available at www.politics.co.uk/comment-analysis/2013/07/22/david-cameron-s-porn-speech-in-full, accessed on 7 July 2014.

PPAC (2013) *Somali Project Evaluation – Executive Summary.* London: Lucy Faithfull Foundation.

Radford, L., Corral, S., Bradley, C., Fisher, H. et al. (2011) *Child Abuse and Neglect in the UK Today.* London: NSPCC.

Salter, D., McMillan, D., Richards, M., Talbot, T. *et al.* (2003) 'Development of sexually abusive behavior in sexually victimised males: A longitudinal study.' *Lancet 361*, 471–476.

Scott, T. (2000) 'Rational Choice Theory.' In G. Browning, A. Halcli and F. Webster (eds) *Understanding Contemporary Society: Theories of the Present.* London: Sage.

Skuse, D., Bentovim, A., Hodges, J., Stevenson, J. *et al.* (1998) 'Risk factors for development of sexually abusive behavior in sexually victimized adolescent boys: Cross sectional study.' *BMJ 317*, 175–179.

Smallbone, S. and McKillop, N. (in press) Evidence-informed approaches to preventing sexual violence and abuse. In A. Blockland and P. Lussier (eds) *Sex Offenders: A Criminal Career Approach.* Oxford: Wiley-Blackwell.

Smallbone, S. and Wortley, R. (2004) 'Onset, persistence and versatility of offending among adult males convicted of sexual offenses against children.' *Sexual Abuse: A Journal of Research and Treatment 16*, 285–298.

Smallbone, S., Marshall, W.L. and Wortley, R. (2008) *Preventing Child Sexual Abuse: Evidence, Policy and Practice.* Cullompton: Willan Publishing.

Stop it Now! UK and Ireland (2013) *Helpline and Campaign Report 2002–2012.* London: Lucy Faithfull Foundation.

Stop it Now! Wales (2013) *Six Month Progress Report to the Welsh Government.* London: Lucy Faithfull Foundation.

Wilson, R.J., Cortoni, F. and McWhinnie, A.J. (2009) 'Circles of Support and Accountability: A Canadian national replication of outcome findings.' *Sexual Abuse: A Journal of Research and Treatment 21*, 412–430.

World Health Organization and International Society for Prevention of Child Abuse and Neglect (2006) *Preventing Child Maltreatment: A Guide to Taking Action and Generating Evidence.* Geneva: WHO.

Wortley, R. and Smallbone S. (2006) *Situational Prevention of Child Sexual Abuse. Crime Prevention Studies Volume 19R.* Monsey, NY: Criminal Justice Press.

Chapter 10

REVIEW

Arnon Bentovim and Jenny Gray

Introduction

This review on evaluating an approach to eradicating child maltreatment has taken as its starting point the seminal work of Henry Kempe and his colleagues who described the Battered Child Syndrome in 1962. Their influential paper focused the attention of the professional world and society itself on the phenomenon of child maltreatment and initiated a global process of recognition, response and intervention. In 1978 Henry Kempe's address to the Congress in London organised by the International Society for the Prevention of Child Abuse and Neglect (which he founded) brought together the work he had done since describing the Battered Child Syndrome some 15 years previously (Kempe *et al.* 1962).

Kempe demonstrated that professionals, having begun to recognise the most severe forms of child physical abuse which resulted in fractures and bruises, then began to recognise other forms of maltreatment, including the most pervasive forms – neglect and failure to thrive, contexts where children are emotionally harmed and rejected and, more latterly, sexual abuse. These forms of child maltreatment continue to be the core concerns of practitioners working in the child protection field. Henry Kempe added, prophetically, a final stage of societal development: when the needs of children are well met and they are appropriately cared for and protected from abuse and neglect.

Kempe's latter theme has been central to this collection of chapters, which are intended to reflect on current thinking about the different forms of child maltreatment. Progress has been observed over the 50 years since Henry Kempe first described the Battered Child Syndrome. We can measure how far we have come towards reaching his final stage and consider what we still need to do to achieve his ultimate goal of children being protected, adequately cared for and having their rights respected.

A further key milestone on this journey is the United Nations Secretary-General's *World Report on Violence against Children* (the 'Study') presented in 2006 to the United Nations (UN) by Pinheiro, the independent expert leading the Study. This report included not only the forms of abuse described by Kempe some years earlier but also broadened the concept of child maltreatment to include other acts of violence and exploitation of children. In addition to using the definition of abuse set out in Article 19 of the United Nations Convention on the Rights of the Child (UNCRC 1989) (see Chapter 2): 'all forms of physical or mental violence, injury and abuse, neglect or negligent treatment, maltreatment or exploitation, including sexual abuse', Pinheiro drew on the definition in the *World Report on Violence and Health* (Krug *et al.* 2002):

> *The intentional use of physical force or power, threatened or actual, against a child by an individual or group that either results in, or has a high likelihood of resulting in actual or potential harm to the child's health, survival, development or dignity. (Pinheiro 2006, p.4)*

The Study reflects a *children's rights approach*, which underpins the UNCRC. The UNCRC has now been ratified by nearly every country to ensure children:

▲ are provided with services to meet their needs

▲ participate in society

▲ have rights of protection and care.

The UN Committee on the Rights of the Child ('The Committee') argues that all three types of rights are inseparable and should be implemented as a package rather than selectively. Bringing together the basic concerns about child maltreatment within the family context (the focus of Henry Kempe's work), a child rights perspective and the need to protect all children from violence has extended the concept of child maltreatment. It is now necessary to include children who are exploited, children involved as both victims and perpetrators of conflict, and the many children for whom the context for such violence is the privation still suffered throughout the world.

The broad-ranging UN study has been followed up by a hopeful UNICEF report (2013), *Championing Children's Rights – a Global Study of*

Independent Human Rights Institutions for Children. It reports that the goals achieved since 1989 and the setting up of independent institutions have included influencing government policy, being available to take up the specific concerns of children and families and ensuring that children have an ongoing voice. These are all steps towards promoting an agenda to achieve the eradication of child maltreatment. However, there are continuing challenges to achieving children's rights in a world where views on whether children and women have rights can change dramatically depending on who holds the political and religious power in a country.

Through its programmes, ISPCAN is contributing to this eradication process by, for example, initiating a *Denver Thinking Space* project, *Preventing Child Sexual Abuse: Working with Men and Boys.* This work is intended to assist the international community to respond appropriately to child sexual abuse by gathering and analysing information on evidence-based programmes used around the world to prevent it occurring and to prevent sexually abused children from continuing to suffer harm (ISPCAN 2011, 2013). The project is also considering how best to implement these findings, particularly in developing countries where resources are scarce.

Evidence for preventing maltreatment

A series of seminal articles in *The Lancet* in 2009 and 2012 have provided an extensive scientific review of the field, looking at the burden and consequences of child maltreatment (Gilbert *et al.* 2009a); reviewing the recognition and response to child maltreatment (Gilbert *et al.* 2009b); exploring a children's rights approach (Reading *et al.* 2009); and reviewing the prevention of harm – primary, secondary and tertiary – and the associated impairment of children and young people's health and development (MacMillan *et al.* 2009). This was followed up by an extensive study in high income countries to review whether the rates of child maltreatment had altered over time, identifying factors which appear to promote a decrease in the incidence of maltreatment (Gilbert *et al.* 2012). The conclusion was that a focus on promoting the general welfare of children does seem to be an effective launching pad to the journey to achieve eradication. The researchers expressed concerns about continuing to use the solution of placing a maltreated child in a new family, which should be a final remedy, and therefore not developing work to prevent the recurrence of maltreatment and associated impairment of children's health and development.

The damaging impact of maltreatment on children

The cumulative evidence about the impact of child maltreatment reviewed in Chapter 2 demonstrates beyond reasonable doubt how damaging are the effects of maltreatment and violence against children, and how extensive the associated impairment of health and development. Longitudinal and cross-sectional studies reviewed by Gilbert *et al.* (2009a) provide convincing evidence of harm to all aspects of children's development, education, physical and mental health and the long-term impact it has on their adult functioning. Recent research (Moffitt and the Klaus-Grawe 2012 Think Tank 2012) on the biological underpinnings of these long-term damaging processes has demonstrated how violence in childhood affects basic biological functioning. There is a negative impact on neurological and brain functioning, and the triggering of physical and psychological illnesses. Prolonged defensive processes triggered to combat the intense toxic stress associated with child maltreatment can permanently affect biological coping mechanisms, which in turn undermine the child's resilience, health and development. It is the long-term impact that maltreatment has which makes a programme of eradication absolutely essential.

Costs of maltreatment

Moreover, the cost to society is highly significant (Fang *et al.* 2012). This is both directly, in terms of costs to ameliorate the primary effects on children's health and development, and the secondary costs to address the needs of adults who were subjected to violence as children and now suffer physical and mental ill health and function poorly as partners, parents and in the workplace. With the significant change in population balance between youth and age in many parts of the world, the long-term effects of violence against children have a significant impact on the functioning of society as a whole. There can be no doubt that violence against children is a significant burden not only to individuals and families but also to the wellbeing of society.

In this book we have presented a series of chapters that provide many of the necessary tools and illuminate some of the ways in which the eradicating agenda can be taken forward. The UN Secretary-General's

World Report on Violence Against Children (Pinheiro 2006) made a number of recommendations which brought together thinking from broad ranging international perspectives. These recommendations have been organised with a focus on *policy* and *practice* and used as a framework to organise this conclusions chapter, endorsing and reviewing the steps in the journey towards eradication. The perspective taken here has been to review cutting edge research and the role that such work could take to further the Study's core recommendations and to significantly improve the lives of children.

Key policy recommendations

The UN Secretary General's *World Report on Violence Against Children* (Pinheiro 2006) made the following key policy recommendations exhorting governments and civil society to:

- ⅄ strengthen the national and local commitment to action

- ⅄ prohibit violence against children

- ⅄ promote non-violent values and awareness raising

- ⅄ ensure accountability and end impunity of those who maltreat children

- ⅄ provide accessible and child-friendly reporting systems and services

- ⅄ address the gender dimension of violence against children

- ⅄ develop and implement systemic national data collection and research efforts

- ⅄ strengthen international commitment.

Strengthen the national and local commitment to action

There are many examples of concerted national multi-faceted approaches to combat specific forms of violence against children. For example, growing concern about the sexual exploitation of children has resulted in collaborative work internationally and nationally between children's rights practitioners, children's commissioners, statutory (such as social work, health, education and police) and non-governmental agencies to develop, co-ordinate and deliver a plan of action. Findlater in Chapter 8 presents a comprehensive framework which, although it focuses on child sexual abuse, can provide a blueprint for developing preventative strategies for all types of abuse at individual, family and societal levels. It can also apply to localities, regions and whole countries.

The development of population-based preventative strategies as described by Prinz in Chapter 5 provides a blueprint for a population-based programme of intervention. It is focused at all levels both for parents who are meeting the normal challenges of childhood and those who are having significant difficulties in parenting successfully and safely. The next step for the Triple P programme, which has been demonstrated to be effective at a regional level, would be for it to be adopted and tested at a national and international levels.

Prohibit violence against children

As increasing numbers of forms of behaviour towards children are considered to constitute violence this recognition needs to be reinforced by international recognition, responses and action together with domestic legislation and co-ordinated strategic planning, allied with action to address poverty and privation.

There is growing international and national concern and public discussion about the harmful practice of female genital mutilation, which is leading to a growing demand that action should be taken to promote a broad based programme of legislation and education to end such a significant, harmful practice. However, in implementing these changes it needs to be recognised that when such actions are part of a deeply held belief system, parents may choose to avoid seeking necessary medical treatments from health professionals with deleterious results for infant/ child health.

Children who are trafficked, used in sexual exploitation or involved in conflict as child soldiers are also examples of the complex ways in which children are used and abused. These types of abuse require an internationally co-ordinated, persistent, multi-disciplinary process to bring an end to the violence.

Banning corporal punishment is also regarded as being key to the eradication of violence towards children. In 1979 Sweden was the first country to pass legislation to ban physical punishment, where it seems to have led to positive changes in attitudes and parental behaviours

(Durant 1999). Since then a number of other countries have passed similar legislation (Global Initiative to End Corporal Punishment 2014).

Promote non-violent values and awareness raising

Public education is an essential component of any programme to eradicate child maltreatment. The Prinz population approach, described in Chapter 5 and referred to above, relied on an extensive public education approach to publicise issues concerning good quality parenting, and to enable parents to become involved in the preventative programme.

Findlater in Chapter 8 describes a comprehensive framework to prevent child sexual abuse that also includes an extensive educational approach. It relies on widespread information-giving about the harmful effects of child sexual abuse and awareness raising at all levels if attitudes are to be transformed, including challenging stereotyped gender roles, discrimination and corporal punishment.

ISPCAN (2013) is identifying approaches that are aimed at educating boys and men in how to combat the negative stereotyped responses associated with male violence. However, it is not just men and boys that require access to education programmes and there are many which address also the attitudes and expectations of girls and women. To be effective, these approaches need to be developed as a core aspect of all children and young people's education.

Ensure accountability and end impunity

Co-ordination is necessary between child welfare, family courts and criminal systems to make appropriate decisions on managing allegations about maltreatment and child and family assessments. Subsequent treatment has to focus on resolving the impact of trauma for the victim and addressing the perpetrator's offending behaviour and fostering rehabilitation (Letourneau et al. 2009). Children who are victimised extensively are at risk of externalising behaviour and need help to address both their experiences as a victim and tracing the process which leads to perpetrating behaviour as described by Bentovim (Chapters 6 and 7) and Findlater (Chapter 8). Working with the impact on the family of children victimised by a family member or individual close to the family also needs consideration, as described by Bentovim (Chapters 6 and 7).

As part of a criminal trial children may be required to give evidence and can experience this process as also being abusive. Sensitive, reliable ways of interviewing children and vulnerable adults, and recording evidence, are now available through video and computer programmes such as *In My Shoes* (Calam *et al.* 2000; Grasso, Atkinson and Jimmieson 2013). The use of such approaches facilitates giving evidence in court in ways that minimise the traumatisation of child witnesses (ISPCAN 2011).

Accessible and child-friendly reporting systems and services

There is considerable experience globally with telephone helplines such as ChildLine in the UK, Telephono Azzurro in Italy and Saudi Child Helpline (16199) in the Kingdom of Saudi Arabia (for further information see the following websites: www.childline.org.uk; www.azzurro.it; www.nfsp.org.sa; www.childhelplineinternational.org). Their value in helping children and young people at risk or who are being abused has been recognised and child helplines are an approach which is being widely adopted, for example in the Arab States. Child Helpline International collects and analyses data annually from its member countries and in 2013 it published ten years of data in *The Voices of Children and Young People*. It reported 'the most common issues that children and young people wanted to talk about were peer relationships (17%), abuse and violence (17%), psycho-social mental health (16%), and family relationships (15%)' (p.3).

The development of parent lines and specialist helplines such as those described by Findlater in Chapter 8 as part of a comprehensive approach to prevent sexual abuse is also of considerable value. *Stop it Now* is an example of an approach where individuals and their families who have concerns about sexual behaviour can receive support to intervene to prevent the development of harmful sexual behaviour.

Address the gender dimension of violence against children

It is agreed that anti-violence policies and programmes need to be designed and implemented from a gender perspective. These need to take into account the different risks facing girls and boys and that the human rights of women and girls need to be promoted and all forms of gender discrimination addressed as part of a comprehensive violence prevention strategy.

ISPCAN's project on the prevention of sexual abuse has raised some interesting issues about whether it is appropriate, for all sorts of reasons (such as cultural, religious, age and stage of development), for girls and boys and men and women to be involved in a programme at the same time. It has also raised questions about how men and boys who are victims can be helped, especially where the focus is is on women and girls. The information provided to ISPCAN has shown that primary prevention programmes for children aged under six tend to be provided for both girls and boys but those for older children and especially programmes at a tertiary level are segregated. There is also evidence that preventive programmes for adults tend to be focused on women. This often relates to beliefs about cultural and religious norms. There is, however, little evidence about whether decisions about who to target which programme at are made on the basis of empirical findings or only on accepted beliefs.

Develop and implement systemic national data collection and research efforts

The UK has relatively well-developed systems for collecting data about children who are the subject of both child welfare and child protection concerns (Department for Education 2013; Rogers and Waugh 2013; Scottish Government 2013; Welsh Government 2013) and these statistics are used extensively in both policy-making and research. In England and Wales child protection data have been collected systematically since the Children Act 1989 came into force. In England data are now collected at an individual child level which means that each child's journey within children's social care can be tracked (anonymously) over time irrespective of whether the child is a child in need, the subject of a child protection plan or looked after. Over time this will mean it is possible to better understand what happens to children who are referred to children's social care. At present however it is not legally possible to link children's social care data with that from health as happens, for example, in Western Australia (see Woodman and Gilbert, Chapter 3).

In the UK there is a long tradition of the government commissioning research to evaluate government policies and their impact on children and families as well as organisations. The Safeguarding Children Research Initiative consisted of 15 studies, which have been drawn on in this book, including one on emotional maltreatment by Barlow and Schrader McMillan (2010). The findings provide a wealth of information about how well children are being protected in England. As well as summarising each study, the overview report has also identified what is known about how best to intervene effectively and makes an important contribution to the evidence base which informs the development of policies and practice (Davies and Ward 2012). It also identified that many of the interventions have numerous elements in common and suggested 'it may be possible to develop an approach which distils the common elements from existing evidence-based interventions to address diverse and complex cases' (Davies and Ward 2012, p.144). This approach is set out in *Hope for Children and Families* described by Bentovim in Chapter 7.

Strengthen international commitment

In the UK the UNCRC was ratified on the 16 December 1991 and, in England and Wales, the Children Act 1989 is the key child welfare legislation by which it is enacted. Eradicating child maltreatment requires the UNCRC to be implemented effectively and General Comment 13, issued in 2011 by the UN Committee on the Rights of the Child, provides practical guidance for governments and key stakeholders on how to undertake this responsibility with particular regard to Article 19: *The right of the child to be free from all forms of harm.*

Key practice recommendations

The UN Secretary General's *World Report on Violence Against Children* (Pinheiro 2006) included the following practice recommendations:

- ⋏ prioritisation of prevention

- ⋏ providing recovery and social integration services

- ⋏ enhancing the capacity of all who work with and for children

- ⋏ ensuring the participation of children.

Prevent maltreatment by addressing the underlying causes of violence against children

Gray in her introductory chapter raises the concept of the value of a public health approach, and Bentovim in Chapter 2 describes the way that a public health approach has been enriched by a redefinition of what constitutes child maltreatment, including both a children's rights perspective and children subject to extensive harm through exploitation. Woodman and Gilbert in Chapter 3 present a public health approach applied to health practitioners, Barlow in Chapter 4 focuses on primary prevention both universally to support the growth of attuned parenting and attachments and Prinz in Chapter 5 provides a multi-level blended approach to prevention. Together these different chapters provide a network of tools and evidence-based approaches that can be applied as part of a comprehensive strategy to target the prevention of child maltreatment on a population level.

Provide recovery and social reintegration services

The eco-systemic *Framework for the Assessment of Children in Need and their Families* (the Assessment Framework), pioneered in the UK (Department of Health, Department for Education and Employment and Home Office 2000) and adopted by a number of countries has the potential to provide a template for a multi-faceted and systemic framework to respond to violence against children and can be integrated into national planning strategy. It is intended for use with individual children and families. However, its successful implementation requires an evidence-based strategy which includes adequate resource allocation so that the necessary services are available to meet the identified needs of children and families, competent practitioners skilled in work with individual children, parents (who may be very challenging) and families and ongoing evaluation of whether the services offered are in fact improving outcomes for the children (Cleaver and Walker 2003).

The operational use of the Assessment Framework has been demonstrated by Bentovim in Chapters 7 and 8. It has been used as the basic model for making evidence-based assessments of how well children function, whether their needs are being met, the capacities of parents to meet those needs and individual family and community factors which can have a supportive or negative impact. Evidence-based approaches are used to outline the steps to recognise and respond to child maltreatment, make assessments, analyse the risks of harm to a child if the family remains unchanged, decide on the potential for intervention and design a programme of intervention which can be made widely available.

Bentovim in Chapters 7 and 8 also builds on Chorpita and colleagues' model to develop an approach to secondary and tertiary prevention by distilling the active practice components of evidence-based approaches to a series of modular interventions. The aim is to make such interventions available widely through the web following the PracticeWise model. Findlater in Chapter 8 introduces a framework which can address primary, secondary and tertiary intervention applied to those who perpetrate harmful sexual behaviour, victims and family members, and the situations which put children and young people at risk. These approaches provide a multi-level approach to work with the spectrum of child maltreatment, focusing on the different components, and integrating elements into a protective cycle to combat the negative spiral of risk factors which result in violence against children

Enhance the capacity of all who work with and for children

Traditionally training in the child maltreatment field has stressed both the importance of training individual practitioners in health, social care, education, criminal justice and legal contexts and also multi-disciplinary training (HM Government 2013; ISPCAN 2014). This ensures that there is an integration of approaches by practitioners from different backgrounds who can 'work together' around the needs of maltreated children and the complex set of factors identified in individuals and families which have an impact on the adults' capacities to parent successfully. The *Framework for Assessment of Children in Need and their Families* (Department of Health *et al.* 2000) provides a core framework for professionals to describe children's needs, parenting capacity and family and environmental factors. This enables training to be developed for practitioners from both individual and joint perspectives.

The Child and Family Training evidence-based approach described in Chapter 7 includes a number of questionnaires and scales, the *Home Assessment of the Environment* (Cox and Walker 2002) and the *Family Assessment* (Bentovim and Bingley Miller 2001). It integrates these and makes them available through training programmes for practitioners at all levels of expertise. A 'training the trainers' model is used so that training skills are provided to practitioners in agencies who can then cascade and develop the training extensively to all practitioners within their agency.

The approach described by Chorpita in Chapter 6 can be accessed on the internet, which ensures that extensive evidence-based resources are available to support practitioners in their work with children and families. Chorpita has found that when practitioners read material it can ensure that they will deliver a more effective approach than 'treatment as usual', and that training within agencies and support for practitioners can improve the quality of delivery of services even more effectively.

The Prinz approach described in Chapter 5 included the adoption of a specific approach, Triple Parenting, that can be delivered at a number of levels of parenting difficulties. All practitioners in an area can participate in the training as Triple P has been found to be an effective approach that can be used in different contexts.

The development of approaches to intervene with young children and their parents, to improve and modify attachment insecurity can be trained widely. The aim of Barlow in Chapter 4 and *Hope for Children and Families* in Chapter 7 is to have material widely available through the web, with additional training and cascading of training within agencies. Broadening frontline practitioners access to training, making it available through the internet and linked with e-learning approaches are all part of making good quality evidence-based ways of assessing and intervening available to all practitioners who need to have a good understanding of issues of children's rights and intervene at primary, secondary or tertiary levels.

It is essential that all practitioners working in the child maltreatment field have a capacity to relate to children. As well as working to address abusive and neglectful parenting, a key area in *Hope for Children and Families,* described by Bentovim in Chapters 7 and 8, is working with children, and the resource materials therefore provide a template for how to relate to children. This work provides a base from which to help them understand that maltreatment is not their responsibility, to find safety, develop coping skills, understand what has happened to them and deal with the specific emotional, traumatic and disruptive behaviour, that is, the impairment associated with abusive and neglectful parenting.

Conclusion

Taking Kempe's seminal work on the Battered Child Syndrome as a starting point the current picture has been examined to review how far we have come along the road to the eradication of child maltreatment – Kempe's ultimate vision. The original concept of child maltreatment has been enlarged to include all forms of violence and exploitation of children. Stake-holders who are now involved include international organisations concerned about child maltreatment (ISPCAN), child health (WHO) and the United Nations (UNCRC: children's rights). It is argued that the journey to eradication of maltreatment and violence against children can be undertaken with an approach which brings together an understanding of children's rights, and the best is a Public

Health Approach described in the chapters of this book. There is a need to integrate universal and targeted approaches to prevent maltreatment and violence occurring in the first place, and to apply the range of evidence-based approaches to prevent the recurrence of maltreatment and the associated impairment of children. The road remains long, and there are many obstacles in the way to achieve eradication. However, the effects of maltreatment and violence against children are so devastating, the human and financial costs so great and on such a scale, that the journey must be undertaken with all urgency. The vehicles to achieve this goal are available and need to be utilised universally.

References

Barlow, J. and Schrader McMillan, A. (2010) *Safeguarding Children from Emotional Maltreatment: What Works.* London: Jessica Kingsley Publishers.

Bentovim, A. and Bingley Miller, L. (2001) *The Family Assessment: Assessment of Family Competence, Strengths and Difficulties.* Brighton: Pavilion.

Calam, R.M., Cox, A.D., Glasgow, D.V., Jimmieson, P. and Groth Larsen, S. (2000) 'Assessment and therapy with children: Can computers help?' *Clinical Child Psychology and Psychiatry 5,* 3, 329–343.

Child Helpline International (2013) *The Voices of Children and Young People.* Amsterdam: Child Helpline International.

Cleaver, H. and Walker, S., with Meadows, P. (2003) *Assessing Children's Needs and Circumstances: The Impact of the Assessment Framework.* London: Jessica Kingsley Publishers.

Cox, A. and Walker, S. (2002) *The HOME Inventory: A Training Approach for the UK.* Brighton: Pavilion.

Davies, C. and Ward, H. (2012) *Safeguarding Children across Services: Messages from Research on Identifying and Responding to Child Maltreatment.* London: Jessica Kingsley Publishers.

Department for Education. (2013). Characteristics of Children in Need in England, 2012-13. London: Department for Education. Available at www.gov.uk/government/uploads/system/uploads/attachment_data/file/254084/SFR45-2013_Text.pdf, accessed on 1 August 2014.

Department of Health, Department for Education and Employment and Home Office (2000) *The Framework for the Assessment of Children in Need and their Families.* London: Stationery Office. Available at http://webarchive.nationalarchives.gov.uk/20130401151715/https://www.education.gov.uk/publications/eOrderingDownload/Framework%20for%20the%20assessment%20of%20children%20in%20need%20and%20their%20families.pdf, accessed on 25 April 2014.

Durant, J.E. (1999) 'Evaluating the success of Sweden's corporal punishment ban.' *Child Abuse and Neglect 23,* 5, 435–448.

Fang, X., Brown, D.S., Florence, C.S. and Mercy, J.A. (2012) 'The economic burden of child maltreatment in the United States and implications for prevention.' *Child Abuse and Neglect 36*, 156–165.

Gilbert, R., Fluke, J., O'Donnell, M., Gonzalez-Izquierdo, A.G. *et al.* (2012) 'Child maltreatment: Variation in transient policies in six developed countries.' *Lancet 379*, 758–77.

Gilbert, R., Widom, C., Browne, K., Fergusson, D., Webb, E. and Janson, S. (2009a) 'Child maltreatment 1: Burden and consequences of child maltreatment in high income countries.' *Lancet 373*, 68–81.

Gilbert, R., Kemp, A., Thoburn, J., Sidebotham, P., Radford, L., Glaser, D. and MacMillan, H.L. (2009b) 'Child maltreatment 2: Recognising and responding to child maltreatment.' *Lancet 373*, 167–80.

Global Initiative to End Corporal Punishment (2014) *Countdown to Global Prohibition.* Available at http://www.endcorporalpunishment.org/pages/frame.html?http%3A//www.endcorporalpunishment.org/pages/progress/countdown.html, accessed on 25 April 2014.

Grasso, F., Atkinson, K. and Jimmieson, P. (2013) *In My Shoes – A Computer Assisted Interview for Communicating with Children about Emotions.* Proceedings of the 2013 Humane Association Conference on Affective Computing and Intelligent Interation (ACII 3013), 2–5 September, Geneva: IEEE Press.

Hecht, D.B., Silovsky, J.F., Chaffin, M. and Lutzker, J.R. (2008) 'Project SafeCare: An evidence-base approach to prevent child neglect.' *APSAC Advisor 20*, 1, 14–17.

ISPCAN (2011) *ISPCAN 'Denver Thinking Space 2011': Child Sexual Abuse: An International Perspective on Responding to Child Sexual Abuse. Executive Summary.* Available at http://c.ymcdn.com/sites/www.ispcan.org/resource/resmgr/events/ispcan_denver_thinking_space.pdf, accessed on 25 April 2014.

ISPCAN (2013) *Working with Men and Boys – a Child Protection Strategy. Report of the ISPCAN Denver Thinking Space 2013.* Available at http://c.ymcdn.com/sites/www.ispcan.org/resource/resmgr/report_of_dts_survey_final_p.pdf, accessed on 25 April 2014.

ISPCAN (2014) *The International Training Program of ISPCAN (ITPI).* Denver: ISPCAN. Available online at www.ispcan.org/?page=ITPITraining, accessed on 1 August 2014.

Kempe, H., Silverman, F., Steele, B., Droegemuelle, W. and Silver, H. (1962) 'The Battered Child Syndrome.' *Journal of the American Medical Association 181*, 4–11.

Krug, E.G., Dahlberg, L.L., Mercy, J.A., Zwi, A.B. and Lozano R. (eds) (2002) *World Report on Violence and Health.* Geneva: World Health Organization.

Letourneau, E.J., Henggeler, S.W., Borduin, C.M., Schewe, P.A., McCart, M.R. and Chapman, J.F. (2009) 'Multisystemic therapy for juvenile sexual offenders: 1 year results from a randomised effectiveness trial.' *Journal of Family Psychology 23*, 89–102.

MacMillan, H., Wathen, C.N., Barlow, J., Fergusson, D.M., Leventhal, J.M. and Taussig, H.N. (2009) 'Interventions to prevent child maltreatment and associated impairment.' *Lancet 373*, 250–266.

Moffitt, T.E. and the Klaus-Grawe 2012 Think Tank (2013) 'Childhood exposure to violence and long and life-long health: Clinical Intervention Science and Stress Biology Research joined forces.' *Development and Psychopathology 25*, 1619–1634.

Pinheiro, P.S. (2006) *World Report on Violence Against Children*. Geneva: United Nations.

Reading, R., Bissell, S., Goldhagen, J., Harwin, J. *et al.* (2009) 'Promoting children's rights and preventing child maltreatment.' *Lancet 373*, 332–343.

Rogers, H. and Waugh, I. (2013) *Children's Social Care Statistics for Northern Ireland 2012/13*. Available at www.dhsspsni.gov.uk/index/stats_research/stats-cib-3/statistics_and_research-cib-ub/children_statistics.htm, accessed on 26 April 2014.

Scottish Government (2013) *Children's Social Work Statistics Scotland, 2011–12*. Available at www.scotland.gov.uk/Publications/2013/03/5229, accessed on 26 April 2014.

United Nations Committee on the Rights of the Child. (2011). General comment No. 13 (2011). The right of the child to freedom from all forms of violence. Geneva: United Nations Committee on the Rights of the Child. Available online at www2.ohchr.org/english/bodies/crc/docs/CRC.C.GC.13_en.pdf, accessed on 1 August 2014.

UNICEF Office of Research (2013) *Championing Children's Rights – A Global Study of Independent Human Rights Institutions for Children*. Florence: UNICEF.

Welsh Government (2013) *Children on Child Protection Register by Local Authority, Category of Abuse and Age Group*. Cardiff: StatsWales. Available at https://statswales.wales.gov.uk/Catalogue/Health-and-Social-Care/Social-Services/Childrens-Services/Service-Provision/ChildrenOnChildProtectionRegister-by-LocalAuthority-CategoryOfAbuse-AgeGroup, accessed on 26 April 2014.

LIST OF CONTRIBUTORS

Arnon Bentovim is a child and adolescent psychiatrist, also trained as a psychoanalyst, and family therapist. He is Director of Child and Family Training UK and a visiting professor at Royal Holloway University of London. He was formerly a consultant to Great Ormond Street Children's Hospital and the Tavistock Clinic. He established the sexual abuse assessment and intervention service and child care consultation service at the hospital, and has researched widely in the child maltreatment field. He and his colleagues have been commissioned by the Department of Education to develop evidence-based approaches to assessment, analysis and intervention. He and his colleagues published *Safeguarding Children Living with Trauma and Family Violence* (Jessica Kingsley Publishers 2009).

Bruce F. Chorpita, PhD, is currently Professor of Psychology at the University of California, Los Angeles. He received his PhD in Psychology from the University at Albany, State University of New York and held a faculty position with the Department of Psychology at the University of Hawaii from 1997 to 2008. From 2001 to 2003 Dr Chorpita served as the clinical director of the Hawaii Department of Health's Child and Adolescent Mental Health Division. Dr Chorpita is widely published in the areas of children's mental health services and childhood anxiety disorders, and he has held research and training grants from the National Institute of Mental Health, the Hawaii Departments of Education and Health, the John D. and Catherine T. MacArthur Foundation and the Annie E. Casey Foundation. He published a book on Modular Cognitive Behavior Therapy in 2007 with Guilford Press and recently published the MATCH-ADTC protocol, tested in the Child STEPs multi-site clinical trial.

Eric Daleiden, PhD, is the Chief Operating Officer of PracticeWise, LLC. He has worked extensively in strategic and operational management and has held leadership positions in the academy, government, and the private sector. Eric received his PhD from Ohio State University.

Donald Findlater is Director of Research and Development with UK-based child protection charity, the Lucy Faithfull Foundation. A qualified social worker and probation officer, he managed the Wolvercote Clinic residential assessment and treatment programme for adult male sex offenders for seven years before establishing and helping to develop the Foundation's primary prevention activities from 2002. His current work involves supporting agencies in East Africa, Eastern Europe and Australia to develop and implement a public health approach to child sexual abuse prevention.

Jenny Gray, OBE, is a social work consultant and President of the International Society for the Prevention of Child Abuse and Neglect. From 1995–2012 she was professional adviser to the British government on safeguarding children, firstly in the Department of Health and then in the Department for Education. In this capacity she led policy development on the assessment of children in need, reviews of serious cases and child deaths and the commissioning of safeguarding children research.

Ruth Gilbert is a qualified paediatrician and epidemiologist. She leads the Healthcare Provision theme of the Children's Policy Research Unit, funded by the Department of Health, which includes studies on healthcare use by children exposed to maltreatment and other forms of adversity in the UK and elsewhere. Much of her research uses administrative data and she leads the maternal and child health theme for the Farr Institute of Health Informatics Research – London and is deputy director for the Administrative Data Research Centre – England.

Alayna L. Park, BA, is a doctoral student in the Clinical Psychology program at the University of California, Los Angeles. Previously she served as a research coordinator for the Child System and Treatment Enhancement Projects' (STEPs) multi-site, randomised clinical trial funded by the John D. and Catherine T. MacArthur Foundation. Her research currently focuses on the dissemination and implementation of evidence-based psychotherapies for children and adolescents within community mental health settings.

Ron Prinz, PhD, is currently Carolina Distinguished Professor in Psychology at the University of South Carolina. He received his BA and PhD in Psychology from the University of California at Berkeley and the State University of New York at Stony Brook, respectively.

He directs both the Parenting & Family Research Center and the Research Consortium on Children and Families at the University of South Carolina. He is lead editor of *Clinical Child and Family Psychology Review* and is widely published in the areas of children's mental health, parenting and family intervention and prevention of child maltreatment. He directs clinical trials and associated research grants from the National Institute of Mental Health and the National Institute on Drug Abuse. Prinz also co-directs an interdisciplinary NIH-funded research training endeavour called the Behavioral-Biomedical Interface Program.

Jenny Woodman is a public health researcher trained in epidemiology and qualitative methods, with a specialist interest in combing the two (mixed methods research). Her research has addressed the role of healthcare services in identifying and responding to child maltreatment, with a particular focus on the role of the GP for maltreated children and their families.

Subject Index

Author Index